UNREASON
WITHIN
REASON

UNREASON WITHIN REASON

ESSAYS ON THE OUTSKIRTS OF RATIONALITY

A.C. GRAHAM

FOREWORD BY
DAVID LYNN HALL

OPEN  COURT

LASALLE, ILLINOIS

OPEN COURT and the above logo are registered in the U.S. Patent and Trademark Office.

© 1992 by Open Court Publishing Company

First printing 1992

Printed and bound in the United States of America.

Library of Congress Cataloging-in-Publication Data

Graham, A. C. (Angus Charles)
    Unreason within reason: essays on the outskirts of rationality / A.C. Graham: foreword by David Lynn Hall.
        p.   cm.
    Includes bibliographical references and index.
    ISBN 0-8126-9166-0 (cloth).—ISBN 0-8126-9167-9 (paper)
    1. Philosophy. 2. Reason. 3. Values. 4. Philosophy, Chinese.
    I. Title.
    B1626.G7U67   1992
    192—dc20   92-24269
                                               CIP

... el pensamiento tiene arrabales donde el filósofo es
devorado por los chinos y las orugas.

FEDERICO GARCÍA LORCA
Panorama ciego de Nuevo York

CONTENTS

Foreword

Almost a year before his death in March, 1991, I escorted Angus Graham on a tour of my home environs in the southwestern United States. He very quickly became fascinated by the desert ambiance, assaulting me with a variety of observations and questions about the numerous types of cacti, the desert wildlife, geological formations, meteorological conditions, characteristics of the Hispanic language, culture, and cuisine—the cumulative effect of which was to instruct me as to how little I really knew about the place I have chosen to live for the greater part of my life.

Such were all my encounters with A. C. Graham. His curiosity and attentiveness, his innocent openness to the world about him, allowed him a level of awareness that never failed to impress and to enlighten those with whom he came into contact. This awareness was both cause and consequence of a refusal to filter out in advance any of the welter of images, sensations, desires, aversions, beliefs, and bemusements that characterize our initial response to our surroundings.

Angus's encyclopedic approach to experiencing the world was evidenced in his reading interests as well. An inventory of his desk top on any given day might lead to a list like the following: Alasdair MacIntyre's *Three Rival Traditions of Moral Inquiry*, G. E. R. Lloyd's *Magic, Reason and Experience*, a paperback copy of *Classic Mummy Tales*, the typescript of a novel offered him for his criticisms, and the Chinese text of the *Ho Kuan-Tzu*. His musical interests were as seemingly disparate. When travelling he often carried his own entertainment—a miscellany of tapes which might include selections of Balinese music along with the latest album of the rock group, U-2.

Angus was a signal exception to the presumption that undisciplined enthusiasms of the sort he evidenced are seldom combined with a rigorous critical sense. For when he set about to criticize, whether in informal converation or through his scholarly writings, he did so with a guileless candor which unmasked cant and obfuscation not only in his intellectual adversaries, but in his most sympathetic allies as well. In fact, Angus had the wisdom to realize that his closest colleagues, those with whom he had the greatest opportunities for dialectical engagement, would likely benefit most from his constructive reproaches. Thus, friends presented with a new book or article from Angus's hand learned to approach the index or footnotes with some trepidation.

Angus's critical spirit was not diminished in the least with respect to his own thinking. Were one to enter his office unannounced it would not be unusual to see him engrossed in one of his own books. It soon became clear that this self-interest was due, not entirely to vanity, but to the need continually to bring his present thinking to bear on that of his immediate past in such a way as to improve both the quality of his insights and the manner of their expression.

His desire to remain open to the flux of experience led Angus to forbear the comforts of both a single-minded philosophical perspective and a single disciplinary interest. His principal philosophical work, *Reason and Spontaneity*,[1] offers an approach to the fact/value dichotomy which seeks to bypass the Enlightenment heritage still haunted by the warring ghosts of rationalists and empiricists. This same happy refusal to respect the bifurcation of reason and experience was evidenced in the manner he parsed his sinological energies almost equally between the dry, logical works of the Mohist School in classical Chinese philosophy,[2] and the lively experiential richness of the Taoist, Chuang-tzu,[3] and the poets of the T'ang dynasty.[4]

Angus's acknowledged mastery of the extremes of Chinese thought was responsible for the highly balanced interpretation of Chinese philosophy contained in his *Disputers of the Tao*.[5] And this interpretation, in turn, provided him with, what he calls in the *Introduction* to this volume, his "peculiar slant on Western philosophy," a slant which permitted him to celebrate the mutual relevance of analytic thinkers such as Moore, Ryle, Wittgenstein, R. M. Hare, and "anti-rationalists" such as Breton, Marinetti, and Bataille.

The writings in this volume illustrate the breadth of Angus's concerns for comparative Chinese and Western philosophy and should provide both an extension and a recontextualization of the most important of his views. I needn't discuss the essays themselves since the author has provided an excellent introduction. I wish merely to supplement his introductory comments by further anticipating the sort of difficulty some readers may encounter in approaching this text.

The best preparation for understanding an author's work is to follow the route he travelled in producing it. Angus details that route in his introductory comments. Essentially, it involves approaching Western philosophical issues and problems with a background in Classical Chinese thought. This would be a much too daunting path for most of us to follow. Fortunately, rather recent changes in the Western philosophic scene have made it somewhat easier for Anglo-European philosophers to gain access to Angus's work.

The narrower forms of logical and linguistic analysis no longer monopolize the profession; post-analytic pragmatists and continental thinkers of the post-structuralist and deconstructionist perspective have carried further the critique of representationalist thinking begun with Dewey, Heidegger, and Wittgenstein. These alterations have called the Enlightenment sense of rationality into question in such a way as to increase the general level of sympathy for alternative senses of "thinking." Thus, we are far better prepared than just a few years ago to respond to the force and originality of *Reason and Spontaneity*.

The most direct access to Angus Graham's constructive philosophic thinking, as well as his distinctive interpretations of Chinese philosophy, may be gained by perusing the growing literature which contrasts what he terms "pre-logical" or "correlative" thinking with "reason" and "rationality".

It isn't clear where the notion of correlative thinking originates. Speaking generally, it may be traced to Marcel Granet's *La Pensée Chinoise*,[6] written in 1934 wherein correlativity is taken to be a characteristic of the "Chinese Mind." Chang Tung-sun, in an article appearing in China in *Sociological World* under the title, "Thought, Language and Culture"[7] contrasts a Western "logic of identity" with a Chinese "logic of correlation" which is neither monistic, nor dualistic, nor reductionistic. In his *Philosophy of Symbolic Forms*, Ernst Cassirer discusses "pre-logical" thinking within the context of mythopoesis.[8] Lévi-Strauss significantly expands the notion of "correlativity" in his *La Pensée Sauvage*.[9] Lévi-Strauss drew his initial inspiration from Marcel

Granet's work, employing Roman Jakobson's metaphoric/metonymic distinction to consider relationships other than the strictly "rational" and "causal".

Joseph Needham,[10] John B. Henderson,[11] and Benjamin Schwartz,[12] provide treatments of the Chinese employment of correlative procedures in the construction of general cosmologies. Fernand Hallyn's *The Poetic Structure of the World—Copernicus and Kepler*[13] demonstrates the use of "pre-logical" thinking in the cosmological theories of the early Modern period. An extremely enlightening work which assays the exercise of "pre-logical" thinking with reference primarily to Western thought is P. K. Feyerabend's *Farewell to Reason.*[14] Here correlative operations are characterized simply as "empirical thinking".

G. E. R. Lloyd's *Polarity and Analogy: Two Types of Argumentation in Early Greek Thought*[15] and *Magic, Reason and Experience: Studies in the Origin and Development of Greek Science*[16] provide discussions of the relationships in classical Greek thought between the modes of thinking Angus and others designate "correlative" and "rational". Angus had become very much interested in Lloyd's work just prior to his death and had interpolated new references to his thinking in several of the essays appearing in this volume.

The most sophisticated philosophical treatment of "pre-logical" thinking is provided by Angus Graham himself. In *Reason and Spontaneity*, the term "analogical thinking" is used to describe the correlative method. He is influenced by Lévi-Strauss's structuralism in developing his mature approach to correlativity found in his *Yin-Yang and the Nature of Correlative Thinking*,[17] *Disputers of the Tao*, and several of the essays in this volume.

Those interested in critical assessment of Graham's thinking, particularly as it bears upon the issues discussed in this volume, should see the essays by Herbert Fingarette and Henry Rosemont, Jr. in *Chinese Texts and Philosophical Contexts: Essays Dedicated to Angus C. Graham*,[18] and Graham's replies to these essays.

• • •

I have made very few alterations in Angus's text; most of them concern the organization of paragraphs in the *Introduction*, and corrections of minor textual infelicities. The greater part of my efforts were spent attempting to insure proper placement in the text for the myriad handwritten and typed emendations that marched out from between the lines and staggered pell mell up and down the margins of his manuscript.

The only substantive alteration concerns the title of this work. At the time of his death, Angus was not satisfied with the subtitle: "The Less Than Logical in Rationality". He had discussed many alternatives with colleagues, but no final choice was ever made. I have elected to keep the intentionally ambiguous main title which tells us both that "unreason" is a constitutive element in reason, and that the resort to unreason ought always be undertaken in a "reasonable" manner. In selecting the new subtitle—"Essays on the Outskirts of Rationality"—I have meant to reinforce the relevance to Angus's arguments of the Lorca citation he had selected for the frontispiece. In English, the passage reads: "The mind has outskirts where the philosopher is devoured by Chinese and caterpillars".

DAVID LYNN HALL
The University of Texas at El Paso
November 15, 1991

NOTES

1. London: Curzon Press, 1985.
2. *Later Mohist Logic, Ethics and Science* (Hong Kong: Chinese University Press; London School of Oriental and African Studies, 1978).
3. *Chuang-tzu: The Seven Inner Chapters and Other Writings from the Book 'Chuang-tzu'* (London: Allen and Unwin, 1981).
4. *Poems of the Late T'ang* (London: Penguin Classics, 1965).
5. La Salle, Illinois: Open Court, 1989.
6. Paris: Albin Michel, 1934.
7. X, June, 1938. The essay also appears under the title, "A Chinese Philosopher's Theory of Knowledge," in S. I. Hayakawa (ed.), *Our Language and Our World* (New York: Harper, 1959), pp. 299–324.
8. See *Philosophy of Symbolic Forms*, Vol. 2 (New Haven: Yale University Press, 1955), *Mythical Thought*.
9. *The Savage Mind* (Chicago: University of Chicago Press, 1966).
10. *Science and Civilisation in China.* See Vol. 2. (Cambridge: Cambridge University Press, 1956), pp. 253–345 *passim*.

11. *The Development and Decline of Chinese Cosmology* (New York: Columbia University Press, 1984).

12. *The World of Thought in Ancient China* (Cambridge: Harvard University Press, 1985).

13. New York: Zone Books, 1990.

14. New York: Verso Press, 1987.

15. Cambridge University Press, 1966. (Reprinted by Bristol Classical Press, 1987).

16. Cambridge University Press, 1979.

17. The Institute of East Asian Philosophies, 1986.

18. Ed. Henry Rosemont, La Salle, Ill.: Open Court, 1991.

ACKNOWLEDGMENTS

Chapter 1, "Value, Fact and Facing Facts," is a revised version of an article originally published in *Journal of Value Inquiry* 19 (1985): 35–41. © Martinus Nijhoff Publishers, Dordrecht.

Chapter 2, "Perspectivism vs. Relativism in Nietzsche," appears in print here for the first time.

Chapter 3, "Natural Goodness and Original Sin," is reprinted from *Rationalist Annual 1963*, ed. Hector Hawton. London: Barry and Rockliff, 1963.

Chapter 4, "Conceptual Schemes and Linguistic Relativism in Relation to Chinese," is a revised version of an article that originally appeared in *Synthesis Philosophica* 4/2 (1989): 713–32. It has also appeared in *Culture and Modernity*, ed. Eliot Deutsch. Honolulu: University of Hawaii Press, 1991.

Chapter 5, " 'Being' in Linguistics and Philosophy," is reprinted from *Foundations of Language* 1 (1965): 223–31. It has also appeared in *Foundations of Language Supplementary Series* 14 ("The Verb 'to be' and Its Synonyms 1, v. 5), 1972, 225–33.

Chapter 6, "Rationalism and Anti-Rationalism in Pre-Buddhist China," is reprinted from *Rationality in Question: On Eastern and Western Views of Rationality*, ed. Shlomo Biderman and Ben-Ami Scharfstein. Leiden: E. J. Brill, 1989. Reprinted by permission of the publisher.

Chapter 7, "A Chinese Approach to Philosophy of Value: *Ho-kuan-tzu*," is reprinted from *Epistemological Issues in Classical Chinese Philosophy*, ed. Hans Lenk and Gregor Paul, by permission of the State University of New York Press. © 1992 SUNY Press.

Chapter 8, "China, Europe, and the Origins of Modern Science: Needham's *The Grand Titration*," is reprinted from *Asia Minor* NS, 16 (1971): 178–96, by permission of the editor and publishers. It has also appeared in *Chinese Science*, ed. Shigeru Nakayama and Nathan Sivin. Cambridge: MIT Press, 1973.

Chapter 9, "Liberty and Equality," reprinted from *Mind* 74, no. 293 (January 1965) by permission.

Chapter 10, "The Question behind Marx's Concept of Alienation," appears in print here for the first time.

Chapter 11, "Poetic and Mythic Varieties of Correlative Thinking," appears in print here for the first time.

Chapter 12, "Bataille as Myth-Maker and as Philosopher of Value," appears in print here for the first time.

Chapter 13, "Two Perspectives on Present Mythopoeia," has not appeared in English or in this expanded form before. Part 2 was published as "Vampiri in uno solo morso," in *Il Manifesto*, Rome, Sept. 1, 1986.

Chapter 14, "Mysticism and the Question of Private Access," is reprinted from *Rules, Rituals, and Responsibility: Essays Dedicated to Herbert Fingarette*, ed. Mary I. Bockover. La Salle, IL: Open Court, 1991.

Abbreviations of Frequently-cited Works by the Author

R & S   *Reason and Spontaneity*, London, Curzon Press, 1985.

DT   *Disputers of the Tao: Philosophical Argument in Ancient China*, La Salle, IL, Open Court, 1989.

SCP   *Studies in Chinese Philosophy and Philosophical Literature*, Albany, NY, State University of New York Press, 1990.

INTRODUCTION

It has been suggested to me that a collection which ranges so widely between analytic philosophy and discussions of myth and mysticism, with such an unusual slant on Western philosophy and such unaccustomed respect for Chinese, needs some sort of autobiographical sketch to explain where I come from.

My personal pressure to philosophise began in 1940 with the loss of religious faith, a month or two after getting a degree in theology at Oxford. Although I had taken theology for the sake of a grant without intending to enter the Church, spending most of my time on literature and Marxist politics, and my dim Protestantism had amounted to little more than an assumption that the current British moral code had the authority of a rewarding and punishing God, the emotional security of it had filled a need; I felt a compulsion to find new intellectual support for values, exacerbated when the reading of A. J. Ayer's *Language, Truth and Logic* frightened me with the thought that value utterances are neither true nor false, just expressions of emotion. I. A. Richards's *Principles of Literary Criticism* and *Science and Poetry* persuaded me that truth belongs to the language of science, value of the arts, and the need is for a theory which will ground values as firmly as truths without confusing them. Richards's anti-metaphysical combination of empiricism with aestheticism has marked me for life, but his own psychological theory of values was itself open to the objection that it derived value from factual truths.

The fact/value dichotomy introduced to me by Ayer seemed to imply that, while fact can be tested by observation, value cannot be tested except by other value judgments, which leads to an infinite regress. It was also worrying that, even if one were content to act out desires without bothering that in theory value cannot be derived from the fact of desire, philosophy provided no reason for respecting the desires of others. More recent British philosophers wrote as though they had left these beginners' doubts behind them, but seemed only to be excluding them from philosophy as questions it cannot answer.

After the war, having been trained as a Japanese interpreter, I took a degree in Chinese at the School of Oriental and African Studies in London University, where I was to teach Classical Chinese from 1950 until retirement in 1984, with some interludes in American universities. Not only my thinking but most of my fruitful experience has ever since been inseparable from Oriental studies and travels. A reluctance to take on Sanskrit and Pali has unfortunately stopped me exploring the philosophy and literature of India, a culture of which the improvised music in particular has deeply affected my tastes (I remain ignorant of Buddhism even in China and Japan). I forgot the little New Testament Greek required for theology, and ignored Greek civilization until long after acquiring expertise in Chinese; only in middle age did I relearn some Greek and discover the philosophers and poets, with the excitement of making a marvellous addition to my cultural worlds. This may have something to do with my impression (shared, however, by Nietzsche, who began as a classical philologist) that Greece is not part of *our* civilization, but, like Israel, one of the alien cultures of the East Mediterranean which contributed to its beginnings. The interest in China sprang from the romantic appeal of the exotic, but also from the desire to view the two things most important to me, philosophy and the arts, from a perspective from outside Europe. Meanwhile my first answers to the fundamental questions of philosophy of value were sorting themselves out. I had some contact with H. J. Paton, who accepted *The Problem of Value* (1961) for Hutchinson's University Library, and with Gilbert Ryle, who criticised the manuscript and also took "Liberty and Equality" (reprinted here) for publication in *Mind* in 1965. *The Problem of Value* was hardly noticed, but satisfied for a time my personal need to solve the problems which troubled me, and the pressure to philosophise relaxed. I have never established more than occasional contact with later generations of British philosophers, who were much less tolerant than Paton or Ryle of untrained outsiders who read what they please, least of all if one's field is the mystic Orient.

My interest centered increasingly on research into Chinese thought and into the many still unsolved textual and grammatical problems involved in understanding it, the intellectual fascination of which often kept me submerged in the detail of pure scholarship. D. C. Lau, then also at the school, a Chinese who unlike myself had a professional training in Western philosophy, taught me the value of the then current "linguistic philosophy" (or "modern" or "Oxford" or later "analytic") for the scrutiny of Chinese concepts. The deepest satisfaction was in working one's way inside a conceptual scheme so remote from our own, the focus of attention always on distinctions rather than resemblances, distinctions sometimes deep in the structures of the Chinese and Indo-European languages, and in discovering how they undermine one's own presuppositions. The ideas of another culture are for me never directly borrowable, but have complex and indirect influences on oneself which one is in no position to analyze; it comes as a surprise to me when, as sometimes happens, I am said to be a Taoist. (This immersion in China, by the way, is bookish rather than lived; I did not get to mainland China, long closed to Westerners, until 1980, and even my wife Der Pao, whom I met in Hong Kong in 1954, has never been able to get me speaking Chinese well.)

Of interest also was the variety of modes of thinking inside the tradition, in particular the extremes of rationalism in the Later Mohists and anti-rationalism in Chuang-tzu, and the explicitly correlative instead of analytic thinking of Yin-Yang philosophy. Progress in understanding seemed to threaten a relativistic chaos, but the effect was rather a multi-perspectival view in which things seemed to show up more clearly than when seeing from the perspective of the West alone. The fear of relativism diminished, but I can still say with Hugo Ball, founder of Dada: "I have examined myself carefully. I could never bid chaos welcome".[1]

From 1967, after running into hippies in San Francisco and Kyoto, the counterculture and student activism recalled me to the present day, and shook up my values, tastes, and thoughts. It became vaguely apparent that the *Problem of Value* was not the last word, but the compulsion to philosophise for myself did not yet revive. On 14 November 1970, while experimenting with a mixture of black coffee and hashish recommended as having interesting effects by a friend experienced in psychedelics, a vague and mystical meditation on consciousness evoked a visual image of light fluctuating in all directions from and back to a point at the centre of a sphere. The point was myself, the sphere the body, the light a unification of willing and knowing; good was the impulse outward to irradiate the body and the objects beyond it, bad was the contrary impulse to flinch back to the point. The stream of thoughts springing from this image, instead of turning out to be nonsense, quickly became clearer and more rational, and obsessed me for ten days. This characteristic example of Popper's "irrational element" deserves mention because for myself it was a dramatic illustration of the sub-rational beginnings of rational thought, and the date is noted here because it was the clearly defined start of all my thinking about awareness and spontaneity, and of my second solution of the two problems (fact/value, egoism/altruism) which continued to be central to me. In my attempts to discuss these matters with professional philosophers I found most of them happier to hear about my sinological work, rather as Groucho Marx on meeting T. S. Eliot found him much more interested in his films than in his prepared comments on *The Wasteland,* and the evolution of the idea over the next decade (side by side with research on the Mohist *Canons* and later on Chuang-tzu) was in almost complete isolation, although there came to be a few professional philosophers, such as my good friend Henry Rosemont, who crossed the wall separating university departments of philosophy and of Oriental studies sometimes geographically only a few hundred yards apart. The original essay after my hashish revelation in 1970, unrecognisable through its transformations, finally became "Value, Fact and Facing Facts", published by the *Journal of Value Inquiry* in 1985, and reprinted here with a few more retouches. My thinking was further isolated from what was going on in contemporary philosophy by my having lost interest in the analytic school, which seemed to be finally reducing the Love of Wisdom to an unnecessary branch of modern technology, but without my yet having outgrown its distrust of contemporary continental schools. (How extraordinary that I remain more receptive to the most far out of Taoists than to Heidegger, whom I still cannot read!) Eventually I settled down to write *Reason and Spontaneity* (1985) as, like Nietzsche's *Zarathustra,* "a book for everyone and no one". I was beginning to notice continental hermeneutics and deconstruction but did not want to rethink fundamentals again too soon, and put off reading Gadamer and Derrida until the book was in the press. There are both advantages and disadvantages in coming from outside professional philosophy; which of them prevail in *Reason and Spontaneity,* and in the present book, it is for others to judge. The same line of thought opened the way to a history of early Chinese philosophy from a new direction, *Disputers of the Tao: Philosophical Argument in Ancient China* (1989), which had the authority of my acknowledged competence. In 1989 and 1990, during semesters in the Philosophy Department of the University of Hawaii, one of the few where East and West come together, I was pleasantly surprised to find myself working with professional philosophers who took both books seriously.

• • •

The present book is a collection of independent papers, published or unpublished, on a wide variety of themes. Most of them, however, approach from one direction or other the relation between the logical and the pre-logical. Several contrast the Western and Chinese traditions, which employ logical and pre-logical thinking in very different proportions.

Karl Popper in *The Logic of Scientific Discovery* wrote that the validity of a theory has nothing to do with its origin and depends solely on its survival of stringent tests. "There is no such thing as a logical method of having new ideas . . . every discovery contains an 'irrational element', or 'a creative intuition' in Bergson's sense".[2] The scientist starts from "the stimulation and release of an inspiration," but in establishing the truth of the theory "he critically judges, alters and rejects his own inspiration." Only the tests of the theory belong to the logic of knowledge; its origin is to be relegated to the psychology of knowledge.

It may occur to one that this claim might be put in very different terms. There may be an indefinite variety of modes of thinking by which we arrive at knowledge; among these the logical, the analytic, "reason" in its narrow sense, the only one which concerns Popper, has the humble task of formulating and testing the results of the rest, and also of showing how their various functions are related within a psychology of knowledge. But in that case it may be necessary, even in philosophy, to take account of the thinking which is pre-logical, on which reason depends if it is to have anything but its own malfunctions to test, in order to view reason itself from a wider perspective. It might be that some of the problems of philosophy arise from treating logical operations as a self-contained realm independent of the hit-or-miss thinking with which we conduct so much of our lives.

Thus analytic thinking strives to define its terms by each other, pursuing identity/difference and dismissing the relatively similar to the loose argument from analogy on the borders of logic, and to the similes and metaphors of poetry. When it discovers that the ideal of full mutual definability is unattainable outside logic and mathematics, and that it must work with terms based on classifications by vague and shifting similarities which are often Wittgensteinian "family resemblances" in which *A* is like *B* and *B* like *C* but *C* not like *A,* it may seem that all the structures it erects are built on quicksand. But if we proceed up to the logical instead of down to the pre-logical, and observe how words assume their meanings, in constant change without our noticing, by the continuing and spontaneous process of assimilating and contrasting, linking and detaching, and structuring by correlation of the similar/contrasting and contiguous/remote which Jakobson finds at the roots of language,[3] with analysis for the most part entering only to clarify muddled concepts, we may wonder why reason has ever entertained ambitions above even its high station to operate exclusively with terms spun out of itself. We may suspect also that it is not only at the level of the words from which it starts that reason is playing on the surface of correlative thinking; the logical in general may be dependent on the pre-logical, in relative security as long as it remains on the alert to test it wherever it may be going wrong, to test, for example, respects in which things are similar. The suspicion is confirmed when we find ourselves forced to concede that science is not built on reason and observation alone but presupposes the similarity of a problem to cases it takes as paradigmatic, and that even when failure to reach a solution suggests that the similarity does not hold, it cannot infer a new Kuhnian paradigm, can only await a spontaneous paradigm-switch set off by the "irrational element" in some innovating scientist's creative thought. Science as a self-contained system, if it cannot be sure of its presuppositions, or even what they are, seems to float in a void. But the proto-science which prevailed before Galileo was still a pre-logical structuring of a cosmos by correlation of the similar/contrasting and contiguous/remote; and if we see modern science as not necessarily any different in the course of its creative thinking but distinguished by testing results by more stringent criteria, science is relieved of the duty of eliminating unproved presuppositions. It is not a matter of groundlessly presupposing, but of there being pre-logical stages in the thought which reason at the last stage formulates and tests. Or again, analytic thinking cannot relate statements in different languages unless the languages are intertranslatable; when it is seen that the relativity of similarity/contrast allows different languages to classify differently, imposing conceptual schemes which cut up the world into pieces of different shapes, the faith in intertranslatability collapses, and it appears that the truth of a proposition presupposes the validity of the scheme to which it belongs, yet no scheme has a better claim to validity than another. But speaking and understanding are by a spontaneous correlative process interrupted only when an occasion for analysis arises, to resolve some terminological, grammatical, or other doubt; and we understand other languages by the same process, replaced by translation only when one fails to understand. If one starts from the correlative stage which precedes analysis, it no longer seems that there is an ungrounded presupposition behind acceptance of a proposition as true. Confirmation by reason and observation of statements in different languages also confirms that the initial classifications, although different, were equally adequate for arriving at these particular true statements, irrespective of whether the languages are intertranslatable. The relativity of

8

similarity/contrast implies rather that one needs more than one classification, and that the more perspectives from which one views by multiplying languages the better one will see; if all languages were intertranslatable we would all be trapped in a single classification, which might prove permanently inadequate to the solution of problems to which it is unfitted.

Turning now to philosophy of value, for analytic thinking my knowledge of myself and my situation has first to be laid down in factual propositions. These could include propositions about desires and aversions, and also about changes in them caused by changing knowledge of self and situation, and about changes in my eagerness or reluctance to know. But none of these propositions answers the question "What shall I do?", for which I need prudential or moral standards. These, however, remain unsupported unless value can be derived in some other way from fact, or from a standard valid a priori. For those who deny both possibilities, reason isolated from other thinking leaves one of its realms, the logic of value judgments, dangling without support. However, things look different if we treat analysis as not sufficient to itself but as starting from and testing pre-logical kinds of awareness. It is plain that my awareness of myself is not entirely a matter of accepting propositions about myself. The same applies even to awareness of my situation; my likes and dislikes veer with fine discriminations of smell, taste, figure, and colour, which are prior to the broader contrasts marked by the vocabulary of my language. In the simplest case, where I am nearest to the animal, my thinking, if one can yet call it thinking, is becoming alert and focussing attention where it is attracted, withdrawing it where it is repelled, with my desires and aversions changing as I become aware of change, or myself change between welcoming and shrinking from awareness. I am unquestionably thinking when I use all my resources, including logic, if necessary, to extend and intensify awareness of my situation or of my own obscure or suppressed preferences; but my changing inclinations to act one way or another may still remain spontaneous, not deliberated but caused by the objects of awareness. If I now ask myself whether the goal to which I find myself moved is a good one, or of two alternatives the right one, whether therefore it is an end to which it is rational to choose means, an answer will follow from the mere acknowledgment that it is better to choose in awareness than in ignorance; the only test required will be whether or not further scrutiny reveals something overlooked which would have made me react differently. Whether value can be derived from fact is here irrelevant; instead of a presumed logical connexion between described fact and prescribed act, we have a causal connexion between becoming aware and being moved to act (being moved at least incipiently is the consequence of becoming aware, letting myself be so moved is a condition of becoming aware). The value of the goal to which I am moved then follows directly from the value of awareness, which will be the same as the value which in analysing propositions I ascribe to truth. This is not to be dismissed as a marginal case, it seems on the contrary to be the representative one. In general we do acknowledge that even in the most rational persons changes in values and tastes are largely spontaneous (they may be unnoticed by oneself until past behaviour begins to be recollected as silly or immature), and judge that when they follow increasing knowledge and experience they are changes *for the better,* without insisting that they follow logically rather than causally. Without this pre-logical thinking behind it analysis would have nothing to start from. If the situation which moves me is a recurrent one, I may lay down the course on which it moves me as to be followed again if it recurs, which is to formulate a standard. It is only at this stage that I can make decisions by analytic thinking alone, from the logical implications of standards combined with factual propositions. But in practical thinking we seldom appeal to prudential standards, we ponder only the situation and leave motivations to action to take care of themselves; the solution by analytic thinking alone is the exception rather than the norm.

Analytic thinking which relies on its resources alone has a further difficulty in passing from prudence to morals. It can take account of one's awareness of other people only as the knowledge of propositions about them. My own ends provide good reason for choosing my means, factual propositions about others' ends provide no reason for me to choose means to them; and if it happens that I do adopt their ends as my own that is an accidental fact about me. Moral philosophy thus becomes another realm of thought loosed from any moorings, reserved for those (the majority admittedly) who do sometimes do things for other people. This is once again to uproot the logical from its soil in the pre-logical. The assimilating and contrasting from which thinking starts includes the incipient simulation, turning observed behaviour inside out, by which we try to understand others from within, and view ourselves as we look from outside. Observation and reason test and train this erratic awareness through simulation, in which we think, feel, and in consequence, are moved to act from other viewpoints; pre-logical as it is, it cannot simply be replaced by the propositional knowledge required by analysis. When therefore I begin to analyse, the goals which in a particular situation I select as ends, the ones to which I find myself more inclined the more aware I become, will be the ones to which I incline from all the viewpoints I assume in becoming aware of the others involved in the situation, not merely from my own. There is then no logically unbridgeable gap between the ends of self and others. If a child behaves selfishly, and one asks, "How would you like it if someone did that to you?", a question crucially important in elevating moral education above a mere training in obedience, it may seem that one is only speaking emotively to excite unselfish reactions. But one is asking him to *think*, to put himself in the other person's place, the cognitive act without which knowledge of others would be solely of external behaviour, and then discover for himself how his selfish impulse is modified by his dislike of it from the other's point of view. If we exclude this indispensable kind of thinking from moral philosophy, and insist on purely logical demonstrations, we are left with nothing to start from but the standards which we happen to have been trained to obey.

Even in philosophy the pre-logical is not always a buried layer to be uncovered; there are fields where it still obstinately refuses to be trodden under. We may instance the prolonged efforts of moral philosophers to reformulate the Golden Rule of Jesus: "Therefore all things whatsoever ye would men should do to you, do ye even so to them", or "And as ye would that men should do to you, do ye also to them likewise".[4] Since they are compelled to understand the "even so" (*houtōs*), "as" (*kathōs*), and "likewise" (*homoiōs*) as affirming not similarity but identity, they find the Golden Rule open to such objections as that people may want things which are bad for them, and that others may not want what you want. It has proved extremely difficult to find a formula which escapes the objections, as the attempts of Kant and his successors illustrate, so that a rule which has been guiding moral discourse for a couple of thousand years becomes for the analytic mind a principle so muddled that it seems a mystery how it can ever have been usable. But a rule laid down by Jesus, with Confucius and Gautama as his predecessors, and never noticed by the Greeks, will be assuming similarity rather than identity. It will not have transcended the pre-logical weighing of disparate goals, by letting conflicting impulses interact and converge on new goals; this, to the extent that one is aware of the situation to which one is responding, is an intelligent process which analysis helps to discipline but cannot supersede, since the "weighing" is of factors to which we are sensitive and responsive but which are only very crudely enumerable or measurable. In a multi-perspectival view proportioned to the actual goals of all concerned, impulses from different viewpoints will in interacting diverge from their own goals but correlate with them in the ratio: "What I am moved to do to others : their goals :: what I am moved to demand from others : my goals."

This suggests an explanation of why the Golden Rule is in practice easily comprehensible. We understand it as correlative: "Let what you do to others be to what they want as what you demand from others is to what you want." Loosely expressed in such a form as "Do as you would be done by", it carries conviction to all who do recognise that thinking about people includes "putting oneself in their places" in order to "understand their points of view", and do as a fact of experience correlate thus when becoming aware from other people's viewpoints. We suggest that an analysis of pre-logical thinking by simulation and correlation justifies this conviction, while an analysis detached from the pre-logical, which collapses all the similarities into identities ("Do to others what you demand of them that they do to you"), and then tries to avoid objections by a more refined formula such as Kant's ("Act only on that maxim through which you can at the same time will that it should be a universal law"), neither arrives at a satisfactory imperative nor gives us any reason to make the jump from selfish to altruistic ends. This failure is inevitable as long as analytic thinking remains incestuous, refusing intercourse with the pre-logical as not its kin.

One further example before leaving this preliminary sketch of arguments most of which will be developed further in the course of the book. The project of Descartes was to establish all truths by logic alone, employing sense perception, of course, but only after deducing a priori that the senses do not deceive us. For a long time, however, we have dispensed with this proviso, content to acknowledge that reason can function outside logic and mathematics only by building on the evidence of the senses, which it questions and criticises only when this evidence is contradictory. This is precisely the relation to reason which we propose to extend from perception to other kinds of thinking than the logical, from which, however, perception has been presumed to differ in affording a direct access to the object prior to judgments of relative similarity and contrast. Although it has long been recognised that perception combines sensation with interpretation, this did not threaten the autonomy of analytic thinking as long as it was assumed that the interpretation was itself a submerged logical inference. But by now it has become impossible to draw a line between perception and the kinds of thinking we call pre-logical. Without attempting a full account of the synthesising of the evidence of the senses into wholes, gestalts, it will be sufficient to stick to our recurrent theme, and note that in perceiving we are already classifying on the dimensions not only of contiguity/remoteness but of similarity/contrast. This is plain, for example, from the ambiguous figures studied in the psychology of perception, such as the one interpretable as the head either of a duck or of a rabbit[5]; not only are we guided by the similarities to both figures to *see* it alternately as one or the other, we find it impossible to see the shape neutrally, as neither. There is a corresponding switch on the dimension of contiguity/ remoteness; an inconspicuous mark which does not belong to the figure of the duck becomes the mouth of the rabbit. When we look at the constellation Orion, we know that we see a constellation only because the stars are contiguous from a viewpoint on earth, and that a sufficiently ancient Greek who believed that the hero Orion ascended into the sky could be led to see him there by the similarity to his belt of a row of bright stars. But if factual knowledge depends on pre-logical assimilation right down to the level of perception, why should we suppose, for example, that moral knowledge can dispense with the assimilation by incipient simulation through which we understand the people to whom we behave morally or immorally?

It may be said that logical thinking supplies "knowledge", pre-logical only untested "opinion". Without quarrelling with this usage of the words, we may notice that the tests which convert opinion into knowledge are sometimes no more than confirmations that the pre-logical thinking which arrived at the opinion is reliable, even that it is more reliable in the given circumstances than logical thinking would be. Thus the insight into similarity, unreliable as it is in fields remote from us, as in proto-scientific cosmologies, is very highly trained for objects of daily experience, as in recognition of a face. When my wife enters the room, a momentary glance takes in the relevant similarities to the woman as I have previously seen her, unerringly dismissing any difference as irrelevant; I know that it is her, not only as a matter of subjective certainty, but because the fact of daily companionship for many years is sufficient evidence that in this case the primal skill at assimilating and contrasting will be very nearly infallible. To analyse the figure I now see, in order to judge whether all relevant parts are identical with hers and identically related, would, even assuming that my memory is sufficient for it, either continue the process of differentiation for ever, or else halt at the roughly identical, which would neither escape the relativity of similarity nor attain the near certainty of instant recognition. I have much better reason for being sure it is my wife than that space-time is curved, which we accept as well-tested knowledge without denying that Einstein's physics may in due course prove inadequate like Newton's. No mode of thinking, poetic, mythic, mystical, whatever you please, is to be called irrational merely because it is pre-logical, but it is irrational to accept it without having a test which it satisfies. Rationality is intelligence excusing none of its varieties from logical tests. Logicality itself is only one of the varieties, and not necessarily the most important for judging someone intelligent. Reason in the narrow sense can presume too much on being the capacity which distinguishes human from animal; an exclusively logical mind, if such is conceivable, would be less than animal, logical operations being the human activity most easily duplicated by a computer. Why should we assume that even in philosophy it is safe to isolate them from the rest of intelligence? As long as we persist in doing so, rationality will seem like a sinking ship in which philosophy goes on finding new leaks, in spite of all the scientific and technological feats which confirm that it is in better shape than ever. We must acknowledge that Popper's "irrational element" is more than an element and unjustly termed irrational, but also learn from him that the kind of rationalism still viable today is his "critical rationalism".

NOTES

1. Hugo Ball, *Flight Out of Time: A Dada Diary* (New York: Viking Press, 1974), p. 19.
2. Karl R. Popper, *The Logic of Scientific Discovery* (London: Hutchinson, revised edition 1972), p. 31f.
3. See chapters 4 and 6 below.
4. *Matthew* 7.12, *Luke* 6.31.
5. Versions of the duck-rabbit figure are reproduced, for example, in Ludwig Wittgenstein, *Philosophical Investigations* (Oxford: Blackwell, 1953), II, xi, and E. H. Gombrich, *Art and Illusion*, 5th ed. (London: Phaidon Press, 1977), p. 4.

Value, Fact and Facing Facts

1

In choosing how to act we are accustomed to recognise an imperative, "Face facts", which imposes itself whenever emotional bias makes us reluctant to acknowledge things as they are. It seems irrelevant to the fundamental problems of ethics, since we would no more expect to derive prudential or moral ends from facts combined with this imperative than from the facts alone. However, the welcoming or resisting of facts is a psychological process in causal interaction with spontaneous inclination; on the one hand bias distorts judgment, on the other desire or aversion veers with additional information. This would appear to be one of the cases in which we have to abandon the generally convenient assumption that the object can be analysed without taking into account its interactions with the subject. It would therefore seem arguable that to let oneself be moved towards one goal rather than another might be a causally necessary condition of obeying "Face facts", in which case this imperative would be sufficient for choosing ends from among spontaneously emerging goals. If so, there may be possibilities of illuminating the relation between fact and value by approaching it from a new direction.

Let us imagine, as the first dawning of objective thought, a child wanting another helping at dinner, remembering what it is like to be sick, and telling himself what he has often been told by his mother, 'Don't, or you'll be ill!' Up to this moment he has always behaved as spontaneously as an animal, surrendering to appetite and vomiting; now for the first time he makes a considered choice. (We describe as "spontaneous" all activity which is not the result of a considered choice.) What will be the logical form of his thought? A common answer would be to fit it into some form of the practical syllogism:

Shall I eat it or not?
You don't want to be sick.
Another helping will make you sick.
Therefore don't eat it.

But this formulation is open to the objection that it appears to derive a prescriptive conclusion from two descriptive premisses. One might avoid the objection, following R. M. Hare (*The Language of Morals*, Oxford, I.3.2), by interpreting 'You don't want to be sick' as itself prescriptive, a logical imperative equivalent to 'Don't get sick' disguised by the grammatically indicative form. On this interpretation, whenever one rejects practical advice by repudiating the assumed end, in the words 'But I don't want that!', one is declaring 'I don't recognise any imperative to do that'. Yet the end would be repudiated even more strongly by a 'But I don't feel the slightest inclination to do that!', which is unmistakably expressive of a spontaneous revulsion. Moreover the interpretation misplaces the centre of imperative force in the child's situation. He does not have to appeal to an imperative obliging him to avoid the sickness from the thought of which he already shrinks in nausea; what he has to force himself to do is hold on to the fact that sickness is the likely outcome if he yields to temptation. Under the pressure of this unwelcome fact, he is being spontaneously pulled between the revulsion when he remembers and the greed when he forgets. In taking this first step to rational choice, the single imperative which imposes itself is none other than "Face facts", which has exerted its authority from his first recognition of the obstinate resistance of external circumstance to his desires. The form of his thought will be something like this:

Overlooking the fact I find myself moved to eat, facing the fact I find myself moved to refrain.
In which direction shall I let myself be moved?
Face facts.
Therefore let yourself be moved to refrain.

This illustration confirms our suspicion that the causal interaction between facing facts and spontaneous inclination renders baseless the assumption that, since no imperative conclusions may be drawn from the facts to be faced, the imperative "Face facts" may be dismissed as trivial. The child's greed is obstructing awareness of consequences the facing of which would cause him to refrain; therefore to let the impulse to refrain prevail over the impulse to eat is a causally necessary condition of obeying the imperative. If he succumbs after all the temptation and suffers the consequences, it would be to the point to say 'You should have known better' or 'You ought to have had more sense', reproaches which derive their authority from "Face facts"; but it would be irrelevant (and exasperating) to say 'You shouldn't have made yourself ill like that', on the authority of the 'You don't want to be sick' of the practical syllogism interpreted as 'Don't get sick'. From the imperative to refrain on this occasion the child may advance, as he observes the situation recur in his own or others' experience, to his first universal principle, 'One ought not to eat too much'; but even this principle would very probably be first encountered by him as 'Sensible people don't eat too much'.

While the first formula (the practical syllogism) served choices of means, the second served choices of ends. The motions in causal interaction with the facing of facts are incipient motions towards goals, spontaneous desires or aversions, and to prefer one inclination in the light of "Face facts" is to choose its goal as an end. At first the prevailing inclination will issue immediately in action, but with increasing rationality the child will learn to suspend action in order to take further goals into account. Later still he may train himself to eradicate the desire or aversion itself, releasing himself from one causally necessary condition of facing facts, so that the formula is no longer directly applicable; but that will be in the service of other ends, and unless he can discover some new way of validating them these will be chosen by applying the same formula to other spontaneous goals. He will also learn to clarify his ends; originally he saw no further than immediate goals, the satisfaction of hunger and the relief from nausea; later he conceptualizes the nourishing of the body by food and the danger to health of overeating, and it is towards or away from these that he now finds himself spontaneously pulled.

Of the second formula, we may observe:

1. It applies "Face facts" to a particular choice, without assuming any other universal imperative; but the imperative may also be applied to a

19

general choice for a recurring situation, which is to ordain a standard ('One ought not to eat too much'). Such standards, like factual generalisations, will always be criticisable by reference to particular cases.

2. It chooses as ends only particular and transitory goals, to which one is spontaneously moved; but it allows generalisation from them to more general and long-term ends (such as nourishing the body).

3. It does not require any principle for weighing spontaneous inclinations, for example a hedonist principle by which vomiting is to be avoided as unpleasant. One is simply moved one way or the other in greater or lesser awareness. If we are to use the metaphor of weighing, in choices of means the agent is the weigher, but in choices of ends he is the arm of the balance itself.

4. It requires no criterion for the relevance of facts which is not implicit in the formula itself. The 'fact' of the first premiss covers all fact awareness of which would modify spontaneous reactions to the particular issue in question; "Face facts" will be applicable to the issue only within the scope of this information. The test of relevance will be whether awareness of a fact does act causally on spontaneous inclination. That the dish is tasty and that another helping will upset the stomach are relevant facts because they do modify inclination; that it is a rainy or a sunny day and that the wallpaper is yellow or white are irrelevant because they do not move the child in either direction.

5. Different though it is from the practical syllogism, it resembles it in that its conclusions are always revisable in the light of further information, which imposes itself as relevant whenever it does turn out to alter spontaneous reaction.

As the child matures in rationality he will arrive at further standards of the type of 'One ought not to eat too much', by choosing between his long-term inclinations, in general and recurring situations, whether confirming the standards externally imposed on him or discovering new ones of his own, until he has developed a code of conduct with more or less consistent principles; but however logically the code is elaborated it will never, unless he can find new grounds for imperatives, have any other authority than his choices between spontaneous tendencies in the light of "Face facts". Is it possible to find such new grounds? Throughout the history of ethical thinking there have of course been many attempts to detach imperatives wholly from inclination and back them by divine authority, or validate them a priori, or derive them from psychological, sociological, or biological generalisations at the cost of a leap from "is" to "ought". But if, as we shall assume, all such attempts have failed, it must be acknowledged that we can never escape from the child's limitation of having no grounds for rational choice except between directions in which he is already being spontaneously pulled. To some this limitation may seem incompatible with the autonomy of the fully rational agent, but it may be questioned whether this impression has anything more behind it than an unexamined habit of thought. Rational people do in general pursue, and at their more moral help each other to pursue, what they spontaneously want, or are expected to want in fuller awareness of themselves and their conditions; the liberal and rationalist tradition even tends to reject as irrational any standard which requires us to act otherwise.

It is time to look more closely at the imperative for which we have so far been getting along on a rough formulation, "Face facts". Since we are using it to infer ends, we cannot treat it simply as prescribing a means necessary to achievement of one's ends whatever they may be, which is what the admonishment rather suggests in ordinary discourse (with the implication 'If you don't you'll suffer for it'). The imperative we require is the one implicit in "X is real", "X exists", "'X' is true", judgments which commit one to taking X into account in choices. We may formulate it as "Be aware of X", and define "aware" as being disposed to take into account in choices. We speak of "awareness" rather than "knowledge" because what concerns us is a highly variable capacity to take facts, sensations, and inclinations into account, by no means guaranteed by knowing in the abstract. Although one can speak also of being aware of the value of something, it will be essential to confine our usage to awareness of the existing, of persons, things, events. We shall then have a bridge between fact and value which does not, as in naturalistic theories of morals, depend on trying to derive the latter from the former. Since it is a contradiction to say that something exists yet need not be taken into account in choices to which if existing it is relevant, "Be aware of everything relevant to the issue" is valid a priori. (This would not exclude the possibility that, as a matter of psychological fact, awareness of something may interfere causally with awareness of something else, so that a local unawareness may be a causally necessary condition of obeying "Be aware".) We shall require a corresponding adaptation of the second formula, which we put in quasi-syllogistic form.

In awareness of everything relevant to the issue (= everything which would spontaneously move me one way or the other), I find myself moved towards X, overlooking something relevant I find myself moved towards Y.

Be aware of everything relevant to the issue.

Therefore let yourself be moved towards X (= choose X as an end).

One would commit oneself to being aware of *everything* relevant as one does to "All men are mortal" in the classical syllogism, for example, by Popper's criterion, a continued failure to refute.

One consequence of basing an ethic on "Be aware" will be to extend to value the neutrality as to spatial, temporal, and personal viewpoints which is claimed for fact. I make myself aware of a three-dimensional object by synthesising what I perceive from here with what I imagine from there, of a continuing event by synthesising what I perceive now with what I remember from past and anticipate from future viewpoints; and in either case "Be aware" obliges me to let myself be moved from the different viewpoints, as a causally necessary condition of becoming aware from them. In choosing between the goals towards which I spontaneously tend, I may find myself being excited more strongly by what I perceive here and now than by what I imagine from other viewpoints, so that, for example, a present amusement obliterates awareness of a future danger. Then "Be aware" prescribes awareness from the future viewpoint, and letting myself be moved to avert the danger. Now awareness of other persons similarly depends on synthesising perception of their bodies with imagining and feeling from their viewpoints, and awareness of myself on synthesising imagination of my body from other viewpoints with perceiving and feeling from my own; otherwise I would become, to vary Ryle's metaphor, a ghost in the company of machines, no longer aware that I resemble other people in the respects in which they resemble each other. "Be aware" therefore prescribes the same neutrality as to personal as to spatial and temporal viewpoints; it refuses a privileged status to "I" as to "here" and "now". But if "Be aware" requires me to be aware both of you and of myself both from your viewpoint and from mine, it requires me also to be moved towards both your goals and mine, as a necessary condition of becoming aware from both viewpoints. We may therefore propose as a specialisation of our quasi-syllogism:

> In awareness from all spatial, temporal and personal viewpoints which are relevant to the issue (= viewpoints from which I do find myself spontaneously moved in one direction or the other) I find myself moved towards X, overlooking a relevant viewpoint I find myself moved towards Y.
> Be aware from all relevant viewpoints.
> Therefore let yourself be moved towards X (a goal which may be here or there, now or then, yours or mine).

Here the prospect of building an ethic on spontaneity and awareness reveals an unexpected advantage. Moral philosophy more usually starts from the individual pursuing his own ends, and is at once confronted by the question, which it finds extremely difficult to answer, of why he should care for any ends but his own; but the present approach abolishes the priority of the self and shifts the burden of proof to the egoist. An egoist who tries to ground his ethic on "Be aware" would have to break down the analogy between personal and other viewpoints; and to do so he could not appeal to the most obvious difference, that while "here" and "there" are exchanged by the agent's movements, and "now" is continuously changing into "then", he remains to himself unalterably "I". The requirement to perceive or imagine from all relevant viewpoints is wholly independent of whether the viewpoint to which one is confined in perceiving is freely mobile, carried forward by time, or permanently fixed.

The first question which an egoist might raise is why it should be assumed that I cannot be aware from another's viewpoint without being moved towards his goals. The other perceives, I merely imagine; he suffers, I merely simulate his distress by letting myself be moved by what I imagine. He himself is moved to relieve his distress, but why should my imaginative simulation move me to do the same? This objection, it will be noticed, assumes a difference between the emotion and the simulation corresponding to that between perception and imagination. But to simulate a feeling is to feel similarly, just as to simulate a process of thought is to think similarly. When trying to guess where someone went when I missed him at the airport I do not imagine his thoughts, I try to imagine his situation as someone like him would see it, and think; if he tells me he has just learned he has cancer I may hear in imagination the doctor's grave voice, but I do not imagine the fear, I feel the chill of it; if I see him cut his finger I do not imagine the pain as something objective before my "mind's eye", either I look on as though the knife were cutting through cheese or I incipiently wince. Provided that an object is conceived to be real, reactions to it are the same in kind whether one happens to be perceiving or imagining it; and if in the latter case one reacts less strongly, that is because one is also less aware of it. If I explore in imagination a coming danger, I cannot simulate my future fear without already being afraid, and moved to avert the danger. Here the analogy of personal to temporal viewpoints plainly holds. That being moved by imagining from a sufferer's viewpoint does draw me towards his goals is sufficiently shown by my impulse to shrink from imagining, as painful in itself, and liable to draw me into action against my own interests. If there is such a thing as a simulation in the same relation to suffering as imagination to perception, it is in response not to a real but to a fictitious situation; it is the emotion of the actor revelling in the part of a tragic hero.

The egoist might raise a further objection: granted that I do indeed suffer from a sufferer's viewpoint, I generally feel very much less from other viewpoints than from my own: then will not the inclinations I choose in obedience to "Be aware" tend to be self-centered, even if they do not quite fulfill the requirements of a pure philosophical egoism? But to choose the action to which I am moved when most aware it is enough that I find myself so moved when most aware from his viewpoint as well as mine, however briefly; and there will be no need even at that moment to feel his pain as intensely as he does, since a further intensification would not discredit the choice but only move me more strongly in the same direction. In the case of temporal viewpoints this point will be easily conceded. My fear of a remote danger may be almost driven from mind by current emotions; but to decide to take precautions I need no more than the faint tremor as I glimpse what the consequences of neglect would be like, I do not have to attempt a full imaginative realisation of the possible outcome, still less maintain the stimulus to action by living in constant terror until the danger is past. Similarly it may take no more than a momentary pang of empathetic distress to move me spontaneously to give help even at my own cost. That will be sufficient to oblige me to choose the inclination which prevailed while I felt the pang, and which I felt increasing *pari passu* with intensifying awareness, after which choice there will be no need to go on agonising over his plight, which might even impair my efficiency as a helper. I can recognise the choice as right (as I would the choice to prepare for coming danger) however strongly I am inclined to shut off the brief glimpse in order not to be distracted from present and selfish goals. Superficially it may seem reasonable to prefer a firmly held end to a faint altruistic stirring which is easily dismissed. But in the course of developing our case we have found no grounds upon which I could have validly chosen my present ends except that they are the ones to which I spontaneously tended when most aware; on what grounds then could I persist in preferring these ends to a further advance in awareness which would undermine them?

The egoist might now appeal to the difference between awareness and attentiveness. Granted that "*X* exists" or "*X* is real" implies "Be aware of *X*" (= "Be disposed to take *X* into account in choices"), it certainly does not imply "Remain attentive to *X*". But it is only while attentive to someone's suffering that one is distressed by it. The egoist might concede that, since in choosing means to his own ends he has to try to predict others' behaviour, he does find it a practical necessity at times to imagine from their viewpoints at the cost of transiently feeling himself moved in altruistic directions. However, after attention lapses he can retain his insights into another person, and use them in choices of means, without abandoning his long-term egoistic ends for the altruistic goals to which he briefly felt himself drawn; he can therefore claim to have obeyed "Be aware" without ceasing to be an egoist. But awareness outlasts attention (although arrived at, maintained, and renewed by it), and although the distress may cease the motivation to action while attentive lasts as long as one stays aware. Even if it is only for one moment that a spasm in your face draws my attention to the intensity of your pain, a glimpse from which I flinch back into insensibility, it is during that moment that a choice between my conflicting pulls to help and to ignore will be made in fullest awareness; and unless the awareness fades and in obedience to "Be aware" I have to renew it, I need never again revive that excruciating memory.

It is essential to the present argument that the only acceptable reason for pursuing a goal which serves no further end is that, even after emotion fades or attention flags, one continues to be so moved in present awareness: it cannot be merely the *fact* that one was so moved at a moment of exceptional awareness, and *would* be so moved if one were equally aware now. Our quasi-syllogism requires that to choose I have to be aware, not, of course, of all the thoughts and feelings of everyone involved, but of the relatively little about them relevant to the choice— primarily, of how from each viewpoint I find myself moved to act. In my own case, the intensity of present emotion may confuse me about the direction in which, and the extent to which, I am moved, and it may be clear to others that I will not do what in the heat of the moment I promise or threaten; it may be necessary, in order to clarify self-awareness, to resist present emotion and try to see myself through others' eyes as an aid to discovering my genuine inclination. In the case of other persons, the simulation by which I feel from their viewpoints may be confused by the complex emotions it arouses in me, pity, gratitude, envy, cruelty, some of which pull me towards and others against their goals. To become aware of all involved in a situation, whether to make a selfish or unselfish choice or simply to predict their actions, I have to let myself be moved from different viewpoints, including my own, in the same proportions as the agents themselves; it would not be enough to compare external behaviour, since I cannot fully duplicate my self-awareness by observing myself from outside. If another person is more strongly inclined to his goal than I am to mine, I learn it by dismissing irrelevant emotions and discovering myself to be less moved from my own viewpoint than from his. There is no contradiction between saying that I feel my own headache less than your broken leg, but also *feel* more inclined to help you to a doctor than to take an aspirin and lie down. For weighing goals against each other, we are best placed when narrowing attention to the bare consciousness of to what and how much each of us is being moved.

An advantage of this approach is that, although it bases morality on a spontaneous unselfishness when aware from others' viewpoints, the spontaneity assumed is like that of the inclination to prefer long-term to present goals when aware from future viewpoints, so that it raises no questions about human nature; it no more requires us to suppose ourselves naturally altruistic rather than egoistic, than far-sighted rather than improvident. It by-passes the whole question of how far people are in fact capable of awareness of each other and of future prospects, or able to resist the psychological pressures to shrink from such awareness as they have.

We conclude that it is possible to build an ethic on the single imperative "Be aware" applied to particular and general choices between spontaneous inclinations. Its standards would derive from the general choices, but remain provisional and criticisable in terms of the particular.[1]

NOTE

1. This paper, which benefitted from criticisms by Peter Winch and Henry Rosemont, Jr., was first published in 1985 in *Journal of Value Inquiry*. The argument is much more fully developed in *Reason and Spontaneity* (pp. 1–51); the paper is reprinted here as a convenient summary of a thesis assumed throughout the present volume, and also to make revisions to avoid an objection raised by Herbert Fingarette (that I allowed inference to right action from the *fact* that one would be moved to it if more aware) in *Chinese Texts and Philosophical Contexts*, edited by Henry Rosemont, Jr. (La Salle, Illinois: Open Court, 1991), cf. pp. 209–25. A further modification is the expansion of the major premiss of the quasi-syllogism from "Be aware" to the explicitly quantified "Be aware of everything relevant to the issue".

Perspectivism vs. Relativism in Nietzsche

2

The new interest in Nietzsche as epistemologist raised the possibility that his perspectivism offered a way out of the dichotomy of absolutism and relativism. I wish to show that it does indeed offer a way out, more promising than that of more recent pluralisms which no longer call themselves 'relativism'.

Alexander Nehamas twice appeals to a passage in the *Gay Science*[1] which dismisses moral absolutism and relativism as "equally childish".[2] Yet it is at first sight by no means obvious that this expresses more than a pious hope of Nietzsche, even that it is more than an excuse for embracing relativism without abandoning the privilege of affirming his own perspective like an absolutist. Nehamas writes that "Perspectivism does not result in the relativism that holds that any view is as good as any other; it holds that one's own views are the best for oneself without implying that they need be good for anyone else".[3] But to affirm that the massacre of whole peoples is right for me as a Nazi although wrong for you as a Christian or a liberal is surely what is commonly understood by relativism; no relativist can get through life without adopting some code of values as appropriate to himself. If all moral judgments are relative to different codes as measurements are relative to the lengths chosen for yard or meter, then in the former as in the latter case standards are not absolute, yet among people with shared standards an action is indeed right or wrong as the distance from here to there is indeed one hundred yards. We seem to be in some danger of merely renaming "perspectivism" what was formerly relativism, and reserving the latter term for the extreme claim that no one has good reason for judging anything right or wrong even from his own viewpoint, a purely theoretical position like solipsism which we do not expect to meet in practice; then by a mere change of verbal fashion we lose sight of a persisting problem. The promise or the threat in Nietzsche's perspectivism is in his insistence that philosophy can establish an "order of rank" by which the perspective of the Christian or the liberal is revealed as inferior, not indeed to Nazism, but to his own "immoralism". His introduction to the argument of *Genealogy of Morals* culminates in this declaration: "*All* sciences have from now on to prepare the way for the future task of the philosophers: this task understood as the solution of the *problem of value,* the determination of the *order of rank* among values".[4]

This paper will concentrate on the one among Nietzsche's various lines of thought for which perspectivism clearly distinguishes itself from relativism. The justification for distinguishing perspectivism derives from the analogy of knowledge to sight, an analogy which underlies so much of cognitive vocabulary. Observer *A* sees one man, observer *B* sees two, one of whom is from *A*'s viewpoint hidden behind the other. *A* says there is one man, *B* says there are two; shall I as a relativist say that there is indeed one for *A* and two for *B*? No, being familiar with visual perspective I shall judge, having assumed both viewpoints, that *A* is wrong and *B* is right. Throughout much of his work Nietzsche is faithful to the visual analogy, and assumes that the wider the range of perspectives from which one views the better one knows, the nearer one approaches the only kind of objectivity which he recognizes:

> ... "objectivity"—the latter understood not as "contemplation without interest" (which is a nonsensical absurdity), but as the ability *to control* one's Pro and Con and to dispose of them, so that one knows how to employ a *variety* of perspectives and affective interpretations in the service of knowledge ...
>
> There is *only* a perspective seeing, *only* a perspective "knowing"; and the *more* affects we allow to speak about one thing, the *more* eyes, different eyes, we can use to observe one thing, the more complete will our "concept" of this thing, our "objectivity" be.[5]

Thus, in *Ecce Homo* Nietzsche boasts of having "an eye beyond all merely local, merely nationally conditioned perspectives; it is not difficult for me to be a 'good European' ",[6] and declares that "not only have the German historians utterly lost the *great perspective* for the course and the values of culture. . . . they have actually *proscribed* this great perspective. One must first be 'German' and have 'race', then one can decide about all values and disvalues *in historicis*—one *determines* them".[7] Valuation from the perspective of the good European is *superior* to that from the restricted perspective of the German nationalist; it is not simply that their valuations are relative to their viewpoints.

It is inherent in the visual analogy that perspectives are related, not to the persisting and self-centered viewpoints of individuals or communities, but to the vantage-points towards which, as with spatial positions, they direct themselves in order to get the most informative view of the scene. Nietzsche is always searching for the unnoticed perspective from which what he has himself said is revealed to be inadequate; and this constant requestioning is for him not a plunge into skepticism but a strengthening and enriching of knowledge. We learn new viewpoints, not only from the propounding by philosophers of supposedly objective truths, but from the arts and even from the gross errors of religion. Without "the art of staging and watching ourselves", cultivated above all in the theatre, "we would be nothing but foreground and live entirely in the spell of that perspective which makes what is closest at hand and most vulgar appear as if it were vast, and reality itself".[8] We learn even from the misleading viewpoint of a religion which makes us "see the sinfulness of every single individual through a magnifying glass"; "by surrounding him with eternal perspectives, it taught man to see himself from a distance and as something past and whole".[9] The idea of the Eternal Return, of such crucial importance to Nietzsche, springs from the struggle to acknowledge *"the most dangerous point of view"*, from which one sees even the most trivial act as influencing everything to come, so that I can say "Yes" to no moment of my life unless I say it to everything and welcome reliving every moment; "in this tremendous perspective of effectiveness all actions appear equally great and small".[10]

In his very varied discussions of truth and knowledge, Nietzsche may be seen as ranging between two poles; at one he rejects their very possibility, at the other he dismisses the all-or-nothing truths affirmed from single perspectives only to insist on the more-or-less of truth in multi-perspectival views. A passage which actually uses the term "perspectivism *(perspektivismus)*" declares that "we simply lack any organ for knowledge, for 'truth'; we 'know' (or believe, or imagine) just as much as may be *useful* in the interests of the human herd, the species"[11]—and goes on to pronounce even the utility imaginary too. This approach is especially prominent in the notes, not necessarily fully considered for publication, which were posthumously collected as *The Will to Power;* these detach the order of rank among values from any relation to truth ("What determines rank, sets off rank, is only quanta of power and nothing else".)[12] But it is the second approach which prevails in *Ecce Homo,* Nietzsche's final summing-up of his intellectual history:

> How much truth does a spirit *endure,* how much truth does it *dare?* More and more that became for me the real measure of value. . . . *Nitimur in vetitum:* in this sign my philosophy will triumph some day, for what one has forbidden so far as a matter of principle has always been—truth alone.[13]

> This ultimate, most joyous, most wantonly extravagant Yes to life represents not only the highest insight but also the *deepest,* that which is most strictly confirmed and born out by truth and science. Nothing in existence may be subtracted, nothing is dispensable—those aspects of existence which Christians and other nihilists repudiate are actually on an infinitely higher level in the order of rank among values than that which the instinct of decadence could approve and call good. To comprehend this requires courage and, as a condition of that, an excess of strength: for precisely as far as courage may venture forward, precisely according to that measure of strength one approaches the truth. Knowledge, saying Yes to reality, is just as necessary for the strong as cowardice and the flight from reality—as the "ideal" is for the weak, who are inspired by weakness.[14]

The two approaches are not at bottom incompatible; one of them repudiates the "knowledge" and "truth" of metaphysics, credited with objectivity in the sense of 'contemplation without interest';[15] the other acknowledges the subjective/objective distinction as we draw it in practical life, where, whatever my philosophy, how much money I have left in the bank is an objective fact which may be obscured for me by subjective factors (wishful thinking, absence of mind). But it is only through the latter approach that perspectivism is seen to diverge from relativism. Another passage which in the standard translation uses the term "perspectivism" (this time for *das perspektivische)* equates the order of rank among values with the degree to which the urge to life escapes from narrow into wider perspectives:

You shall learn to grasp the sense of perspective in every value judgment—the displacement, distortion, and merely apparent teleology of horizons and whatever else pertains to perspectivism; also the quantum of stupidity which resides in antitheses of values and the whole intellectual loss which every For, every Against costs us. You shall learn to grasp the *necessary* injustice in every For and Against, injustice as inseparable from life, life itself as *conditioned* by the sense of perspective and its injustice. You shall above all see with your own eyes where injustice is always at its greatest: where life has developed at its smallest, narrowest, neediest, most incipient, and yet cannot avoid taking *itself* as the goal and measure of things and for the sake of its own preservation secretly and meanly and ceaselessly crumbling away and calling into question the higher, greater, richer—you shall see with your own eyes the problem of *order of rank,* and how power and right and spaciousness of perspective grow into the heights together.[16]

Nothing in Nietzsche's philosophy is so unusual as the frankness with which he flaunts his own personal tastes; it might seem that no thinker could sink more openly into subjectivism. He derides the old saw *De gustibus non disputandum,* affirms that on the contrary only tastes are worth disputing over. But this open appeal to his own likes and dislikes is possible because he does not think of preferences as inferred from principles but as springing from the force of life which he comes to identify as the Will to Power, and as driving us towards one or other perspective but themselves spontaneously changing direction with changes of information and of perspective. When we decide to suppress a drive "our intellect is only the blind instrument of *another drive* which is the *rival* of the drive whose vehemence is tormenting us", and *"that* one *desires* to combat the vehemence of a drive at all, however, does not stand within our own power".[17] Before decisions we ponder the consequences of alternative courses, and find "in our *picture of the consequences* of a certain action a *motive* for performing this action, yes! *one* motive!"; but at the same time "there come into play motives in part unknown to us, in part known very ill, which we can *never* take account of *beforehand",* so that "although I certainly learn what I finally *do,* I do not learn which motive has therewith actually proved victorious".[18] Since reason can in any case do no more than alter the balance of spontaneous and partially hidden forces, it is pointless to lament the loss of firm principles of action since the death of God: *"To reassure the sceptic.—*'I have no idea how I am *acting!* I have no idea how I *ought to act!'*—You are right, but be sure of this: *you will be acted upon!* at every moment! Mankind has in all ages confused the active and the passive: it is their everlasting grammatical blunder".[19]

This position has become a commonplace since Freud, but without its radical implications being drawn. However rationally, against the grain of all my prejudices, I develop a "picture of the consequences of a certain action", if at the deep springs of motivation I shall still simply be reacting to it spontaneously, then to let myself react at least incipiently in whichever direction it moves me will be a causally necessary condition of coming to picture the consequences; a mere imperative to know these consequences will, other things being equal, commit me to prefer this course, and the fact/value distinction is by-passed. Nietzsche is not, therefore, trusting irrationally to his own tastes; granted the value of truth and objectivity, in the senses which his second approach recognises, his spontaneous preferences have *improved* as he progressed to a wider and more fully informed perspective. This way of grounding valuation, quite foreign to the philosophical mainstream which runs through Kant, is implicit in others who refuse to detach thinking from feeling; I argue elsewhere that it underlies, for example, the whole tradition of Chinese philosophy, and that it has a hidden logic which may be uncovered and put in quasi-syllogistic form.[20]

We may now understand why the perspectivism of *Genealogy of Morals*, whatever our objections to the argument, is not to be confused with relativism. Nietzsche insists in the first place that an inquiry into morals requires a tremendous quantity of information, from history, linguistics, physiology, medicine.

> The question: what is the *value* of this or that table of values and "morals"? should be viewed from the most divers perspectives; for the problem "Value *for what?*" cannot be examined too subtly. . . . The well-being of the majority and the well-being of the few are opposite viewpoints of value; to consider the former *a priori* of higher value may be left to the naiveté of English biologists.[21]

He proceeds to argue that Christian and liberal values are desirable only from the viewpoint of the majority, the weak, who are disposed to hate life because they are losers in the struggle for power; from the perspective of the few, the strong, who can love life because it favors them, these values are contemptible. In exploring from both directions, he comes to approve the values of the lovers of life, enriched however by insights from the subtle intelligence evolved by the weak in defending themselves against their oppressors. The reader is *not* asked to become a simple convert to Nietzsche's values, which spring from a blending of perspectives unique to himself. However, the reader cannot accept the argument without himself transcending what he must then regard as the restricted perspective of the majority, his Christian or liberal values will fall away from him, and whatever the direction he himself takes he will acknowledge Nietzsche's values as superior to them although without absolute authority for himself. We may admit then that Nietzsche, as long as he remains faithful to this approach, is justified in dismissing absolutism and relativism as equally childish.

Perspectivism is a concept with an indefinite boundary. It depends for its coherence on the visual analogy; but beyond a certain point there is nothing to tell us how far to press the analogy and in what direction to press it. Nietzsche seems faithful to the analogy when he says, "There is *only* a perspective seeing, there is *only* a perspective knowing". But one might well interpret the analogy differently; we judge between visual perspectives by appeal to tests independent of visual perspective, and similarly require generalizations about perspective knowing (for example, that we learn more from multiple than single and wider than narrower perspectives) which are not themselves perspectival. It seems pointless to become involved in a paradox of self-reference ("Is perspectivism itself affirmed only from a perspective?"), since at this extreme the analogy has broken down and the concept is incoherent.

In particular, perspectivism is distinguishable from relativism only as long as one is assumed to prefer knowledge to ignorance. To allow the weak, the majority, the haters of life, to say, "But why shouldn't I prefer my restricted perspective?" would be to fall back into relativism. Here Nietzsche has a line of argument (summed up in the slogan he coined for the Assassins, "Nothing is true, everything is permitted"[22]) which does revert to relativism: he allows the question: "Suppose we want truth: *why not rather* untruth? and uncertainty? even ignorance?"[23]

At first sight he seems merely to be making a new move in the perspectivist dance, opening up a new perspective from which the faith in truth is seen to be itself perspective-bound and so inadequate. But a viewpoint from which one doesn't see, or sees a blur or something that isn't there, is not an overlooked viewpoint which has to be taken into account to achieve a full view; and to *want* one or other of these perspectives is not itself a perspective at all. With this departure from the visual analogy on which perspectivism depends for its meaning, Nietzsche undermines his whole position. Generally if we listen to him it is because of his incomparable tough-mindedness, mercilessly forcing us to confront the harshest realities, the most unwelcome truths. Unlike modern perspectivists, in whom (as in idealists) one may at times suspect an eagerness to escape from reality into the insubstantial pageant of interpretations, Nietzsche is very conscious of how obstinately reality forces itself on us however we may interpret it. (Witness some passages from *Ecce Homo* quoted above.) His commitment to the kind of objectivity achieved by multiplying viewpoints is in no way weakened by his denial of the possibility of objective truth and knowledge as philosophers have hitherto conceived them, nor by his insistence that there is an economy by which man achieves knowledge in one direction only at the cost of falsehood and ignorance in others. But when the commitment does weaken, we find him entitling us to choose truth or falsehood, to open or close perspectives, in the service of values affirmed only from his own perspective, such as power, life, individuality. No longer a perspectivist, he is now either an absolutist who wants to bind us to his own values or a relativist who leaves us free to evaluate as we please.

> The falseness of a judgment is not for us necessarily an objection to a judgment. . . . The question is to what extent it is life-promoting, life-preserving, species-preserving, perhaps even species-cultivating.[24]

> Ultimately the point is to what *end* a lie is told. That "holy" ends are lacking in Christianity is *my* objection to its means. Only *bad* ends: the poisoning, slandering, denying of life. . . .[25]

We do not find Nietzsche pressing his perspectivist questioning to ask, "Suppose we want life, why not rather death?", which should be a very real question for a former disciple of Schopenhauer. One might have thought however that the question he leaves open, "Suppose we want truth, why not rather untruth?" does permit only one answer. However much I deceive myself, or recognize that delusions now seen through benefitted me in the past, or suspect that there are others not yet diagnosed which are benefitting me now, I cannot explicitly pose the issue as whether to believe a falsehood without ceasing to believe it, and so preferring truth. It is when Nietzsche judges men by whether they say "Yes!" to truth rather than to life that his perspectivism transcends the difference between absolutism and relativism, with valuation springing from feeling as it spontaneously adapts to increasing knowledge.

> What distinguishes the higher human beings from the lower is that the former see and hear immeasurably more, and see and hear thoughtfully. . . . We who think and feel at the same time are those who really continually *fashion* something that had not been there before, the whole eternally growing world of valuations, colors, accents, perspectives, scales, affirmations and negations.[26]

By allowing the question, "Why not rather untruth?" Nietzsche also discredits an alternative escape route from relativism, the attempt to ground values in the supposed fact of a universal will to power. This interests us less because it is in the style of familiar psychological theories of value such as hedonism and has nothing to do with perspectivism. On this line of thought the order of rank is determined, not by the wider or narrower perspectives opened up by different trends of life, but by a trend supposedly common to all life ("What determines rank . . . is only quanta of power.")[27] Granted that it is a psychological fact that my own choices and everyone else's, however we may interpret them, are ultimately motivated by the will to power, and granted that *there is a universal obligation to acknowledge the truth about oneself,* then we should all adopt power as our conscious end, and degrees of power (like degrees of pleasure for a hedonist) become the universal measure of value. Here the obligation to be aware questioned by, "Why not rather untruth?" is indispensable to transfer the will to power from the plane of fact to that of value.[28] The vagueness of Nietzsche's concept of power makes this measure of value difficult to apply, but we may admit for the sake of argument that on a crude definition (which is not, of course, Nietzsche's) we would have grounds for a universal consensus that, for example, Stalin was the noblest man of the twentieth century. However, Nietzsche's deduction from an untestable generalization about the direction of all life assumed the obligation to self-knowledge. When Nietzsche values intensity and fullness of life above truth, he seems to forget he can no longer ground that value in a supposed psychological fact which he is entitling us to ignore, and is now simply affirming it from his own perspective, which is after all clearly recognizable as that of late nineteenth-century vitalism and individualism.

A suspicious feature of the slackening demand for truth which undermines perspectivism is that we meet it just when the commitment to truth would conflict with Nietzsche's dearest project, his "immoralism" discrediting the ranking of altruism above egoism. The issue of egoism is the only one on which he refuses to recognise single perspectives as limiting and imprisoning. The embarrassing implications for him of being a consistent perspectivist here may be sensed in an aphorism from the *Gay Science: "Egoism*. Egoism is the law of perspective applied to feelings: what is closest appears large and weighty, and as one moves farther away size and weight decrease."[29]

On Nietzsche's most characteristic approach to perspectives, this should imply that the egoist has a single and restricted perspective, to be corrected by learning to see—and *feel*—from other viewpoints. Nietzsche does in fact hold that understanding of others requires empathetic feeling, stimulated either by imagining what they are reacting to or by mimicking their behaviour.

Empathy. To understand another person, that is, *to imitate his feelings in ourselves*, we do indeed often go back to the *reason* for his feeling thus or thus and ask for example: *why* is he troubled?—so as then for the same reason to become troubled ourselves; but it is much more usual to omit to do this and instead to produce the feeling in ourselves after the *effects* it exerts and displays on the other person by imitating with our own body the expression of his eyes, his voice, his walk, his bearing (or even their reflection in word, picture, music). Then a similar feeling arises in us in consequence of an ancient association between movement and sensation, which has been trained to move backwards or forwards in either direction. We have brought our skill in understanding the feelings of others to a high state of perfection and in the presence of another person we are always almost involuntarily practicing this skill; one should observe especially the play on the faces of women and how they quiver and glitter in continual imitation and reflexion of what is felt to be going on around them.[30]

Should it not follow that in exploring other perspectives we have to feel from and so be moved from them, letting ourselves be drawn from egoism towards altruism? It begins to look as though the demand for Nietzsche's kind of objectivity, the multi-perspectival vision which escapes what metaphorically he called the 'injustice' of limited perspectives, will amount to a quite literal demand for justice, and do some of the work of the Categorical Imperative. But no conclusion could be less welcome to Nietzsche as immoralist, for whom altruism is a major virtue only from the restricted perspective of the weak. To some extent he is protected by a false sense of security, seeing empathetic understanding as independent of pity except for idiots who imagine that *"pity* makes two beings into one and in this way makes possible the immediate understanding of the one by the other".[31] Empathy is often "far from being harmless or sympathetic or kind", as he remarks in a penetrating analysis of how the striving for distinction, for making an impression on others, "keeps a constant eye on the next man and wants to know what his feelings are".[32] The strongest motive to empathy is fear.

> . . . man, as the most timid of all creatures on account of his subtle and fragile nature, has in his *timidity* the instructor in that empathy, that quick understanding of the feelings of another (and of animals). Through long millennia he saw in everything strange and lively a danger; at the sight of it he at once imitated the expression of the features and the bearing and drew his conclusion as to the kind of evil intention behind these features and this bearing. . . . The capacity for understanding—which, as we have seen, depends on the capacity for *rapid dissimulation* declines in proud, arrogant men and peoples because they have less fear; on the other hand every kind of understanding and self-dissembling is at home among timid peoples; here is also the rightful home of the imitative arts and of the higher intelligence.[33]

However, one must insist against Nietzsche that the example of fear by no means implies that one can incipiently mimic another without being incipiently moved from his viewpoint—a reaction which may harmonise with or clash with and be suppressed by the reaction from one's own, or blend variously with it to generate such compound attitudes as pride, cruelty, envy, or pity. It may even be doubted whether there are any specifically human desires (as distinct from the hunger and sexual appetite shared with animals) which do not involve reacting from another, as well as from one's own, perspective.[34] There can of course be a limited understanding of the other by thinking without feeling from his perspective; a fugitive inspired by fear may put himself in his enemy's place to ask of himself 'Where will he hide?', with the intention of hiding somewhere else. But if he wants to measure the lengths to which his enemy will go to catch or punish him, he has to feel at least momentarily the blast of hatred and vengefulness directed at himself. This could be deeply unsettling, because the clash with how he feels about himself calls into question his own self-valuation. Nor is his own viewpoint bound to prevail in such a clash. When the fear is of an established master the subject may for most of the time prefer to look down on himself from his master's viewpoint and estimate himself as inferior.

Reactions such as pity and cruelty fluctuate spontaneously between our own and other viewpoints; but a multi-perspectival vision which escapes the 'injustice' of limited viewpoints would separate them and give them equal weight, and clarify and steady reactions from each. The intensity or duration of feelings would be irrelevant to its valuations. Viewing things in proportion might involve finding our own sufferings less important rather than feeling those of others more intensely. Oddly enough Nietzsche almost says all this, unaware of any threat to his immoralism except from an over-valuation of pity.

> To view our own experiences with the eyes with which we are accustomed to view them when they are the experiences of others—this is very comforting and a medicine to be recommended. On the other hand, to view and imbibe the experiences of others *as if they were ours*—as is the demand of a philosophy of pity—this would destroy us, and in a very short time; but just try the experiment of doing it, and fantasise no longer! Moreover the former maxim is certainly *more in accord* with reason and the will to rationality, for we adjudge the value and meaning of an event more objectively when it happens to another than we do when it happens to us: the value, for example, of a death, or a money-loss, or a slander.[35]

In spite of his many psychologically very acute criticisms of the value of pity, Nietzsche does know that the commitment to open oneself to and feel from all perspectives would oblige him to prefer altruism to egoism. But as immoralist he wants the strong to feel sympathy primarily for their peers; he is driven to concede that in order to close themselves to the pity which would disadvantage them against the weak they must refuse to see from the perspective of the weak. Nietzsche experiences pity as an overwhelmingly powerful feeling, Zarathustra's last temptation, which can infect the strong and healthy like a sickness, and emasculate them by making them doubt their own right to happiness. "That the sick should *not* make the healthy sick—and this is what such an emasculation would involve—should surely be our supreme concern on earth; but this requires above all that the healthy should be *segregated* from the sick, guarded even from the sight of the sick, that they may not confound themselves with the sick."[36]

Nietzsche admits freely that the self-closure of the strong to the perspectives of the weak involves a degree of self-delusion, although less than does the vengeful fantasizing of the weak against the strong.

> When the noble mode of valuation blunders and sins against reality, it does so in respect of the sphere with which it is *not* sufficiently familiar, against a real knowledge of which it has indeed inflexibly guarded itself: in some circumstances it misunderstands the sphere it despises, that of the common man, of the lower orders; on the other hand one should remember that, even supposing that the affect of contempt, of looking down from a superior height, *falsifies* the image of that which it despises, it will at any rate still be a much less serious falsification than that perpetrated on its opponent—*in effigie* of course—by the submerged hatred, the vengefulness of the impotent.[37]

In another of his sallies against pity he goes as far as to say: "I know just as certainly that I only need to expose myself to the sight of some genuine distress and I am lost".[38]

How is one to reconcile an inflexible self-defense against a real knowledge of the majority of mankind, shutting oneself off from the very sight of sickness or of genuine distress, with the declaration in *Ecce Homo* that "Nothing in existence may be subtracted, nothing is dispensable"?[39] There he was insisting on the tremendous effort of courage required to view reality as comprehensively as he does. But does his immoralism appeal to our courage or to our cowardice?

The timing of intellectual fashion has linked the Nietzschean revival and the vogue of perspectivism with structuralist and post-structuralist literary criticism. But if we detach perspectivism from immoralism it seems to belong rather with the moralistic criticism of a generation ago, at its most severe in the *Scrutiny* school of F. R. Leavis. The air of satisfaction with one's own maturity which nowadays makes so much of this criticism seem ridiculous need not deter us from rediscovering its relevence. It identified literary value with a moral sensitivity at its most refined in highly integrated works of art such as the novels of Henry James. It assumed that moral sensitivity is at its height when we abandon our personal viewpoints and fixed standards to discover how our sympathies and antipathies develop as we view the self-contained situation of the story from the perspectives of all the interacting characters. Even if the author makes the error of taste of exhibiting explicit moral judgments we should ignore them, as crude simplifications inadequate to the fineness of his moral vision (D. H. Lawrence's "Never trust the teller, trust the tale"). There is no question of moral absolutism here, since there is no appeal to standards whatever. But neither is this relativism; readers, however much they may continue to disagree with each other, recognize that the reactions of each one of them to the behavior of the characters becomes morally more discriminating the more deeply and impartially he enters into their contrasting perspectives. Novel and drama can provide a moral training, for those who want it, by enabling sympathies and antipathies to clarify and refine themselves in situations more coherent, from the perspectives of characters more transparent, than we expect to meet outside books.

Of special interest in this connection are novels about clashes between cultures. The issue of absolutism and relativism is never more acute than when we confront the values of an alien society. Shall we say simply that slavery, human sacrifice, or widow-burning is wrong for us but right for them? If not, on what grounds am I to affirm that it is our code which is right and theirs which is wrong? But if we look at such a novel as the Nigerian Chinua Achebe's *Things Fall Apart*[40] we see that this is a false dichotomy. Achebe, without ever intruding his own moral judgments, makes us feel the dignity of the traditional way of life in a pre-colonial African village. But at two points we come on behavior which offends our Western sensibilities. The wife of a man in Okonkwo's village is killed in another village, which compensates for the killing with a woman and a boy whom Okonkwo's village may deal with as it pleases. Okonkwo brings up the boy Ikemefuna in his own family, but the village oracle finally pronounces that he must be killed. As the boy is attacked he cries out, "My father, they have killed me!", but Okonkwo joins in striking him down. Afterwards he "did not taste any food for two days" and "drank palm wine from morning to night". He takes a sombre pride in his victory over womanish feelings, but a friend reproaches him. " 'If I were you I would have stayed at home. What you have done will not please the Earth. It is the kind of action for which the goddess wipes out whole families. . . . If the Oracle said that my son should be killed I would neither dispute it nor be the one to do it.' "

The second issue is the exposure of twins, who as monstrosities are left to die in the forest. When passers-by hear the infants wailing they fall silent and hurry away. Okonkwo's own son is deeply troubled by both experiences; "something seemed to give way inside him, like the snapping of a tightened bow". When the first missionaries arrive the son is quickly converted, to the disgust of his father. "The poetry of the new religion, something felt in the marrow . . . seemed to answer a vague and persistent question that haunted his young soul—the question of the twins crying in the bush and of Ikemefuna who was killed". The novel proceeds to show how "things fall apart" when an alien religion disrupts a traditional code, in particular by the catastrophic discrediting of factual assumptions; thus the Christians do not, as confidently expected, die within twenty-eight days when they ignorantly build their church in the Evil Forest. Achebe never tells us whether he prefers the traditional or the Christian code. Does he then allow us to take the relativist position, that the deaths of the twins and of Ikemefuna are right by one code but wrong by another? But we see that observers of the old code have to close themselves deliberately to the perspectives of the victims; Okonkwo gets drunk for two days, and people who hear the twins crying hurry past. Granted the dire consequences supposed to follow the rearing of twins or disobedience to the Oracle, they have the right to harden themselves in

43

this way; to surrender to pity would be sentimentality. But these consequences are illusory, and the factual mistake is discoverable by the villagers just as in the case of the Evil Forest. Without making any general claims for the Christian code, whether as having absolute authority or even an overall superiority to the African, the son who throws off these illusions and lets himself be moved to pity from the perspectives of the victims is in these matters morally more educated than his father.

NOTES

This paper has benefitted from criticism by Graham Parkes, and from many illuminating conversations with him about Nietzsche.

1. Friedrich Nietzsche, *The Gay Science (GS)*, trans. Walter Kaufmann (New York: Vintage Press, 1974), 345.
2. Alexander Nehamas, *Nietzsche: Life as Literature* (Cambridge, Massachusetts: Harvard University Press, 1985), 36, 209. Nehamas notes (ut sup. 242 n. 5) that Nietzsche took the term "perspectivism" from his former colleague at Basel Gustav Teichmüller. It may be mentioned that the word *Bildungsphilister* (cultural philistine) which Nietzsche prided himself on having introduced into the German language was also picked up from Teichmüller, *Ecce Homo (EH)*, trans. Walter Kaufmann, (New York: Vintage Press, 1968), U2 and n. 2).
3. Nehamas, 72.
4. Nietzsche, *On the Genealogy of Morals (GM)*, trans. Walter Kaufmann and R. J. Hollingdale (New York: Vintage Press, 1968), 1/17.
5. *GM*, 3/12.
6. *EH*, 1/3.
7. *EH*, W2.
8. *GS*, 78.
9. *GS*, 78.
10. *GS*, 233, cf. 341.
11. *GS*, 354.
12. Nietzsche, *The Will to Power (WP)*, trans. Walter Kaufmann and R. J. Hollingdale (New York: Vintage Press, 1968), 855.
13. *EH*, P 3.
14. *EH*, BT 2.
15. Cf. the two senses of "objectivity" distinguished in *GM* 3/12, quoted above.

16. Nietzsche, *Human-All-Too-Human*, trans. R. J. Hollingdale (Cambridge University Press, 1986), Preface 6.

17. Nietzsche, *Daybreak (D)*, trans. R. J. Hollingdale (Cambridge University Press: 1982), 109.

18. *D*, 129.

19. *D*, 120.

20. Cf. ch. 1 above, ch. 14 below.

21. *GM*, 1/17.

22. *GM*, 3/24. Nietzsche's slogan rephrases a *description* of the Assassins in Joseph von Hammer, *Die Geschichte der Assassinen* (Stuttgart and Tübingen, 1818, p. 56), "since they consider everything [in religion] a cheat and nothing forbidden . . .".

23. Nietzsche, *Beyond Good and Evil (BGE)*, trans. R. J. Hollingdale, (London: Penguin Books, 1973), 1.

24. *BGE*, 4.

25. Nietzsche, *The Anti-Christ*, trans. R. J. Hollingdale (Penguin Classics), 56.

26. *GS*, 301.

27. *WP*, 855, quoted above.

28. Cf. the quasi-syllogism discussed in Chap. 1 above.

29. *GS*, 162.

30. *D*, 142.

31. *D*, 90.

32. *D*, 113.

33. *D*, 142.

34. Cf. my *R & S*, 20–24.

35. *D*, 137.

36. *GM*, 3/14.

37. *GM*, 1/10.

38. *GS*, 338.

39. *EH*, *BT*, 2, quoted above.

40. Chinua Achebe, *Things Fall Apart* (London: Heinemann, 1958).

Natural Goodness and Original Sin

3

In the eighteenth century the doctrine of natural goodness was a favourite weapon of Reason against the pretensions of priests and kings. With the decline of liberalism, belief in original sin recovered the offensive, backed by some very unpleasant twentieth-century reminders of the atrocities of which men are capable. What is this controversy about?

Let us begin by putting the issue in its traditional form. Has human nature been corrupt since some primal Fall, so that we are capable of good only to the extent that we are disciplined by authority or strengthened by divine grace? Or shall we say that human nature is good, and seems otherwise only because social institutions hide, suppress, and distort the natural promptings of the heart? The use of such moral terms as 'good' and 'corrupt' in posing the question does not quite exclude the possibility that the question is primarily one of fact; for it is clear that when people argue over the goodness or badness of human nature they are seldom disagreeing only over the value of what they agree to be natural. Someone who regards sexual desire as inherently sinful and obedience to authority as the ground of all virtue is admittedly more likely to believe in original sin than someone who takes the quality of his orgasm and the degree of his personal liberty as the two main tests of his success in life. However, people seldom argue about original sin and natural goodness unless they share certain moral assumptions, and they support their claims by appealing not to moral standards but to supposed facts about behaviour. It is not difficult to formulate the problem in ways which bypass considerations of value. Is it when I am in the mood to be kind, generous, and self-sacrificing that I am following the bent of human nature, or when I am selfish, cruel, vindictive? If we could remove the external checks to natural inclinations, would the effect be social disruption or closer harmony?

What cannot be bypassed, of course, is the problem of what we mean by 'nature'. There is no space here to analyze in detail the various tests on which this word depends for its various meanings; it is enough for our purposes to point out that the more obvious at least of these tests do not apply to social behaviour. For example, we can easily find criteria for deciding whether it is natural for a baby to suck the nipple. We can say that the tendency is innate, unlearned, because we observe it in children who have not been taught it and who lack models from whom they could have imitated it. We can also say that the tendency is characteristic of human beings and of mammals in general, not because it is found in every individual—a few exceptions might not refute the claim—but because the functioning of the mammalian organism depends on it, both to empty the mother's breasts and to sustain the infant before it can seek other nourishment. But we can apply neither test to men's behaviour towards each other. To use the second we should have to replace the mammalian organism by a concept of social man which would assume all that the test was to help us to discover. As for the first, we can never show that the disposition to any kind of social conduct is innate, because all who display it belong to society and may therefore have learned it from others.

Rousseau, in the *Discours sur l'origine de l'inégalité*, tried to identify the moral potentialities of man in the pre-social state, the state of Nature. But if in the state of Nature men live in isolation from each other, they cannot exhibit either social virtues or social vices; if they live together in harmony, they already form a society; if there is a war of all against all, each has all the rest as models from whom he could have learned his predatory behaviour, and as enemies among whom he cannot survive unless he does learn it. It might be supposed that an isolated individual entering society for the first time would show his natural reactions to others before he had time to learn from them, and that we are all in this position in early childhood. But the child's consciousness of other people begins as consciousness of the mother's breast; he takes time to discover even his mother's bodily wholeness and separateness, and cannot be credited with kindness or ingratitude, pity or cruelty, until he perceives her not only as a body but as a person into whose feelings he can enter.

To discover the individual's natural reaction to others from the example of the child we should have to find one who can already put himself in the place of others and anticipate the consequences of his own actions, yet has never learned from others' instruction or example.

The difficulty is often obscured by a facile identification of the claim that men are by nature good or evil with the quite different claim that they are predominantly decent or wicked in practice. Yet any amount of actual evil might be the effect of bad institutions perverting our natural ability, and any amount of actual good might be credited to God's grace enabling us to defeat our fallen nature. A common objection to Calvinism—that if God elects some to salvation by his irresistible grace, it is unjust of him not to save us all—shows vividly that it would be possible to affirm the total depravity of human nature even if in practice all men were saints. In any case, even if we could accept the relevance of such generalizations, the people who make them seem always to be judging by some subjective standard of comparison. Each man has a private estimate of how much decency he can reasonably expect from others, an estimate which rises and falls with chance circumstances; a trusted friend betrays him and he 'loses his faith in human nature'; a stranger goes out of his way to help him, and his faith is restored. A thinker impressed by the eternal wickedness of man seems often to have at the back of his mind nothing more significant than the observation that torture and mass murder were more common in mid-century than they were in the last decades before 1914, or even that the world is a dirtier place than he supposed before moving from a day to a public school. The popularity of natural goodness in the eighteenth and nineteenth centuries, when material and spiritual progress seemed to go side by side, and the revival of original sin after the Holocaust and Stalin's purges, suggest that for most people the standard is an unconscious estimate of the average moral level of the previous generation.

There are other arguments employed in this controversy which do profess to distinguish between natural and other types of behaviour. A Christian sets himself an ideal of conduct which he strives to attain. He is always aware of the conflict between principle and certain inclinations which he fights, sometimes conquers, but cannot abolish by any act of will; and if in course of time some of these inclinations diminish in strength, he knows that the process is largely independent of his own efforts and gives the credit for it to God's grace. Is it not clear, he is likely to insist, that we do good by an effort of will, and relapse into evil as soon as the will slackens? The concept of original sin is deeply rooted in an unquestionable psychological fact, that a man who believes himself the creature of a just and almighty God can be certain that a desire is absolutely evil, understand that the trivial pleasure of its temporary satisfaction is nothing compared with the salvation which it threatens, concentrate all the strength of his will to suppress it, yet still feel it rising up from the most intimate part of him. This gap between moral understanding and the vitiated will has been a theme for tormented eloquence from Ovid's *"Video meliora proboque, deteriora sequor"* ("I see and approve the better, I follow the worse"), that favourite tag of classically educated believers in original sin, to such elaborations as this, the source of which I prefer for the moment not to identify: *"Non, l'homme n'est point un: je veux et je ne veux pas, je me sens á la fois esclave et libre; je vois le bien, je l'aime, et je fais le mal. . . ."*

But this aspect of moral experience seems to justify conclusions about human nature only to those entangled in at least three different kinds of confusion:

(i) The desires which conflict with principle are 'natural' in the sense that they are spontaneous, independent of conscious decision, and not eradicable by it. This is a common use of the word, to which there is no reason to object. But we can call a desire natural in this sense even if we know that it is not innate but an effect of conditioning which has become 'second nature', for example the drunkard's need of alcohol. It is therefore a mistake to assume that the desires which rise in revolt against moral principle, being natural in the first sense, must be rooted too deep to be touched by such facile methods as social reform and psychoanalysis. A personal discovery of the limits of voluntary control, undermining faith in the possibility of a fully self-dependent moral life, leads some to dependence on God, others to the transfer of large areas of conduct from the scope of morals to that of psychiatry. Nothing in the psychological facts discredits even belief in natural goodness. (The second of the quotations just given was from Rousseau's *Profession de foi du vicaire savoyard* in *Émile.*)

(ii) Granted that we identify the natural with the spontaneous, it is not true that Nature rebels against the Good; Nature rebels against any ideal which we choose to pursue, whatever its value. The revolutionary who lets sentiment interfere with his long-range calculations, the ex-Puritan whose inherent prudery still hinders him after his conversion to hedonism, Sade's squeamishness in the French Revolution, the pity which made it painful for Nietzsche to read *Don Quixote*, Huckleberry Finn helping his friend the runaway slave, are all examples of the Old Adam in revolt against consciously imposed principle. The effort and conflict involved in disciplining inclinations which run counter to one's overriding purpose have nothing to do with the worth either of the inclinations or of the purpose.

(iii) Allowing that some evil is natural, what is there to show that evil is more natural than good? A man aiming at moral self-improvement is no doubt conscious particularly of the evil in his natural inclinations, since his nature hinders advance and threatens regress, and the good in it has sufficed only to raise him to a level with which he is dissatisfied. Moreover, it is an important part of his tactics not to tempt his vanity and laziness by dwelling on his own virtues. Nothing, however, is involved here except the direction in which he finds it useful to turn his attention; the fact remains that some virtues come easily to him even if others do not. But unless the evil in us is in some sense more natural than the good, and we can distinguish between the source of evil in the depths of our corrupted nature and the external source of good promptings in the grace of God, the idea of original sin loses the whole of its challenge. Theologians admittedly differ as to the degree to which human nature was corrupted after the Fall. But there would be no point in arguing with an opponent who maintained merely that *some* natural inclinations are evil, since he would need to postulate corruption and the Fall only on the assumption that a being created by a perfectly good God cannot originally have been inclined to evil; the dispute would immediately shift its ground from human nature to the existence of God.

Defenders of natural goodness are as unsuccessful as their opponents in providing tests by which one kind of social behaviour can be shown to be more natural than another. There are several lines of thought in the liberal and humanist tradition which may tempt towards the conclusion that human nature is good. The Christian starts from an absolute moral law to which the desires must always be referred, not necessarily for condemnation, but at any rate for judgment. A humanist starts from the desires and criticizes traditional morality in relation to them, rejecting all prohibitions which seem to him not to further human happiness, and questioning the appropriateness of simple repression even when he still disapproves. This approach has both encouraged and drawn encouragement from the doctrine of natural goodness; for the assumption that the satisfaction of desires is the test of value can easily become the claim that the desires are inherently good, and at every point at which a traditional prohibition is rejected rebellious human nature is justified against the standards which have been invoked to condemn it. From this point of view desires are evil only when they are socially harmful, in conflict with the desires of others; and the discovery of the immense variety of behaviour in different kinds of society has contributed to the hope that anti-social desires are accidentals which a suitable change of institutions can eliminate. Yet none of these considerations gives us any reason to suppose that socially beneficial impulses are natural in any sense in which anti-social impulses are not, or, on the other hand, that it is any easier to root out the latter by suitable institutions than the former by unsuitable ones. The stress on human malleability leads rather to another thesis which has been as potent in the humanist tradition as that of natural goodness, the claim that there is no human nature good or bad, and that men are as good or bad as the societies which form them.

Without a criterion for the natural the assertion that human nature is good or bad tells us nothing at all about men. People sometimes act well and sometimes badly; neither doctrine helps us to discover when they will act one way rather than the other, or even, as we have seen, that one alternative is the more frequent. Original sin has often been used as a weapon against democracy, as a proof that the masses are too wicked and stupid to govern themselves. It may be used equally plausibly to argue that no authority can be trusted to rule to the common advantage, that there must be institutions to defend the masses against rulers whom power will corrupt and absolute power will corrupt absolutely. There is the same arbitrariness about all attempts to apply these doctrines to particular cases. From 'Human nature is evil' one can no more deduce that there will always be wars than that there will always be blood-feuds or duels, the impossibility of social equality than the impossibility of equality before the law, the inevitability of prostitution than the inevitability of polygamy or the Right of the First Night. An agreeable sophistry would be to put original sin in the service of the Materialist Conception of History. It is surely unduly charitable to human frailty to suppose that most men can be persuaded by a religion or philosophy or political programme which does not appeal to some material interest. But the Augustinian would be the last person to accept this particular insult to our nature.

It may be objected that even if doctrines of human nature tell us nothing directly about human behaviour, they certainly do in some way help or hinder our recognition of facts. The quantity or degree of actual evil may have no theoretical bearing on the question: yet it is plain enough that such events as the Nazi massacres of the Jews came as a considerable shock to believers in natural goodness, while believers in original sin were able to say 'I told you so'. At this point it becomes necessary to take a second look at the observation with which this essay began, that the use of moral terms does not necessarily forbid us to discuss the question as one of fact. This observation does not entitle us to translate 'Human nature is good' directly into, let us say, 'It is men's socially beneficial inclinations which are natural'; 'good' is a word used to recommend, and the function of the sentence is not to describe human nature but to recommend us to act in accordance with it. Its connection with fact is that it is a hypothetical imperative, a type of imperative which is justified by factual evidence that the means is suited to the end. The end assumed in this case is the speaker's conception of the Good Life; if social harmony is part of this conception, and a situation in which each man follows his own nature in fact leads to anarchy, then the advice is mistaken.

Now as long as we understand 'Human nature is good' as a maxim of conduct and not as a descriptive statement, the meaning of 'nature' does not give trouble. If 'Human nature is good' advises us to act in a certain way, then the word 'nature' tells us what this way is; it does not inform us that the tendency to act in this way is innate and not learned. Indeed, when we use the word to characterize actions the adverbial form 'naturally' loses its connection with innateness and becomes nearly synonymous with 'spontaneously'. We take 'Human nature is corrupt' or 'Human nature is good' as a call to discipline or spontaneity, self-control or self-expression, punishment or an appeal to the offender's 'better nature', on the assumption that men are behaving naturally to the extent that they are unconstrained by inwardly accepted principles and by external laws and conventions. In every situation which presents such a pair of alternatives the choice between them depends on one's answer to the factual question 'Is order possible in this case without control?'; and an overall choice between the two maxims depends on a general estimate of the degree to which people deserve trust. Such estimates of course vary with the temperaments and circumstances of individuals. If events since 1914 have disillusioned many believers in natural goodness, it is by disappointing expectations which several centuries of apparent progress had seemed to confirm.

If *X* claims that human nature is good and *Y* that it is bad, they seem to contradict each other as drastically as any two opponents can possibly do. The difference between them is real enough, in that they recommend conflicting attitudes of trust and mistrust of unschooled and undisciplined impulse, but it is a difference of degree only. Both agree in the last resort that expression and repression are alike indispensable; *X* dislikes spontaneous reactions which he regards as perversions of Nature by social conditioning, while *Y* commends spontaneous motions of the soul which he interprets as the workings not of Nature but of divine grace, the ambiguity of 'natural' allowing both contestants to retreat in case of emergency from the sense of 'spontaneous' to the sense of 'innate'. It would be as useless to insist that one attitude is absolutely the right one as it would be in the case of conservatism and radicalism or optimism and pessimism, and as pointless to ask outside a context 'Should we express or repress?' as 'Should things change or stay the same?' and 'Are hopes fulfilled or disappointed?'. In all these cases we are concerned with pairs of contrasting attitudes to experience, suited to different temperaments and conditions, within which either attitude is as realistic or unrealistic as the person who assumes it.

Proceeding to a specific case, suppose that *X* claims that a certain young criminal can be reformed by giving him the love which his parents denied him, *Y* that the boy will commit crimes until convinced by severe punishment that it does not pay to do so. The evidence relevant to a decision consists of facts about the offender's personality and background, and about the results hitherto of treating him in one way or the other. 'Human nature is good' and 'Human nature is bad' contribute nothing to this evidence, but they point to attitudes which incline *X* towards one solution and *Y* towards the other, and which have been nourished by the outcome of such cases in the past. Similarly, on many particular issues over the last couple of centuries, belief in original sin has inclined people to dread the risk of opening the floodgates, while belief in natural goodness has encouraged them to remove political controls in the confidence that freedom will not lead to anarchy. The doctrine of natural goodness has acted as a force on the side of political, social, and intellectual liberty, and up to 1914 events tended to support the confidence it encourages that people will co-operate without being forced to do so; modern states combined a perhaps unprecedented degree of public order with a weakening of sanctions and authorities in the democracies which has an equally good claim to be judged unprecedented. The facts can tell in favour of a doctrine of human nature, but only in the way that they can tell, for example, in favour of optimism or pessimism—temporarily and locally.

Rousseau's vision of an instinctively noble being perverted by society is only one of several concepts of Man which have appeared as successors to the Christian picture of a corrupted and redeemable creature of God. There is another which conceives individuals as rational egoists incapable of disinterested goodwill towards each other, but at the same time assumes that it should not be beyond our wits to find some deal to the mutual advantage of all. Yet another denies that there is any human nature and conceives man as infinitely malleable by social institutions. Sartre's type of existentialism attacks human nature from another direction; what I am I choose to be, and to say that I cannot help doing what it is my nature to do is an evasion of responsibility. Finally, there is a conception which appears in different forms in, for example, Freud's *Beyond the Pleasure Principle*, Lawrence's *Women in Love,* and Mann's *Magic Mountain*, of Man as a battleground between not Good and Evil but Life and Death, a demarcation cutting across moral distinctions in that the urge to self-preservation or self-destruction is treated as closely inter-connected with the urge to preserve or destroy others. Although this last model of Man has no more claim to final validity than the rest, it may be suggested that it renders the habit of thinking in terms of natural goodness or corruption obsolete, by calling attention to two important aspects of behaviour which on those terms are hard to reconcile.

In the first place, we have become very conscious of the element of irrational, motiveless cruelty and destructiveness in man. Freud demon-strated this destructiveness in theory and the Nazis in practice; we can trace the awareness of it backwards through the great explorers of the dark regions of the mind in nineteenth-century literature to those two French aristocratic brothers-under-the-skin at the end of the preceding century, the atheist and revolutionary Sade and the Catholic and reactionary Joseph de Maistre. This uncovering of a motiveless appetite for pain and death is not the rediscovery of something always known before humanists chose to avert their eyes from it. Up to the eighteenth century sin appeared as a compound of selfishness, rebelliousness, carnal lust, from which the element of pure destructiveness was hardly detached when it was recognized at all. Hobbes, whom no one reproaches for sentimentality, includes among his definitions of the passions: "*Con-tempt,* or little sense of the calamity of others, is that which men call CRUELTY; proceeding from security of their own fortune. For, that any man should take pleasure in other men's great harmes, without other end of his own, I do not conceive it possible" (Hobbes's *Leviathan,* Part I, Ch. 6).

The extent to which we have come to accept a view of man in this respect actually darker than that of Hobbes or of the Age of Faith can be seen in the manner in which cruelty has insensibly shifted its place from a marginal to the basic moral evil, in the gradual exclusion of mere callousness and brutality from the definition of 'cruelty', in the new coinage 'sadism' to distinguish disinterested cruelty both within and outside the sexual sphere.

Yet psychoanalysis has shown the necessity of combining a recogni-tion of human destructiveness which makes nonsense of any faith in natural goodness with a relaxation of inhibitions which entirely contra-dicts the practical conclusions commonly drawn from original sin. Freud put a whole armoury of new weapons in the hands of those who, often inspired by the slogan of natural goodness, had insisted that the recovery of spontaneity is a side of moral self-development as important as the cultivation of self-control, and that envy and hate can breed from the refusal of pleasure, charity and generosity from affirmation of one's own right to happiness. We now recognize that a narrow line separates conscious self-control from unconscious inhibitions which wither, pervert, and disease, that when we pride ourselves on controlling inclination for the sake of principle we are often merely repressing from irrational and unavowed motives, that to weaken the grip of the repressive system is an essential step in winning well-being both for oneself and for others. But the most remarkable innovation in this moral revolution is Freud's identification, anticipated in Nietzsche's *Genealogy of Morals*, of the repressive forces within and the destructive forces turned outwards against others. It amounts to the assertion, which would surely have been unintelligible to almost anyone before the nineteenth century, that when an ascetic struggles to obey the voice of God calling on him to mortify his carnal desires, and when he resists the voice of Satan tempting him to injure others, he is in fact listening to the same voice, that of Thanatos countering the pull of Eros.

There is no contradiction between the two aspects of the psychoanalytic image of Man. The extent to which spontaneous passions are anarchic and malevolent is one question, whether and when it is best to cope with them by threats of hell, hanging and flogging, self-discipline, self-expression, social reform, or psychiatric treatment is quite another question; and the traditional doctrines of human nature have always confused the two.

Conceptual Schemes and Linguistic Relativism in Relation to Chinese

4

Philosophers discussing conceptual schemes seem generally to treat them as assumptions in propositional form behind the thought of different cultures, cosmologies, or phases in the history of science. On the one hand, conceptual schemes appear as conflicting systems of assumed truths which are only imperfectly testable by observation, and bring us uncomfortably near to epistemological chaos; on the other, suspicion arises that the notion of a conceptual scheme may not be coherent at all. As Donald Davidson argues in his paper, "On the Very Idea of a Conceptual Scheme", we seem to end up with nothing definite but "the simple thought that something is an acceptable conceptual scheme or theory if it is true."[1] For inquirers into the thought and language of other cultures, the issue is inescapable. That very idea is one of their indispensable tools, to which Davidson's objections do not directly apply, since their own tendency is to think of it in terms, not of propositions,[2] but of classification by naming, and perhaps of syntactic structures. I wish to argue that examination of their usage can open up a different perspective on the philosophical problems. At the roots of the systems of propositions called 'conceptual schemes' by philosophers there are patterns of naming, pre-logical in the same sense as patterns of perception are pre-logical, and I shall myself use the term exclusively of these. As an example of the usage I quote a few paragraphs written by myself before having read Davidson.[3]

"That all thinking is grounded in analogization shows up especially clearly when we try to come to grips with the thought of another civilization. The concepts which it assumes as self-evident, until persistent failure to solve a problem calls attention to them, appear to an outsider as strange metaphorical structures to be examined and re-examined as he learns to find his way around the conceptual scheme. To take an example from my own professional field, sinology, the first Christian missionaries in China were confronted with the neo-Confucian cosmology, for which the universe is composed of something called *ch'i* and ordered by something called *li*. *Ch'i* is a universal fluid out of which bodies condense and into which they dissolve. At its densest, as in a stone, it is inert, but the more tenuous it is the more freely it moves, for example, as the air we breathe; even the void is *ch'i* at the ultimate degree of rarification. Inside the denser *ch'i* of the living body flow more rarified currents which circulate and activate it, moving freely as breath, less freely as blood. The concrete meaning of the word in ordinary language is in fact 'breath', and the alternations of breathing out and in are the paradigms for the *ch'i* in its active phase moving, expanding, rarifying as the 'Yang', and in its passive phase reverting to stillness, contracting, solidifying as the 'Yin'. This duality accounts for the generation and alternation of opposites throughout nature, light and dark, moving and still, male and female. Since *ch'i* occupies the place in Chinese cosmology corresponding to matter in ours, Westerners took a long time to grasp how very different it is from what we understand by matter. Early in the present century S. Le Gall was still translating *ch'i* by *matière*. A passage by the neo-Confucian Chang Tsai (1020–1077), translatable as

> The assembly and dispersal of the *ch'i* in the *T'ai-hsü* ("Supreme Void") is like ice congealing and melting in water

is rendered by Le Gall

> La condensation et les dispersions *des atômes* (my italics) dans la T'ai-hiu peuvent se comparer a la fonte de la glace dans l'eau.

Although Chang Tsai's comparison with water shows clearly that the *ch'i* is a continuum and not an aggregate of atoms, the analogy with matter is so deep in Le Gall's preconceptions that he assumes the component atoms to be implicit in the word *ch'i* of the Chinese text. A reader asking the important question, 'Is there atomism in Chinese philosophy?' would find the wrong answer embedded in an actual quotation from a Chinese philosopher.

"As for *li*, it is pattern, structure, order; the concrete uses of the word are for veins in jade and the grain of wood. The *li* as a whole is the cosmic pattern which lays down the lines along which nature and man move, which harmonises opposites with complementary functions, Yang and Yin, ruler and subject, father and son, and alternates day and night, birth and death, the rise and fall of dynasties, in regular cycles, diverging downwards to the minutest detail of texture and converging upwards to the unity in which everything is interrelated. The *li* is not obeyed or defied like a law, one goes either with or against the grain of it, as in chopping wood. Le Gall translated it by *forme*, thus by the choice of two words remoulding the whole neo-Confucian cosmology after the analogy of Aristotelian form and matter. J. Percy Bruce chose for his equivalent 'law', and so incorporated into the neo-Confucian terminology itself the wrong answer to the question, 'Are there laws of nature in China?', a misunderstanding which Joseph Needham in elucidating the concepts of Chinese science had to analyse at length. But to think of Le Gall and Bruce as making mistakes which we now avoid would miss the whole point. There are no exact equivalents for *li* and *ch'i* among our concepts, and there is no way of approaching them except by breaking out from or awakening to one analogy after another.

"Approaching this cosmology, it is natural for an outsider to suppose that the Chinese can think only concretely, after the analogies of breathing or the veins in jade (a supposition encouraged by misunderstandings of Chinese script as a kind of picture writing), while he thinks abstractly; that the Chinese are wrong and he is right (for is not the universe in fact composed of matter obeying the laws of nature?); that the Chinese are trapped within an unchanging conceptual scheme while he is free to go wherever reason bids. However, to take the first point first, the Chinese concepts appear concrete to us only because the inquiring outsider, unlike the insider who habitually thinks with them, needs to fix his attention on their metaphorical roots. He is much less conscious of the metaphors behind his own 'matter' and 'law', which, however, he must rediscover if he wants to explore the differences to the bottom. He himself thinks of matter after the analogy, if not actually of the timber which is the concrete meaning of Greek *hule* and Latin *materia,* at any rate of the 'materials' utilized in making an artifact; and the usage of 'matter' has behind it a larger model, of a universe created by God for a purpose, from which the transparently metaphorical 'laws of nature' also derive. Indeed, we no longer employ the word with full assurance, or are confident of what we mean by philosophical 'materialism', now that we are forbidden to think of atoms as little balls out of which a universe could be constructed; twentieth-century physics has less substantial entities which would slip through one's fingers. As for the metaphor of 'law', its persisting power is evident whenever someone, pondering the determinist thesis that even his own actions are 'bound by', are 'subject to', 'obey' the laws of nature, finds himself thinking as though he ought to be conscious of his own resisting will, as he is when submitting to human laws."

To approach the pre-logical patterning of names we require in the first place the tools not of philosophy but of semiology. The most useful for our purposes are Roman Jakobson's 'paradigm/syntagm' and 'metaphor/metonym'.[4] A sentence is formed, on the one hand by selecting words, on the other by combining them. Words relate 'paradigmatically' in the sets from which they are selected, 'syntagmatically' in the phrases or sentences which combine them.

	A	B	Paradigm
1	He	They	
2	posted	collected	
3	a	the	
4	letter.	mail.	

Syntagm

Verbal thinking draws from a stock of paradigms already grouping syntagmatically in chains of oppositions which at their simplest are binary. The following chain (in which we number only for convenience) guides the formation of such English compound words as 'daylight' and such formulas as 'the light of knowledge' or 'the darkness of evil' before they enter into sentences.

	A	B	Paradigm
1	Day	Night	
2	Light	Darkness	
3	Knowledge	Ignorance	
4	Good	Evil	

Syntagm

In Jakobson's terminology, paradigmatic relations are of 'similarity/contrast', syntagmatic of 'contiguity/remoteness'. There are consequently two kinds of proportional opposition guiding our thinking:

A 1 : B 1 :: A 2 : B 2 (Day compares with night as light with darkness)

A 1 : A 2 :: B 1 : B 2 (Day connects with light as night with darkness).

When relations tend to similarity rather than contrast, contiguity rather than remoteness, one of a pair may substitute for the other, by the figures of speech called 'metaphor' and 'metonymy'.

	A	B	Paradigm	A	B
1	King	Lion		King	Chairman
2	Man	Beast		Throne	Chair

Syntagm

King compares with Lion as men with beasts, so by metaphor the lion is king of the beasts and the king is a lion among men. King connects with throne as chairman with chair, so by metonymy the monarchy is called the throne and the chairmanship the chair.

In these chains of oppositions we find the beginnings of a conceptual scheme, in which the thinking we shall call 'correlative' in contrast with 'analytic' will tend to fill a vacancy by its place in the pattern. We conceive it as spontaneous and pre-logical, the completion of a *Gestalt* as in perception, indispensable at the foundations of thought but requiring analytic thinking to test it. It is at this level that one would begin a comparison of Western with Chinese conceptual schemes. The relevance of chains of oppositions, easily overlooked when we try to uncover our own preconceptions, is immediately obvious when examining Chinese thought, since the structures are exposed nakedly by the tendency to parallelism in the classical language, and are overtly formulated in the Yin-Yang cosmological scheme.

A	B
Yang	Yin[5]
Light	Darkness
Motion	Stillness
Heaven	Earth
Male	Female
Ruler	Subject

It is this scheme which has called attention to the most often noticed difference between Western and Chinese thinking, that the Western tends to centre on conflicting opposites (truth/falsehood, good/evil), the Chinese on complementary polarities. We may illustrate the latter tendency from *Chuang-tzu*[6]:

> If then we say 'Why not take the right as our authority and do without the wrong, take the ordered as our authority and do away with the disordered, this is failing to understand the pattern of heaven and earth, and the myriad things as they essentially are. It is as though you were to take heaven as your authority and do without earth, take the Yin as your authority and do without the Yang; that it is impracticable is plain enough.

Some of the English chain of oppositions with which we started (day/night, light/darkness . . .) fits neatly into a Yang/Yin scheme; but in the latter A and B are interdependent with A only relatively superior, and the chain does not lead to 'good/evil'. Here our conceptual schemes differ, not in assuming the truth of contradictory propositions, but in including or excluding different pairs of words. That the Western chains of oppositions, like the Chinese, are right at the foundations of thought, has only been suspected quite recently. For Derrida[7] our 'logocentric' tradition has a chain in which it strives to abolish B and leave only A, 'signified/signifier, speech/writing, reality/appearance, nature/culture, life/death, good/evil . . .'. Contemplating it, one begins to see an affinity, for example, between Western positions as far apart as the Christian faith in the immortality of the soul and the scientist's (before quantum mechanics) in universal causation; given the pairs 'life/death' and 'necessity/chance', the West struggles to eliminate B in favour of A. More recently David Hall and Roger Ames[8] have directly contrasted Western and Chinese oppositions, with the West habitually treating A as 'transcendent' in the sense that A is conceivable without B but not B without A; for Westerners there could be God without world, reality without appearance, good without evil.

On the paradigmatic dimension vocabularies class as similar or contrasting each in its own way; to the extent that languages are like English and Chinese in lacking a common ancestor, words will approach synonymy only when, in our Jakobsonian terminology, they name things closely similar to each other and distinctly, remote from everything else, such as organisms and human artifacts. If for example an English speaker says, 'The cat sat on the mat', and a Chinese, *Mao wo tsai hsi-tzu-shang*, only the cat is satisfying these conditions. For the English its posture is similar to a man sitting in a chair, for the Chinese to a man lying *(wo)* whether face forward or on his back. As for the mat, we cannot expect an unrelated language to share precisely our classification of floor coverings as mats, rugs, carpets; *hsi-tzu* is used of straw mats. In addition, the verb is tensed in English but not in Chinese. The sentences are not, therefore, fully intertranslatable, do not express the same proposition; *Mao wo tsai hsi-tzu-shang* is true even if the cat has never before now sat on the mat, false if it sat on a cloth mat. That Chinese and English divide up and organise the world differently shows up still more clearly in the classical language, with its neat parallelism and explicit classifications. For 'Grass is green' one might find *Ts'ao ch'ing*, at any rate where a two-word parallel excluded the need for grammatical particles. Here the meaning of *ts'ao* depends on a division of vegetation into *ts'ao mu* 'grass and trees', implying a wider scope than our 'grass'. *Ch'ing* is one of the Five Colours, the blue-green which contrasts equally with red, yellow, white, and black. If grass were blue 'Grass is green' would be false but *Ts'ao ch'ing* would be true. It will be said perhaps that anything factual may be translated into any language by expanding with qualifications. But this claim, besides being unprovable by any number of examples, seems to assume that there are indeed atomic divisions in nature and culture which will impose themselves on the speakers of all languages.

Synonymy will of course be even harder to find in the terminology of philosophy and morals. We might say that apparently synonymous words will be like exactly equal lines; with a further focussing of the microscope a difference will appear. When a discipline is borrowed from another culture precise equivalents may be stipulated (the names of the elements in physics will in any language have the same Latin formations or assigned native words), but this consideration does not apply to ancient China. Since logical operations are independent of language structure—a point to which we shall return later[9]—we might expect true synonymy among logical and mathematical terms; we can hardly deny that the numbers are the same, or that the Mohists' *Huo yeh che pu chin yeh*[10] is if correctly then exactly translated, " 'Some' is not all". But in philosophical terminology, even when there are commonly agreed equivalents, *Tao* 'Way', *hsing* 'nature', *T'ien* 'heaven', there can be no question of perfect synonymy; they are satisfactory because if used consistently they enable the reader of a translation in which they recur to develop a sense of how they are diverging from the same words in an English context, an insight which is no more than assisted by the explanations in the introduction or notes of the book. Students of the ethical, political, scientific, or philosophical thinking of China are often amazed to discover that some crucial Western concept ('truth', 'being', 'liberty') is missing in this civilization; but granted that the classical language has no exact synonyms for the words, neither has it for 'ethics', 'politics', 'science', 'philosophy', or 'civilization'. The point is always to compare and contrast Chinese concepts with our own, not go looking for our own in other cultures.

It may seem that these proposals commit us to an extreme form of linguistic relativism. Of *Ts'ao ch'ing* and 'Grass is green' neither entails the other, since there is *ts'ao* which is not grass and *ch'ing* which is not green; nothing said in Chinese can imply or contradict anything said in

English, and likewise with all conceptual schemes. Since schemes overlap and run into each other, and each person has his own continually changing blend, the result should be epistemological chaos. Plainly we have to respect the evidence of experience that in international and other intercourse we do succeed in exchanging facts, and do know how to take into account that the other person is not saying quite the same thing. Whatever explanation we give for making this concession to common sense will apply also to statements within philosophical and scientific schemes. On the present line of argument the explanation will be that we come to understand the words by correlation within the scheme, a pre-logical process which analysis assists but cannot replace. We are in command of English only when we have stopped analysing and applying a rule for singular and plural, and the gap in the chain 'dog/dogs, tree/trees, house/ . . . . ' spontaneously fills with 'houses'. Learning Chinese we start by translating with equivalents from the dictionary: *an* 'Quiet, still. Peace, tranquility': *wei* 'Dangerous; perilous. Lofty'. But we are at home with these words only when we have become acquainted with them in different contextual patterns, in particular when we notice that, as we would never have guessed from these entries in Mathews's dictionary, *an* and *wei* are opposites. We may think of them as basically 'secure/insecure', but our analyses of the words never catch up with our understanding of them in context. But if I learn the words primarily by correlating them, with analysis secondary even if employed at all, I understand the Chinese as I understand the English, and can confirm the truth of either *Ts'ao ch'ing* or 'Grass is green' by looking at grass and other herbs without bothering about translatability. If in a particular context a Chinese reports what he saw by *Mao wo tsai hsi-tzu-shang,* I am oriented towards what he saw as towards things I have seen myself, possibly but not necessarily by visually imagining as in my own case I visually remember. I can then say, 'The cat sat on the mat', as I might say, 'You still have that cat then', responding to the event which he observed without concern for whether I am saying what he said. I do have to co-ordinate the Chinese and English sentences, but will do so most accurately by correlation sensitive to more difference and similarity than I can analyse; there is no need to relate them logically because if I want to infer from one of them it will be in the same language. On this account the only connexion between truth and translatability, *pace* Davidson,[11] will be that *if* a true statement does have a translation equivalent (as with scientific statements using stipulated equivalents), the latter will be true as well.

To think of the conceptual scheme as a pre-logical pattern of names—understanding by 'names' the products of the classifying act of naming, not the singular terms of logic—does not have the revolutionary consequences of treating it as a system of logically related propositions. The position remains the same as with dating by a calendar. That for a Muslim this is not the year 1988 does not open up the terrifying thought that in another conceptual scheme I am living hundreds of years ago; having compared the Muslim and Christian calendars I find that we agree. If there is a single goat in plain sight, and *X* says *Yu yang* 'There is a *yang* (conventionally translated 'sheep')' and *Y* 'There is no sheep', I may be startled if I fail to appreciate that *yang* include goats as *shan yang* 'mountain *yang*'; but for anyone who has fully correlated the Chinese and English words the observation confirms both sentences. Davidson offers a similar case of agreement disguised by different usages of 'yawl' and 'ketch'[12]; our account, however, differs from his in not having to assume (even if it is indeed the case) that the extensions of *yang* and 'sheep and goats' precisely coincide, that they are intertranslatable like the dates of the two calendars. When reading explanations in two languages of a vocabulary difference between them one is positively grateful that they do not say exactly the same thing, much as when collecting information about an incident one wants photographs taken from different angles at different moments. Davidson remarks that, "Whorf, wanting to demonstrate that Hopi incorporates a metaphysics so alien to ours that Hopi and English cannot, as he puts it, be 'calibrated', uses English to convey the contents of sample Hopi sentences",[13] but there is no paradox here; Whorf would hardly have denied that bilingual readers would be clearer about the divergence with an equally sophisticated Hopi account to compare with his.

Our account of the incommensurability of statements in English and Chinese may seem at first sight to have the same consequences as Feyerabend's of the incommensurability of some scientific theories, according to which a crucial experiment cannot refute an old theory and confirm a new one because terms change in meaning with the change of context; the reason for going over to the new theory is that the experiment described in relation to the old is incompatible with the old but in relation to the new is compatible with the new.[14] Agreeing with Kuhn that, of Popper's methods of rationalizing science, "the one that can be applied, refutation, is greatly reduced in strength", he draws a more radical conclusion than Kuhn's, that "what remains are aesthetic judgements, judgements of taste, and our own subjective wishes".[15] Our present approach, without necessarily excluding his epistemological anarchism, does not in itself imply more than we already know, that to confirm or refute requires, not only logic and observation, but checking whether words have the same sense and whether the calendar is Christian or Muslim. What distinguishes our approach from Feyerabend's is that as long as the scheme is conceived as propositional all truth dissolves into 'verisimilitude', but when it is conceived as a pattern of names we have two clearly defined poles, with truth irrelevant to the pre-logical pattern and required for the observation statements; we ignore for the moment what lies in between.[16]

To treat the schemes as systems of propositions makes it hard to interpret those paradigm switches by which, according to Kuhn,[17] science moves from an old one to a new. Davidson's abolition of the conceptual scheme is already implicit in his own description of the supposed switches: "We get a new out of an old scheme when the speakers of a language come to accept as true an important range of sentences they previously took to be false (and of course vice versa)", but with the meanings of the sentences changed.[18] But granted that Kuhn's paradigms are not Jakobson's, and that they are disciplinary matrices with the theories inside them, his choice of the term 'paradigm' calls attention to the point he takes as crucial, that a scientific theory is not fully intelligible outside the practice in which the experimenter assumes his problem to be *similar* to those of classic cases taken as exemplary. A crisis comes when scientists lose faith in the similarity, leading in due course to the sudden insight which shifts the classification of the similar and the contrasting. On Kuhn's account as on ours the switch is pre-logical, like the flash of metaphor in a poem. The conceptual scheme as pattern of the matrix as a whole is of course neither true nor false, but the truth of predictions which follow from the old and new theories can be checked as one checks the Chinese and English sentences against the cat on the mat, the green grass, the goat in the field.

As the paradigm for the paradigm shift we may take the argument of Ryle's *Concept of Mind,* and restate it in terms of the proportional ratios of our semiological description.[19] Ryle sets out to discredit the dichotomy of a body which is extended in space and a mind which is not. He points out that to assume that mind is different in kind from, yet interacts with, the body which is a machine, implies crediting it with a similarity, that its activities like the body's have causes and effects. The mind as 'ghost in the machine' has to be conceived as a 'spectral machine'. This leads to familiar difficulties; how can willing, which is non-spatial, cause the limbs to move in space, or the mind's perception of a colour be the effect of a process in the optic nerve? Ryle sees the problem as arising from an improper correlation in the metaphorising at the back of thought, 'Mind : head, hands, feet : : ruler : subjects' (the 'parapolitical myth'), adjusted after the advent of mechanistic science to '. . . . : : governor engine : other engines' (the 'para-mechanical myth'). He invites us instead to try out other correlations: 'Mind : head, hands, feet : : University : colleges, libraries, playing fields', or '. . . . : : the British constitution : Parliament, judiciary, Church of England'. It is implied that the correlations deposited by habit or initiated by fresh insights are prior to the possibility of logical demonstration; when a new one occurs to the philosopher he chooses which to prefer by whether the arguments which start from them lead into or avoid logical difficulties.

Ryle's change of approach is not a matter of questioning the *proposition* 'Mind is to head, hands, feet, as ruler is to subjects'. We may illustrate this point, and also the fluidity which makes the paradigm switch possible, by adding two more pairs to the chain with which we started.

	A	B
1	Day	Night
2	Light	Darkness
3	Knowledge	Ignorance
4	Good	Evil
5	White man	Black man
6	Blonde	Brunette

The scheme does impose a pressure to think of white man as contrasting with black as day and good with night and evil, of black man as connecting with ignorance and evil as white with knowledge and good. Someone who yields to it may formulate a couple of the syntagmatic connexions (B 5 with B 3 and 4) in the sentences 'Black men are ignorant' and 'Black men are evil'. But even the least rational of racialists guided by the correlation is unlikely to base his case on, or even to accept, the propositionalised 'White man is to black man as. . . . '; he will offer examples to prove 'Black men are ignorant' and 'Black men are evil'. Or again, in responding to certain kinds of art and entertainment, we allow ourselves to expect that the blonde girl will be the heroine and the brunette the villainess; but not only have we never formulated 'Blondes are to brunettes as . . .', we do not in ordinary life expect blonde girls to be sweet and innocent, and brunettes sultry and dangerous. The propositions from which our rational thinking starts do not belong to the conceptual scheme as we are using the term, they are formulations of syntagmatic connexions within it. Once formulated, they can be tested by observation from within the scheme, which confirms that there is generally light by day and darkness by night, but not that white men are generally good and black evil, and forces ejection of the penultimate pair from the scheme.

Let us suppose that in X's scheme propositions formulating syntagmatic connexions have grown into a magical system which entitles him to predict that by reciting certain spells the ritually pure become invulnerable to bullets, in Y's into a scientific system entitling him to predict that they will be as vulnerable as anyone else. X, seeing his comrades fall, assumes that they have ritually defiled themselves, until finally the slaughter compels him to admit that in this case his system has no predictive value. Then X and Y agree in assenting both to X's 'Your magic is stronger than mine' and Y's 'My science is more effective than your magic', sentences which are not intertranslatable. If we make X speak Chinese and Y English, the words with which they assent will differ in semantic scope, but each if bilingual will respond to X's sentence with *ian* 'so' *hsin* 'trustworthy' (for convenience we make them speak the classical language of Chinese philosophy) and to Y's with 'true'. X is now driven to the conclusion that to defend China it will be necessary to master Western magic; and in doing so he finds himself, at least while utilizing the discipline which he is now coming to conceive as science, forced into a paradigm shift from his own to Y's conceptual scheme. At this point X and Y agree that Y's system of propositions is more adequate for prediction, perhaps also that X's is or was more adequate for integrating a community in harmony with nature. Does it follow that for both of them X's is false and Y's true? That will depend on whether they judge truth solely by utility for prediction. We use the word 'true' unanimously only of factual statements such as 'The cat sat on the mat' and 'No one is invulnerable to bullets'. Its variable metaphorical extensions (different from those of comparable Chinese words), to moral, spiritual, metaphysical, logical, or scientific truths, or to the truth to life or nature of works of art, are a matter of preferred terminology; nowadays one can even accept a religion without insisting on its truth. The issue which concerns us here has nothing to do with whether one decides to apply 'true' to theories only relatively adequate for prediction, which we accept in the expectation of abandoning them when they are superseded by the work of some future Nobel prize winner. To escape the conclusion that all truth is relative to incommensurable conceptual schemes it is enough to show that the schemes themselves are patterns of names neither true nor false, and that factual statements depend on them for their meaning but not for their truth; we need not bother about what lies between these extremes.

We have imagined X and Y as learning each other's languages. The mere fact that they can do so forbids us to suppose that what is true at one end of the Old World may be false at the other, or that schemes being incommensurable an English speaker and a Chinese can never judge the truth of anything the other says. However, it makes no difference whether the schemes belong to different natural languages or to the same. If we make X an English practitioner of modern witchcraft saying 'My magic is stronger than yours' to the man of science Y, the appeal to judgment by results is the same as if we make him Chinese. There is always danger of thinking of language communities with their conceptual schemes as distinct entities like persons, so that getting out of the scheme of one's own seems to raise the same difficulties as escaping

72

solipsism in the case of the individual. But for the philosophical issue it does not matter whether, within language in general, differences are of total vocabulary or of technical terminology or of elevated, colloquial, or slangy levels of speech, any more than it matters for children at the stage when they effortlessly pick up a language and as quickly forget it. (A friend of mine trying to halt the rapid erosion of the Chinese which his children had been speaking before returning to England was asked, "Why do you keep on talking in that funny way?"). For the issue which we are discussing there is no such thing as a monolingual speaker, and the language in which any one person thinks embraces every variety in varying degrees comprehensible to and utilisable by him. If his French is perfect he can no more translate it perfectly into English than his scientific into liturgical language or his poetry into officialese.

As we noticed in the first paragraph of this paper, conceptual schemes may be taken to include, not only the syntagmatic connexions of pairs in a chain, but the syntactic structures which organise them in sentences, although not on our account the sentences themselves. We may see Indo-European and Chinese syntax as converging towards a shared distinction between the nominal and the verbal unit, much as their vocabularies approach synonymy in naming organisms, artifacts, and other 'natural kinds'. On closer inspection of nouns differences appear; Hansen argued that classical Chinese nouns in general are closer to our mass than to our count nouns,[20] Harbsmeier has more recently divided them into three classes:

1. Mass noun, counted with a preceding sortal as in modern Chinese (*yi pei shui* 'one cup of water').
2. Count nouns, counted individually without sortal or with the sortal *following* the noun (*san ma* or *ma san p'i* 'three horses').
3. Generic nouns, with kinds variously divisible and countable without sortals (*ssu min* 'the four [classes of] people').[21]

Hansen argues that Western thought is predisposed by number termination to conceive the world as an aggregate of distinct objects, Chinese by the mass noun to conceive it as a whole variously divisible into parts. Le Gall's inability to understand the *ch'i* except as a collection of atoms[22] would be a good illustration. The hypothesis survives Harbsmeier's classification; most or all philosophical terms would presumably be not count but generic nouns. This is plainly the case with *ch'i*; the *yi ch'i* 'one *ch'i*' divides into the *erh ch'i* 'two (sorts of) *ch'i*' the Yin and Yang, and so on through the *wu ch'i* 'five (sorts of) *ch'i*' down to the *wan wù* 'myriad (sorts of) thing'. That Chinese thought would be conditioned to divide down rather than add up is in any case suggested by other features of the language. In classical Chinese one affirms existence not by '*X* exists' but by *Yu X* '(It) has *X*' (the 'it' of the translation being the stop-gap 'it' of English 'It is raining'), tends to ask of a particular object not *Ho yeh* 'What is it?' but *Ho mu yeh* 'What tree is it?' or *Ho niao yeh* 'What bird is it?', and asks for the agent of an action not with *ho* 'what?' but with *shu* 'which?'.[23] We may even catch out Davidson, that blasphemer against the conceptual scheme, in taking a wrong turning because predisposed by grammatical number to think of the world as an aggregate of constant and discrete units. He is denying the coherence of claiming that a scheme organises "reality (the universe, the world, nature)".

> We cannot attach a clear meaning to the notion of organizing a single object (the world, nature, etc.) unless that object is understood to contain or consist in other objects. Someone who sets out to organize a closet arranges the things in it. If you are told not to organize the shoes and shirts but the closet itself, you would be bewildered. How would you organize the Pacific Ocean? Straighten out its shores perhaps, or relocate its islands, or destroy the fish.
>
> A language may contain simple predicates whose extensions are matched by no simple predicates, or even by any predicates at all, in some other language. What enables us to make this point in particular cases is an ontology common to the two languages, with concepts that individuate the same objects. We can be clear about breakdowns in translation when they are local enough, for a background of generally successful translation provides what is needed to make the failures intelligible.[24]

Here the example of the Pacific Ocean is well chosen. Language divides up and organises its indeterminate parts (its 'seas', its 'shores', its 'bays' unless the shores have been straightened out) and its individual objects ('islands', 'fish'). The differentiation of objects from parts is relative to the degree of Jakobsonian similarity and contiguity; Indo-European languages draw a sharp and at some places arbitrary line between them, preferring for our convenience to treat the Pacific spray with its transient drops, and the sand with its enduring grains, as masses rather than as collections of individuals. Why then does Davidson treat this example as without significant difference from the much less apposite illustration of the closet, of a space occupied by the artifacts (shoes, shirts) which like organisms are especially clearly individuated? Surely because he is thinking in a language which sharply contrasts the singular with the plural, 'the closet itself' with 'the shoes and shirts', 'the Pacific Ocean' with 'its islands' and even 'its shores' (which are parts rather than objects), 'the world, nature, etc.' with 'objects'. There would be no such compulsion to assume the primacy of individuals if English, on the analogy of Classical Chinese, lacked number termination, and we said 'this closet' and 'its shoe and shirt' as we say 'its dust' or 'its smell'. The effect of number termination is such that we cannot even make the simple statement that language classifies things as similar or different without implying in advance that the 'thing-s' are different.

Davidson recognises that different languages may individuate differently over a certain range of words, but sees this as only a local difficulty for translation. That we could not explore such differences without sharing "concepts that individuate the same objects" seems to him self-evident, requiring no further explanation or illustration. But let us suppose, reverting to one of our previous examples, that a Chinese student of English has been assuming that *yang* and 'sheep' are synonymous but begins to doubt it. He points out a sheep and a goat, asks of both 'Is that a sheep?', and in the second case I answer 'No, a goat'. He has no need to guard against the danger that I might take him to be pointing at the horn; I cannot answer 'No, a horn' because 'horn', unlike 'goat' is not on the same paradigmatic level as 'sheep'. It would be less appropriate to his problem to ask the 'What is that?' which allows me to answer 'A horn', forcing him to introduce a shared concept by narrowing his question to something like 'What is that animal?'.

As this criticism of Davidson illustrates, logic is independent of syntactic structure, which in any language is logically untidy, and can guide argument in a direction which irrespective of language may be wrong. An obvious example is the ambiguity of 'or'; the absence of a linguistic marker of the distinction between exclusive and inclusive 'or' has not stopped Westerners from establishing it and Chinese from learning it from them. The mysteries of *Lao-tzu* and the *Yi-ching*, and the systematic but seemingly quite alien thinking of Yin-Yang cosmology, has often tempted Westerners to speculate that Chinese thought has a logic peculiar to itself. But Harbsmeier's examination of Classical Chinese particles from the logician's angle[25] leaves no doubt that logical operations were always the same in China as they are here. Even Yin-Yang thinking, which is pre-logical, is the same elaboration of correlative thinking as that of Western proto-science right up to the Renaissance. Chinese syntax does affect both the subject/predicate distinction and, as I have argued elsewhere,[26] the categories; but we no longer think like Aristotle that these belong to logic. It is convenient to speak of the Chinese *verb* as having a subject, but this refers to the agent of the action rather than the topic of the sentence, and in sentences divisible into topic and comment the verb may have a subject inside the comment. However, Aristotle's assumption that the grammatical subject provides what the sentence is about and the predicate what is said about it does not work well even for Indo-European language ('Who was the writer? *Shakespeare* was the writer'). It is not required for the validity of the syllogism; if asked for an example of a particular which is demonstrably mortal, I could answer 'All *men* are mortal, *Socrates* is a man, therefore *Socrates* is mortal'. When the occasional syllogism with both premisses explicit happens to turn up in early Chinese literature there is no doubt that it is functioning precisely as it would for us, as in this one from Wang Ch'ung (A.D. 27–c. 100): "Man is a thing: though honoured as king or noble, by nature he is no different from other things. No thing does not die, how can man be immortal?"[27]

Here it may be noticed that with the tightening of logical organisation sentences do approach intertranslatability. It would seem pointless to extend our doubts about 'The cat sat on the mat' to 'No thing does not die' as translation of Wang Ch'ung's *Wù wu pu ssu*, which word-for-word is roughly 'Thing not-have not die'. In Chinese as in standard English the double negative amounts to an affirmative (and would be so understood in such a sentence even in languages which are logically less tidy in this respect, such as Greek, in which negatives can pile up without a switch to the affirmative). Doubt as to whether the Chinese sentence can be analysed as subject and predicate does not affect the point that *wù* and *ssu* have the same logical relation as 'thing' and 'die'. *Wù* has a narrower extension than 'thing' (for 'things to do' there is another Chinese word, *shih*), but the logical relation to *ssu* 'die' narrows the extension of each to 'living thing'. Granted that in traditional Chinese medicine there is not even an exact synonymy of *ssu* and 'die', this raises only the same sort of problem as the difficulty of defining clinical death in our own medicine; the general difference between a functioning and decomposing body is among the least impugnable distinctions between natural kinds.

As for the categories, it has been shown by Benveniste[28] and others that Aristotle's relate closely both to the Greek interrogative pronouns, adjectives, and adverbs and to Greek grammatical distinctions. Thus, the last four (posture, state, action, passion) are illustrated by verbs in the middle, perfect, active, and passive respectively; since modern languages lack the middle voice and an equivalent to the Greek perfect, the categories of posture and state are barely intelligible to us. I have tried the experiment of similarly relating Classical Chinese interrogatives and sentence units to the vernacular category-words, and found that the resulting classification often diverges from Aristotle's. Thus, questions such as *Ho jo* 'What is it like?', when asked of a thing, are answered by describing its *chuang* 'appearance, characteristics', comparable with Aristotelian quality. But interrogatives such as *Wu-hu* 'whence, where, whither?' will, depending on the direction implicit in the succeeding verb, ask for the source, position, or destination, in agreement with the common generalization that Chinese thinking is in terms of process rather than of static entities. The corresponding category would have to be much wider than Aristotelian place; it seems to be *tao* 'path, way', with *so* 'place' as a position on it. It is notable that what we would call moral qualities seem never to be included in a person's *chuang*; they belong to his *tao*, the way he acts, and to his personal *te* (variously translated 'virtue, power, potency'), the source from which the action starts.[29] Here we catch a glimpse of answers to such questions as why the Tao is central to Chinese thought, why it is regularly paired with *te*, why it is conceived as the source of all things as well as their path. But although convinced that syntactic structure guides categorization in both Greek and Chinese, I fully agree with Reding's observation[30] that, for example, Aristotle recognises logical relations even when they are not marked by the genitive case which in the Greek distinguishes his initial examples of the category of relation. This would only be further evidence that syntactic structures are logically irregular and have to be tidied up. Since the interrogative words of different languages are not synonymous, and connect with their syntactic structures, it seems inevitable that Aristotle or anyone else asking questions with them will be categorizing along lines initially set by the language in which he thinks.

Introducing syntactic structure into the conceptual scheme does not, therefore, bring us any nearer to epistemological relativism. Truths of fact are independent of the scheme, and so are logical 'truths', if that is what you want to call them. Moral 'truths' we leave out of the present discussion. By 'independent', it may be necessary to repeat, I do not mean that factually true statements are translatable into any natural language, but that to confirm or refute a factual statement by reason and observation you have only to understand its place in the appropriate conceptual scheme, you do not have to share the scheme. Nor do I want to suggest that if schemes could be perfectly corrected by logic and observation they would all become the same. In reading Chinese thinkers, as in reading the poets of unfamiliar literatures, one welcomes —to use the inevitable visual metaphor—looking out on the world from a new perspective, has the impression of seeing the world more clearly the more perspectives are opened. This is not simply because much Chinese philosophising *is* poetry; one has the same impression in reading the great philosophers of the West, who do not, like the great scientists, become obsolete. In treating schemes as equal, with one or other more adequate for solving one or other kind of problem, it becomes possible to use one to criticise something in another, as Fingarette uses Confucius to undermine our inner/outer dichotomy, Rosemont the problematic of moral choice, Hall and Ames the concept of transcendence.[31] Thus, one oddity of the Western tradition, as I have argued elsewhere,[32] is an ontology in which the concept of Being covers the whole range of the Indo-European verb 'to be', the various uses of which are distinguished by different words and constructions in many or most languages, including Chinese. It was in Arabic, which like Chinese has no common word for existence and the copulative functions, that the concepts of existence and essence divided out.[33] Here we have a good instance of a logical distinction which is more visible in one language than in another but is not created or abolished by them. Aristotle, alone among the Greeks, did perceive the distinction between existence and the copulative; and the Latin scholastics did see the point of the Arabic concepts and borrow them, although only to incorporate them into their own concept of Being.

In this example the syntactic structures guiding Chinese thought happen to be logically tidier than the Indo-European guiding ours. Like symbolic logic, Classical Chinese deals differently with existence and the copulas, and although it does not distinguish class membership from class inclusion has from the early centuries A.D. a separate copula *chi* distinguishing identity. The existential *yu X* '(It) has *X*, there is *X*' is analysable as verb-object not subject-verb, so, like the existential quantifier of logic, *yu* cannot be mistaken for the predicate. Again as in logical symbolism, there is no copula linking the subject to what corresponds to our predicative adjective, in Chinese a stative verb as in *Ts'ao ch'ing* 'Grass is-green'. Finally, there is no word for a concept of Being covering all these, any more than there is a symbol for it in logic. That symbolic logic is a Western discovery confirms that our thought has not been permanently imprisoned by Indo-European language structure. Nevertheless, Being has never quite lost its place in our conceptual scheme. Even in refuting the assumption that existence is a predicate, Kant passing from 'God is omnipotent' to 'God is, or there is a God' *(Gott ist, oder es ist ein Gott)* thinks of the 'is' as still the same word positing the subject as previously it posited the predicate in its relation to the subject.[34] Modern languages, unlike Greek and Latin, distinguish existence from the copulative relations almost as clearly as Arabic and Chinese, using 'there is', *il y a* and Kant's *es ist* for existence and reducing 'is' to a copula. However, we still have the abstract noun 'being' embracing all the functions of Greek *einai* and Latin *esse*, now detached from both our natural and our artificial languages, but all that is needed for the ghost of the old concept still to walk.

We may see the question of the conceptual scheme as emerging because in recent thought the relation between correlative and analytic thinking has unobtrusively become a problem. Western philosophy (like one ancient Chinese school, the Later Mohists[35]) strives to detach analytic thinking from correlative and make it the sole authority for knowledge as distinct from opinion. This enterprise has no place for correlative thinking as spontaneous patterning in which a gap is filled by a flash of insight; it has to propositionalize it as the loose inference by analogy outside the bounds of strict logic, allowable for everyday commonsense thinking, where indeed it is indispensable, and in the creative thinking which precedes exact formulation (as Popper affirms, what matters in science is how you test the hypothesis, not how you arrived at it). As for the more exuberant excesses of correlative thinking in the Chinese proto-sciences and in Western up to the sixteenth century, for the seeker of exact knowledge they are not only fallacy-ridden but scarcely intelligible, and thinkers who (like most of the Chinese) seldom analyse except to correct correlations[36] do not count as philosophers at all. However, modern philosophy has to take increasing notice of the models, analogues, metaphors, paradigms, which still refuse to be expelled from its realm. It is driven from several directions (by Wittgenstein, Ryle, Kuhn, Derrida) to admit that if we dig below the surface of our supposedly exact knowledge we still find the correlative at its foundations. This recognition is the same as the sinologist's when in searching for the metaphorical roots of a Chinese concept he discovers that to compare and contrast it with Western concepts he has to explore their roots as well.

But a philosopher habituated to assume the complete independence of analytic thinking cannot fully adapt to this changed situation. A conceptual scheme is intelligible to him only as a system of propositions presupposed as true. In our longest quotation from Davidson[37] it may be noticed that, where we would speak of distinguishing things by naming them 'sheep' and 'goat' or assimilating them by their Chinese name *yang*, Davidson speaks of "simple predicates whose extensions are matched by no simple predicates" (the extension of 'is sheep' or 'is goat' not matching that of *yang yeh* 'is *yang*'). For him the act of naming being outside logic cannot be taken into account. But to accept the idea of the conceptual scheme on these terms has the result that as observational tests become progressively weaker our propositions about the world threaten to become disconnected from the world. In the extreme case of Derrida, the similarities and contrasts between things are wholly excluded from consideration, difference is confined to the 'identity/ difference' of Saussurean linguistics, and language, instead of returning analytic thinking to its correlative roots, breaks out of its bounds to fly away into the void. Then it comes as a relief when Davidson shows that a conceptual scheme conceived as propositional does not even make sense, and we are back where we started.

The solution, I suggest, is to accept and come to terms with the thought that analysis starts from the results of spontaneous correlation. Modern philosophy no longer treats thought as distinct from and 'clothed' by language, modern linguistics confirms our intuition that for the full exercise and understanding of language analysis is insufficient. The thinking which is fully adequate, for linguistic as for other skills, is spontaneous correlation. To the extent that we lose the faith that, by definitions and stipulated translation equivalents, we can detach words from their dependence on variable patterns of syntagm and paradigm, to achieve true intertranslatability, it becomes urgent to recover the engagement of analytic with correlative thinking. It may be humiliating at first for the pure rationalist to admit that reason has never after all escaped dependence on structures maintained by habit or shifted by unanticipated insight. But he is being asked only to relinqish his hope of a knowledge which is more than critically tested opinion; and by now we are all getting used to that. Is not reason more secure when credited only with testing and building on the results of spontaneous patterning which although erratic is corrigible than when, insisting on its independence, it turns against itself, persistently refuting all its traditional supports? Do we not already assume that it does merely test and build on results at the level below perceptual patterning?[38]

NOTES

1. Davidson in *Post-Analytic Philosophy*, ed. John Rajchman and Cornel West (New York: Columbia University Press, 1985), 139.
2. For practical reasons I shall speak of 'propositions' where Davidson and others

say 'sentences', reserving the latter for sentences in natural languages, English, Chinese.

3. *Reason and Spontaneity* (London: Curzon Press, 1985), 57f.

4. Roman Jakobson, "Two Aspects of Language", *Selected Writings*, 2 vols. (The Hague and Paris: Mouton, 1971), 239–59.

5. As Henry Rosemont has pointed out to me, there are few exceptions (such as English 'black and white') to the rule that the preferred member of a pair is said first, and Chinese *Yin Yang* is perhaps the most remarkable.

6. *Chuang-tzu*, ch. 17, trans. A. C. Graham, *Chuang-tzu: The Inner Chapters*, (London: Allen Unwin, 1981), 147; (Unwin Paperbacks, 1986), 147.

7. Jacques Derrida, *On Grammatology*, trans. G. C. Spivak (Baltimore: John Hopkins University Press, 1976).

8. David L. Hall and Roger T. Ames, *Thinking through Confucius* (Albany, NY: State University of New York Press, 1987).

9. Cf. below pp. 75–79.

10. *Mo-tzu*, ch. 45, trans. A. C. Graham, *Later Mohist Logic, Ethics and Science* (London and Hong Kong: The Chinese University Press and School of Oriental Studies 1978), 471.

11. Cf. Davidson's argument that there can be no notion of truth independent of the notion of translation, Davidson, 140.

12. Davidson, 141.

13. Davidson, 130.

14. P. K. Feyerabend, *Problems of Empiricism* (Cambridge University Press, 158f.).

15. Feyerabend, 160.

16. Cf. below pp. 71–73.

17. Thomas S. Kuhn, *The Structure of Scientific Revolutions* (Chicago: University of Chicago Press, 1970).

18. Davidson, 133.

19. Gilbert Ryle, *The Concept of Mind* (London: Hutchinson's University Library, 1949).

20. Chad Hansen, *Language and Logic in Ancient China* (Ann Arbor: University of Michigan Press, 1983).

21. Christoph Harbsmeier, "Language and Logic in Ancient China", in *Science and Civilisation in China*, Vol. 7, part 1, ed. Joseph Needham (Cambridge University Press, forthcoming).

22. Cf. above p. 60.

23. Cf. "Relating Categories to Question Forms in Pre-Han Chinese Thought", in my *Studies in Chinese Philosophy and Philosophical Literature* (Institute of East Asian Philosophies, National University of Singapore, 1986; Albany, NY; State University of New York Press, 1990), 373–78, 380–85.

24. Davidson, 137.

25. Christoph Harbsmeier, *Aspects of Classical Chinese Syntax* (London: Curzon Press, 1981).

26. Graham, "Relating Categories".

27. *Lun Heng*, ch. 24 (*Tao hsu p'ien*), trans. Alfred Forke, *Lun Heng, Essays of Wang Ch'ung*, vol. 1 (New York: Paragon Book Gallery, 1962), 335f.

28. Émile Benveniste, *Problèmes de linguistique générale* (Paris: Gallimard, 1966), 63–74.

29. Graham, "Relating Categories", 385–94, 400–404.

30. Jean-Paul Reding, "Greek and Chinese Categories", *Philosophy East and West* 36, no. 4 (1986): 349–74, criticising Benveniste and myself on this question.

31. Herbert Fingarette, *Confucius—The Secular as Sacred* (New York: Harper Torchbooks, 1972). Henry Rosemont, Jr. "Why Take Rights Seriously? A Confucian Critique", *Human Rights and the World Religions*, ed. L. Rouner (South Bend, 1988). Hall and Ames ut sup.

32. "Being in Western Philosophy Compared with *shih/fei* and *yu/wu* in Chinese Philosophy", *Studies in Chinese Philosophy and Philosophical Literature* (Institute of East Asian Philosophies, National University of Singapore, 1986), 322–59.

33. I discuss the linguistic side of the Greek-Arabic-Latin transmission of Western ontology in "Being in Linguistics and Philosophy", *The Verb 'to Be' and Its Synonyms*, ed. John Verhaar, Foundations of Language Supplementary Series, vol. 5 (Dordrecht, Holland: D. Reidel, 1972), 225–33, reprinted as chapter 5 in this volume. The same series has a version of "Being in Western Philosophy" designed for the non-sinological reader, " 'Being' in Classical Chinese", vol. 1 (1967), 1–39.

34. Cf. "Being in Western Philosophy", *Studies*, 354f.

35. Cf. *Later Mohist Logic*.

36. As in the dialogues of Mencius and Kao-tzu, analysed by D. C. Lau, *Mencius* (Harmondsworth, Middlesex: Penguin Classics, 1970), 235–63.

37. Davidson, 137.

38. For this essay I am indebted to the criticisms of Henry Rosemont.

'Being' in Linguistics and Philosophy

5

The concept of Being is a good test for the thesis of Benjamin Whorf[1] that the grammatical structure of language guides the formation of philosophical concepts. Consider these three facts:

(1) A verb 'to be' which serves both as copula ('*X* is *Y*') and as indicator of existence ('*X* is', 'There is *X*') is almost confined to Indo-European languages.[2]

(2) A concept of Being combining essence (what *X* is *per se*) and existence is confined to philosophies developed in languages of the Indo-European family. In the two major philosophical traditions which developed outside this family, Arabic *wujūd* and Chinese *yu* are not 'being' but 'existence'.[3]

(3) Although the first language of Western philosophy was Greek, its main stream passed through Semitic languages (Syriac, Arabic, Hebrew) before returning to Indo-European languages (scholastic Latin, French, English, German). It was in Arabic, which sharply separates the existential and copulative functions, that the distinction between existence and essence emerged.[4]

An adequate account of the development of the Western concept of Being in its linguistic context would require the co-operation of specialists in many disciplines. But it may be useful to offer a preliminary sketch, as a focus for future criticism and inquiry. I shall therefore cover much ground in a little space, and intrude into several fields within which I am not an authority.

It is well known that Greek philosophy hardly ever distinguishes between the existential and copulative functions of *einai* 'to be'. Thus Plato argues that since everything is double or big or heavy in relation to some things and half or small or light compared with others, we have an equal right to say that it is (exists) or that it is not (does not exist).[5] Aristotle ignores the distinction when he analyses the senses of *einai* in *Metaphysics* V.vii, although he carefully separates being *per se* and *per accidens*, being as 'truth', and potential and actual being, and differentiates being *per se* according to the categories. The great exception is the second book of *Posterior Analytics*, where the question 'whether it is' (*ei esti*) is contrasted with the question 'what it is' (*ti esti*). By 'whether it is' Aristotle means 'whether it exists', but it is interesting to notice that it costs him some trouble to make this plain: "I mean the question whether or not it is absolutely, not whether it is white or not" (τὸ δ' εἰ ἔστιν ἢ μὴ ἁπλῶς λέγω, ἀλλ' οὐκ εἰ λεῦκὸς ἢ μή).[6] He has no verb corresponding to 'exist' and except for *ousia* (which embraces the concepts later distinguished by *essentia* and *substantia*) he has no noun corresponding to 'essence' to replace his *ti esti* ('what *X* is') and *ti ēn einai* ('what it is to be *X*'). Confined to constructions with *einai*, he can distinguish between existential and copulative functions only by such expressions as: "the substance being not this or that but absolutely, or not absolutely but something *per se* or *per accidens*" (. . . τοῦ εἶναι μὴ τοδὶ ἢ τοδὶ ἀλλ' ἁπλῶς τὴν οὐσίαν, ἢ τοῦ μὴ ἁπλῶς ἀλλά τι τῶν καθ' αὑτὸ ἢ κατὰ συμβεβηκός), and "whether it absolutely is, not is one of its attributes, or whether it is one of its attributes" (. . . ἢ ἁπλῶς καὶ μὴ τῶν ὑπαρχόντων τι, ἢ τῶν ὑπαρχόντων).[7]

Whenever Aristotle dispenses with such constructions we are left doubtful whether or not he has lost sight of the distinction, although in many contexts the impossibility of replacing *einai* by the less flexible English 'to be' forces translators to prejudge the issue by resorting to 'to exist'. Thus when Aristotle observes that definition shows what a thing is (*ti esti*) but not 'that it is' (*hori esti*), which is known not by definition but by demonstration, it is convenient and sometimes hardly avoidable to translate *hoti esti* as 'existence', although it certainly embraces not only the existence of *X* but its being in fact what it is defined as being:

ut sup. 92b20–25 φανερὸν δὲ καὶ κατὰ τοὺς νῦν τρόπους τῶν ὅρων ὡς οὐ δεικνύουσιν οἱ ὁριζόμενοι ὅτι ἔστιν. εἰ γὰρ καὶ ἔστιν ἐκ του μέσου τι ἴσον, ἀλλὰ διὰ τί ἔστι τὸ ὁρισθέν; καὶ διὰ τί τοῦτ' ἔστι κύκλος; εἴη γὰρ ἄν καὶ ὀρειχάλκου φάναι εἶναι αὐτόν. οὔτε γὰρ ὅτι δυνατὸν εἶναι τὸ λεγόμενον προσδηλοῦσιν οἱ ὅροι οὔτε ὅτι ἐκεῖνο οὐ φασὶν εἶναι ὁρισμοί, ἀλλ᾽ ἀεὶ ἔξεστι λέγειν το διὰ τί.

> It is evident also from the methods of defining now in use that those who define do not prove *the existence of the definiendum* (*hoti esti*, 'that *X* is'). Even supposing that there is something equidistant from the centre, why *does* the object so defined *exist (esti)?* and why is it a circle? One might equally well assert that it is the definition of mountain-copper. Definitions do not include evidence that it is possible for what they describe *to exist (einai)*, nor that it is identical with that which they claim to define. It is always possible to ask *why* (Tredennick).[8]

Although Tredennick translates *hoti esti* as 'existence' (no doubt because in the second underlined instance it is grammatically impossible to replace *esti* by 'is'), the phrase implies both that something described as equidistant from a centre exists and that it is in fact a circle.

ἔτι ἕτερον τὸ τί ἐστι καὶ ὅτι ἔστι δεῖξαι. ὁ μὲν οὖν ὁρισμὸς τί ἐστι δηλοῖ, ἡ δὲ ἀπόδειξις ὅτι ἐστι τόδε κατὰ τοῦδε ἢ οὐκ ἔστιν. "To reveal the essence of a thing is not the same as to prove a proposition about it; now definition exhibits the essence, but demonstration proves that an attribute is, or is not, predicated of a subject."[9] (Literally: "Moreover to show what it is is different from showing that it is; now definition shows what it is, demonstration on the other hand that with regard to this this is or is not.")

Here the *einai* of *hoti esti* 'that it is' is primarily the copula between subject and predicate; unable to use 'exist', Tredennick is driven in a different direction, and a reader of the English would hardly guess that in both passages Aristotle is discussing the same topic in the same terminology.

While in Greek it is much more difficult than in English to distinguish existential and copulative 'to be', in Arabic there is no convenient word which combines both functions. Arabic has an existential verb *kāna* 'be, become'; but for "*A* is *B*" it uses the sentence pattern "*A* (nominative) *B* (nominative)", or, interposing the third-person pronoun *huwa* (feminine *hiya*), "*A* (nominative) *huwa B* (nominative)", or, with the particle *inna*, "*Inna A* (accusative) *B* (nominative)". The contrast is not quite absolute, for there is also a copulative pattern with *kāna*: "*Kāna A* (nominative) *B* (accusative)". But the Arabic translators

87

did not in fact exploit any possibility there may have been of regularly reproducing *einai* by *kāna*, an unsuitable equivalent in any case because of its suggestion of 'becoming'.[10] The version of Aristotle's *Categories* made by Isḥaq ibn Ḥunayn (died A.D. 910/911), which Khalil Georr has studied in detail,[11] deals with *einai* by the following devices:

(1) Existential *einai* in ordinary contexts is represented by *kāna*, when used technically by the passive of *WaJaDa* 'find', in a usage not unlike that of English "Lions are found in Africa". For *to einai* it uses the infinitive *WuJūD*, for *to on* the passive participle *maWJūD* 'what is found/what exists'.

(2) For "*A is B*" it occasionally uses "*Kāna A B*", but generally "*A B*" or "*A huwa B*". In conjunction with *mā* 'what', the usual formula for *'ti esti . . .*' 'what is . . . ?' is '*mā huwa . . .*' (feminine '*mā hiya . . .*'). The coinage *māhiyyah* 'quiddity', an abstract noun probably formed from *mā hiya*,[12] appears several times in the phrase *māhiyyatu-hu*, 'its quiddity', translating *hoper esti*, 'just what it is'. This became a key term in Arabic philosophy, as did *dhāt*, feminine of *dhū* 'possessor' (used in ordinary Arabic in such phrases as *dhū 'ilmin* 'possessor of learning/learned man'), that to which accidents belong. This appears regularly in the phrase *bi dhāti-hi*, 'in its *dhāt*', translating *kath' hauto (per se)*. The versions of other writings of Aristotle introduce other technical terms; thus in the crucial passage on the different senses of 'Being' in *Metaphysics* V.vii *einai* is represented by *huwiyyah*, an abstract noun formed from the interposed pronoun in "*A huwa B*".[13] It may be noticed that the Arabic 'essence'-words are independent of Greek *ousia* (in imitation of which the Latin *essentia* was formed). The Arabic equivalent of *ousia* is *jawhar* 'substance', believed to be a Pahlawi loan-word.[14]

The Arabic versions of Aristotle are very literal, yet because of the structure of the language they transform him at one stroke into a philosopher who talks sometimes about existence, sometimes about quiddity, *never about being*. In place of the single verb *einai* the Arabs found in Aristotle a set of abstract nouns, each rooted in either the existential verb or the copulative sentence patterns. This deformation often obscured Aristotle's meaning, a fact which some of the Arabs discerned.[15] But it also gave Arabic ontology a fresh start, free from the confusion from which Greek philosophy was barely beginning to find the way out. It is a misplaced compliment to credit Al-Fārābī (died 950) and Ibn Sīnā (Avicenna, 980–1037) with the discovery of the ontological difference between essence and existence; it was impossible for an Arab to confuse them, although he might, as did Ibn Rushd (Averroes, 1126–1193), choose for reasons of his own to identify them. The general assumption of Arab philosophers other than Averroes is that existence cannot belong to the quiddity of anything which does not exist necessarily, from which Avicenna concludes that the existence of things is added to their quiddities by the single necessary existent, God.

The Latin translators of Avicenna and Averroes inherited an ontological vocabulary formed in Roman times by translation from Greek. Standard Latin *esse* cannot reproduce *einai* through the whole range of its forms, since it has no participle and gerund, and there is no Latin article with which to establish the case of *esse* treated as an undeclinable noun. (Contrast Greek *to einai* 'being', *tou einai* 'of being'.) Philosophical Latin filled most gaps by supplying an artificial participle (*ens*) and gerund (*essendum*), and by such constructions as *hoc esse* ('this being') *huius esse* ('of this being'). But since it used *ens* only for the nominal *to on*, it was never able to cope with all uses of the Greek participle, and Latin translators were forced on occasion to use either the indicative or *existens* for *ōn, ousa, on:*

Aristotle, *Categories* 2b, 5, 6: μὴ οὐσῶν οὖν τῶν πρώτων οὐσιῶν ἀδύνατον τῶν ἄλλων τι εἶναι.

Aristoteles latinus 1/1–5 (ed. by L. Minio-Paluello, Oxford 1961) p. 8 (Boethius, c. A.D. 510): Si ergo primae substantiae non sunt, impossibile est aliquid esse ceterorum. p. 49 (Editio composita, before A.D. 822): Non existentibus ergo primis substantiis, impossibile est esse aliquid aliorum. "Therefore were there no primary substances it would be impossible for any of the others to be."

The word *essentia* was coined not later than the first century as Latin equivalent for *ousia*,[16] for which, however, Boethius in his translations preferred *substantia*. For Boethius, who remained the primary authority for the use of the word throughout the early Middle Ages, *essentia* still coincided in meaning with *ousia* and had not contracted to the later sense of 'essence' (what *X* is *per se*, what is presented by its definition):

Contra Eutychen III 29–35[17]: Atque uti Graeca utar oratione in rebus quae a Graecis agitata Latina interpretatione translata sunt: αἱ οὐσίαι ἐν μὲν τοῖς καθόλου εἶναι δύνανται. ἐν δὲ τοῖς ἀτόμοις καὶ κατὰ μέρος μόνοις ὑφίστανται, id est: essentiae in universalibus quidem esse possunt, in solis vero individuis et particularibus substant.

"And, if I may use Greek for matters which raised by the Greeks have been translated into Latin, . . . that is: *essentiae* indeed have potential being in universals, but are substantial in individuals and particulars alone."

In the twelfth and thirteenth centuries translations from Arabic and Hebrew, of the Arabic and Jewish philosophers and of previously unknown writings of Aristotle, contributed to the revival of Aristotelianism in Latin Europe. The translations use the following equivalents (The earlier Greek-Arabic and Greek-Latin equivalents are added in brackets):

wujūd 'existence' *(einai)* . . .	*esse (einai)*, occasionally *existere (einai)*
mawjūd 'existent' *(to on)*	*ens (to on)*
dhāt 'possessor' (—)	*essentia (ousia)*
māhiyyah 'quiddity' (—)	*quidditas* (—), *essentia (ousia)*
jawhar 'substance' *(ousia)*	*substantia (ousia)*.

This word-list invites two comments. In the first place it contains the new word *quidditas* apparently directly modelled on *māhiyyah* (this suggestion would of course be vulnerable to a single example of *quidditas* earlier than the twelfth century) and the old word *essentia* finally detached from its historical connexion with *ousia* and sharply separated from *substantia*. Mediaeval philosophers, for better or for worse, are now like the Arabs equipped to speak of the essence or quiddity of a thing, not merely of what it is *(ti esti)* and what it is to be it *(to ti ēn einai)*. In the second place the sharp Arabic distinction between existence and quiddity is partially obscured; *wujūd* 'existence' is replaced by the more general *esse*, and *dhāt* 'possessor' (etymologically independent of *wujūd)* by *essentia* (etymologically derived from *esse*). We can see the effect of this in the *De ente et essentia* of Aquinas, who follows Avicenna closely yet is radically unlike him in the very starting-point of the inquiry ("Ex significatione entis ad significationem essentie procedendum est",[18] "One should proceed from the meaning of 'being' to the meaning of 'essence'". Cf. the later "Essentia autem est secundum quam res esse dicitur",[19] "But essence is that according to which a thing is said to be"). The Arabic and Greco-Latin ontologies have in fact already been spliced in the process of translation; the mediaeval absorption of essence within the concept of Being is already implicit in the Latin Avicenna and Averroes, just as the Arabic refusal to embrace existence on the one hand and quiddity on the other within any common concept is already implicit in the Arabic Aristotle. We may illustrate this by comparing a passage of Averroes with its thirteenth-century Latin version and with a passage of Aquinas which refers to it:

Averroes, *Tafsīr mā ba'd aṭ-ṭabī'at* (edited by Maurice Bouyges, Beyrouth, vol. 2 [1942] 561): "But you should know in short that the name *huwiyyah* (abstract noun formed from the copula) which indicates the *dhāt* of the thing is other than the name *huwiyyah* which indicates the true, and likewise the name *mawjūd* ('existent') which indicates the *dhāt* of the thing is other than the *mawjūd* which indicates the true".

Aristotelis stagiritae Metaphysicorum libri XIV cum Averrois Corduben-sis in eosdem commentariis (Venice 1552), Book 5, f 55v, left column, ll. 56–58: Sed debes scire universaliter quod hoc nomen ens, quod significat essentiam rei, est aliud ab ente, quod significat verum. (The copulative and existential words are both replaced by *ens*, and the two sentences reduced to one; *dhāt* is replaced by *essentia*).

Aquinas, *De ente et essentia* (edited by M.-D. Roland-Gosselin, Paris 1948) 3, ll. 7–12: Nomen igitur essentie non sumitur ab ente secundo modo dicto . . . sed sumitur essentia ab ente primo modo dicto; unde Commentator in eodem loco dicit quod ens primo modo dictum est quod significat essentiam rei.

"Therefore the name 'essence' is not taken from 'being' (*ens*) used in the second sense . . . but 'essence' is taken from 'being' used in the first sense; whence the Commentator (Averroes) says in the same place that 'being' used in the first sense is what signifies the essence of a thing." (The novelty here is that essence is assumed to *take its name* from the etymologically cognate *ens*).

When philosophers began to write in French and English they treated *être* and 'to be' as synonymous with *einai* and *esse*. But this verb, which is characteristic of the Indo-European family, is unstable even within the

Indo-European family. In Sanskrit and in Russian it is nearly as definitely existential as the Arabic *kāna*; in Greek it is primarily existential and not obligatory as copula; in English and French on the other hand it is almost exclusively the copula, existence being indicated by the formulas 'there is' and *il y a* and by the verbs 'to exist', *exister*, which have entered ordinary language from scholastic Latin. The Latin *exsistere, existere*, ('step out from') settled into its present meaning very gradually. For Alexander of Hales (c. 1175–1245) it was still *ex alio sistere* 'to stand out from the other'[20]; Aquinas (c. 1225–1274) still discusses existence and essence in the terminology of the title of his work. *De ente et essentia;* but by the next century Ockham (c. 1280–c. 1349), for example, is discussing the distinction as between *esse existere* or *existere* and *essentia* or *entitas*.[21] The word 'exist' is perhaps the most valuable legacy of the ontological vocabulary of scholasticism, since it illuminates the distinction at the level of the verb, while *essentia* and *quidditas* are nouns which illuminate it only as a metaphysical distinction between concepts.

The extent of the change is very visible in modern translations from Greek. Although '*X* is' is still intelligible as an archaism, however willing the translator may be to archaise he finds the verb 'to be' grammatically much less flexible than *einai*. We cannot replace "Is there *X?*" and "Does *X* exist?" by "Is *X?*", nor "There is life on Mars" and "Life exists on Mars" by "Life is on Mars" (in which 'is' would be understood as copula). It is therefore not only inconvenient but grammatically impossible to translate *einai* consistently by 'to be', as can be seen in the examples quoted earlier in this article from the *Posterior Analytics*. Forced to substitute 'exist' for *einai*, and for other reasons 'essence' for *to ti ēn einai*, we re-interpret Aristotle in a terminology with fifteen hundred years of further development behind it.

Such formulas as 'There is', *il y a, es gibt*, did not really attract the attention of philosophers until recently, because these formulas cannot be turned into abstract nouns. But philosophers use them and are influenced by them whether they notice them or not; and these formulas, since they cannot without artificiality be grammatically analysed into subject and predicate, undermine the assumption that existence is a logical predicate. (Attacking this assumption, Kant took the example *Gott ist allmächtig* 'God is almighty', cut it down to *Gott ist* 'God is', and immediately added *oder es ist ein Gott* 'or "There is a God" '.[22]) Similarly the contraction of the scope of 'to be' to its copulative function has shifted emphasis away from the existential function; Kant, as we have just noticed, starts his discussion of existence from 'God is almighty'; Hegel actually defines 'Being' in copulative terms, " 'Being' may be defined as *'I = I'*, as absolute indifference, or identity, and so on" ("Sein kann bestimmt werden, als Ich = Ich, als die absolute Indifferenz oder Identität u.s.f.".[23]) If we could wipe out the memory of all past philosophy from a man's mind, and start him thinking afresh in contemporary English, would it not be natural for him to conceive 'Being' as purely copulative, as clearly detached from existence as Arabic *dhāt* and *māhiyyah* from *wujūd?* But in practice of course the continuity of the philosophical tradition makes a final divorce of the two concepts impossible. Kant still supposes that when he replaces "God is almighty" by "God is" he is using 'is' in the same sense as before, philosophers still discuss "I think, therefore I am" without rephrasing it in contemporary English, and the abstract noun 'being' with its plural 'beings' remains primarily existential even in common speech. A philosopher therefore cannot adapt his use of 'Being' to the functions of 'to be' in English grammar; he must either stick bravely to the conviction that there is a single concept of Being behind the different functions of *einai,* which is hidden by the grammars of non-Indo-European languages, and which even among the languages of Western philosophy is perfectly displayed only in Greek and Latin, or he must discard the verbal noun 'being' as incurably ambiguous. However difficult he may find it to choose the second alternative while he is thinking in the living language with its deep roots in the past, the artificial language of symbolic logic enables him to make the choice without even noticing what he is doing. In symbolic logic the verb 'to be' dissolves into the sign of existence (∃), which is not a predicate but a quantifier, and three separate copulae, the signs of identity (=), class membership (ε) and class inclusion (⊂).

NOTES

1. *Language, Thought and Reality* (New York: John Wiley, 1956).

2. Cf. Ernst Locker, "Être et Avoir. Leurs expressions dans les langues", *Anthropos* 49 (1954): 481–510.

3. For *wujūd* cf. pages 88 and 90 below. For *yu* cf. A. C. Graham, "Being in Western Philosophy Compared with *shih/fei* and *yu/wu* in Chinese Philosophy", reprinted Graham, *Studies in Chinese Philosophy and Philosophical Literature* (Institute of East Asian Philosophies, National University of Singapore, 1986), 322–59.

4. Cf. E. Gilson, *Le Thomisme* (Paris 1948), p. 55; M.-D. Roland-Gosselin, *Le 'De ente et essentia' de S. Thomas d' Aquin* (Paris: Librarie philosophique J. Vrin, 1948), pp. xix, xx, 150–56; Soheil M. Afnan, *Avicenna* (London, 1958), pp. 115–21.

5. *Republic*, Book 5, 479. For a much fuller account of Being in Greek, see Charles H. Kahn, *The Verb "Be" in Ancient Greek, Foundations of Language Supplementary Series*, vol. 6 (1973), 1–486.

6. *Posterior Analytics*, 89b 33.

7. *Ut sup.*, 90a 10–2, 33.

8. Hugh Tredennick, *Posterior Analytics* (London and Cambridge, Mass.: Loeb Classical Library, 1960), pp. 197, 199.

9. *Ut sup.*, p. 185.

10. Cf. A.-M. Goichon, *La distinction de l'essence et de l'existence d'après Ibn Sinā* (Paris, 1937), p. 29, note 4. For an examination of this account of Being in Arabic, see Fadlou Shehadi, "Arabic and 'to be'", *Foundations of Language Supplementary Series*, vol. 9 (1969), 112–125. Cf. also Shehadi, "Arabic and the Concept of Being", *Essays on Islamic Philosophy and Science*, ed. George F. Hourani (Albany: State University of New York Press, 1975).

11. *Les catégories d'Aristote dans leurs versions syro-arabes* (Beyrouth Adrien-Maisonneuve, 1948). For the Arabic ontological vocabulary cf. Goichon *ut sup.*, pp. 15–17, 29–49; and *Lexique de la langue philosophique d'Ibn Sina* (Paris, 1939); *Vocabulaires comparés d'Aristote et d'Ibn Sina* (Paris, 1939); Soheil-M. Afnan, *Philosophical Terminology in Arabic and Persian* (Leyden, 1964), pp. 29f, 94–97, 99–102, 117–24. My data are from these authorities (who, of course, bear no responsibility for the conclusions drawn from them), and from my own comparisons, made with a very limited knowledge of Arabic, of the Greek and Arabic texts of samples of Aristotle and the Arabic and Latin texts of samples of Avicenna and Averroes.

12. Cf. Afnan, *loc. cit.*, pp. 117–20.

13. Averroes, *Tafsir mā ba'd aṭ-ṭabi'āt*, ed. by M. Bouyges (Beyrouth: Imrimerie catholique, 1942), pp. 552–63.

14. Afnan, *loc. cit.*, p. 99.

15. Afnan, *loc. cit.*, p. 29; Averroes, *Compendio de metafisica*, edited with Spanish translation by Carlos Quiros Rodriguez (Madrid: Real Academia de ciencias

morales y politicas, 1919), Book 1/21. (Of doubtful authenticity, cf. Bouyges ut sup. LIII–LIV.)

16. Roland-Gosselin, *loc. cit.*, p. 9.
17. H. F. Stewart and E. K. Rand, *Boethius: The Theological Tractates.* (London and Cambridge, Mass.: Loeb Classical Library, 1962), p. 86.
18. Roland-Gosselin, *loc. cit.*, p. 2, ll. 6–7.
19. *Ibidem*, p. 10, ll. 4–5.
20. Gilson, *loc. cit.*, p. 73.
21. Ockham, *Philosophical Writings*, a selection edited and translated by Philotheus Boehner (London: Nelson, 1957), 92–95.
22. *Kritik der reinen Vernunft*, Elementarlehre, Part 2, Division 2, Book 2, Chapter 3, Section 4.
23. *Logik*, 96.

Rationalism and Anti-Rationalism in Pre-Buddhist China

The question whether ancient Chinese thought is rational is generally approached with the preconception that the rationalism we have inherited from the Greeks is either a good thing or a bad thing. If it is a good thing, one dismisses Chinese thought as not philosophy but wisdom, if it is a bad thing one extols the superiority of the aphorisms of *Lao-tzu* and the diagrams of the *Book of Changes*. But the question is much more interesting than that. In China we have a culture in which our various modes of thinking about the world appear in different proportions and relations. The mainstream of thought is correlative thinking tested by analysis when it is seen to be going wrong, interrupted by episodes of pure rationalism, of positive anti-rationalism, of rigidifying correlative cosmos-building, and of system-breaking exercises to recover the freedom to correlate.

G. E. R. Lloyd in his *Polarity and Analogy* discovered something similar in Greek philosophy, which it had been our habit to interpret retrospectively as logical from the beginning; the analytic was at first no more than a play on the surface of correlative thinking, and made its bid for full independence only with Aristotle. Western intellectual traditions, however, tend to have only their beginnings in correlative cosmos-building, Greek philosophy before Socrates, Renaissance philosophy before Descartes, science before Galileo, even socialism before Marx (Fourier's Utopia was fitted into a fantastic scheme of cosmic cycles), and to achieve their takeoff by the turn to analysis. This recurrent victory of analytic reason has opened up prospects unsuspected in traditional China, in particular the accelerating progress of science since the seventeenth century. But it might be that the Chinese and the early Greeks are basically right in treating analytic thinking as ultimately the servant of correlative.

The most familiar texts of Chinese philosophy, the *Analects* of Confucius, *Lao-tzu* and the *Book of Changes,* contain nothing which a Westerner would recognise as rational argument; they may tempt us to see China as the Shangri-La of irrationalism. With a closer look at the literature of the classical period of philosophy (500–200 B.C.) one finds a more complicated situation. Confucius (551–479 B.C.) has no need of rational demonstrations because he is offering in his wise sayings an interpretation of traditional values to him self-evident and not yet questioned. His first rival Mo-tzu (late fifth century B.C.), with his ten new doctrines such as universal love, promotion of worth, rejection of fatalism, reward and punishment by the spirits, already has to defend himself by giving reasons. He introduces the term *pien* 'disputation' (literally, 'distinguishing', arguing to distinguish the right alternative from the wrong), and lays down three tests for judging a doctrine, the authority of the wisest in the past, observation by the eyes and ears of the multitude, and whether consequences are beneficial or harmful.[1] In the core chapters of the corpus of his school (*Mo-tzu*, chs. 8–37) all the ten Mohist doctrines are defended at length in organised essays, appealing to the authority of the sages, to practical consequences, and in the case of factual issues (the existence of spirits and the non-existence of Destiny), to the evidence of common observation. With the appearance of new schools debate intensifies, with neater arguments and more precise definitions; this progress continues down to Hsün-tzu and Han Fei in the third century B.C. In the philosophical mainstream, analysis tends to be of questioned similarities and differences, as in the debates of Mencius and Kao-tzu,[2] suggesting that thought is conceived primarily as a synthesising process which goes wrong when it fails to assimilate and differentiate correctly; we shall return to this point in discussing 'correlative thinking'.[3] Towards the end of the fourth century B.C., however, the Sophists (*Pien-che* 'those who argue out alternatives') are offering paradoxical theses supported by logical demonstration. About 300 B.C. the Later Mohists undertake the enterprise of grounding the whole Mohist ethic in the analysis of moral concepts. This surely is rationalism as we find it in Greece, the plainest example in the Chinese tradition. But the Sophists have already provoked the reaction of the Taoist Chuang-tzu (c. 320 B.C.), who will have a much more lasting influence on Chinese thought. His position, to use a terminology which we shall explain later,[4] is 'anti-rationalism' (denial that reason is the right means to see things as they are) rather than 'irrationalism' (which allows you to see things as you like). After 200 B.C., Chinese thinking channels in the orthodox Confucian direction (ethical, practical, conventional) and the unorthodox Taoist (spontaneous, mystical, disreputable). The former is often 'rational', in that it checks its synthesising by analysis, but not 'rationalistic' in the sense of Later Mohist or Aristotelian thought, which tries to detach rational demonstration wholly from commonsense synthesising; the latter remains anti-rationalist, as philosophical Taoism and its continuation as Ch'an or Zen in Chinese Buddhism. As for true irrationalism, it seems to have no place in Chinese thought; it is never doubted that in the vision of the sage things show up as they are, as clearly as the detail of beard and eyebrows reflected in clear water.

Let us look first at the brief episode of rationalism, which since it failed to take root in China has left only sparse and mutilated literary remains. Of the Sophists we have only paradoxes reported without their explanations by hostile witnesses, and the book *Kung-sun Lung tzu* ascribed to Kung-sun Lung (early third century B.C.). This has turned out to be a forgery from between A.D. 300 and 600, preserving, however, early stories of Kung-sun Lung (ch. 1), and three genuine essays, the "White Horse" (ch. 2), "Pointings and Things" (ch. 3), and probably the "Left and Right" dialogue which introduces ch. 4, the rest of it nonsense.[5] The most accessible essay is the "White Horse", which defends the thesis that 'A white horse is not a horse'. On the class/member analysis natural to a Western reader it seems to start with a *non sequitur* ("By 'horse' we name the shape, by 'white' we name the colour. To name the colour is not to name the shape. Therefore I say a white horse is not a horse") and to continue with a systematic confusion, of identity with class membership, which is ceasing to seem credible as our understanding of Chinese philosophy advances. It has only recently been noticed that Kung-sun Lung seems rather to be thinking in terms of whole/part, with 'white horse' as the combination of 'white' and 'horse', and that the argument becomes fully intelligible as a demonstration that since the whole is not one of its parts the white horse is not the horse which is part of it.[6] It is clear in any case that Kung-sun Lung's demonstrations, however interpreted, are purely analytic, excluding the analogical arguments so common throughout the mainstream philosophical literature.

For the Later Mohists we have a much more substantial literature; it raises complicated textual problems which long deterred students of Chinese thought, but they are by now sufficiently resolved for it to be usable as a source.[7] It is preserved in *Mo-tzu* chs. 40–45.

(1) The *Canons* (chs. 40, 41) and their *Explanations* (chs. 42, 43), divided between a series of seventy-five definitions and twelve analyses of ambiguous terms (A 1–87) and a series of propositions (A 88–B 82).

(2) The *Big Pick* (ch. 44) and the *Little Pick* (ch. 45), collections of fragments from two documents including their titles, *Expounding the Canons* (twelve more canons and explanations) and *Names and Objects*, a consecutive treatise.

There must also have been a lost document defining the words in the formulations of the ten Mohist doctrines, since these crucially important terms are conspicuously absent from the seventy-five defined in the *Canons*.[8]

The organisation of this collection has a considerable bearing on the nature of Later Mohist rationalism. The *Canons* are grouped in sequences with common topics, not marked by titles, but running parallel throughout the two divisions, the definitions and the propositions. Both have a central sequence on the problem of knowledge and change (A 40–51, B 13–16), followed by a sequence on the sciences, geometry, optics, mechanics, and economics (A 52–69, B 17–31), and preceded by a sequence on ethics (A 7–39, and a gap perfectly fillable by *Expounding the Canons*). The first and last sequences of both seem at first sight to be about logic or proto-logic. The interesting point is that the arrangement of the five parts implies that they are conceived as dealing with disciplines as unlike as either is to ethics or science.

(1) A 1–6, A 88–B 12, on the testing of similarities and differences. We are here at the same level of rational discourse as in the philosophical mainstream. *Names and Objects* is an independent treatise on the same discipline. It examines the effects of idiomatic variations on formally parallel sentences, such as: "White horses are horses, riding white horses is riding horses"; "Huo's parent is a person, but Huo serving her parent is not 'serving a person' (*shih jen* 'serving a husband')".

The Mohist criticises a thesis which wrongly assumes parallelism with the first sentence: "Robbers are people, killing robbers (*sha tao* 'executing robbers') is killing people (*sha jen* 'murder')."

This implies that executing robbers is murder. The Mohist's answer is that the true parallelism is with the second sentence, and a series of others with similar idiomatic shifts, so one is entitled to say: "Robbers are people, but killing robbers is not killing people."

Since the argument is about idiomatic sentences, not propositions, it clearly does not belong to logic. Not that it is unsound; if someone objected "Well, I prefer to class with the first sentence and say 'Killing robbers *is* killing people', one would answer 'Certainly, but then it loses its pejorative force by shifting in meaning from 'executing robbers is murder' to the neutral 'killing robbers is killing persons'."

(2) A 70–75, B 32–82, on logical demonstration as we find it in Kung-sun Lung. There is no search for logical forms such as the syllogism, but the demonstrations which multiply in the *Explanations* towards the end of the proposition series are strictly logical. Here is the refutation of an objection to the Mohist doctrine of universal love:

B 73   *(Canon)* Their being limitless is not inconsistent with doing something to the total of them.

(Explanation) (Objection) The south if limited is exhaustible, if limitless is inexhaustible. If whether it is limited or limitless is not yet knowable, then whether it is exhaustible or not, whether men fill it or not, and whether men are exhaustible or not, are likewise not yet knowable, and it is fallacious to treat it as necessary that men can be exhaustively loved.

(Answer) If men do not fill the limitless, men are limited, and there is no difficulty about filling the limited. If they do fill the limitless, the limitless

has been exhausted, and there is no difficulty about exhausting the limitless.

This quite different discipline seems to be *pien* 'disputation' itself, a term defined in this section. The definition is in terms of a corrupt word which we might expect to mean 'contradictory', but if rightly identified as *fan*,[9] a word found only in this document, seems from other contexts to mean 'converse'; if so, the Mohist thinks of calling some objects 'ox' as the converse of calling all the rest 'non-ox'.

> A 74 *(Canon)* Disputation is contending over *fan*. To win in disputation is to fit.
>
> *(Explanation)* One calling it 'ox', the other 'non-ox', is contending over *fan*. Such being the case, they do not both fit; and if they do not both fit, necessarily one of them does not fit. (Not like fitting 'dog').

True *pien* must be over an 'ox or non-ox' issue, not—a point further established elsewhere in the *Canons*[10]—over such an issue as 'Is it a whelp or a dog?', of which both or neither might fit the object. In true *pien* one alternative fits 'necessarily' (*pi*). Inferences are regularly pronounced necessary in this discipline, never in the discipline treated in the first sequence. In an *Explanation* classifying types of connexion we read: "If necessarily there is not one without the other, it is 'necessary'. What is from the sages, employ but do not treat as necessary. The 'necessary', admit and do not doubt."[11]

A central preoccupation of the *Canons* is to arrive at judgments unaffected by change. The middle sequence of definitions concerned with the relation of knowledge and change (A 40–51) concludes with the definition of the 'necessary' as the invulnerable to change.

> A 51 *(Canon)* The necessary is the unending.
>
> *(Explanation)* It is said of cases where the complements are fully formed. Such cases as 'elder brother or younger brother' and 'something so in only one respect or something not so in only one respect' are the necessary and the unnecessary.[12] Being this or not this is necessary.

Pi 'necessary' is used regularly of logical and also causal necessity, in disputation and the sciences, the two disciplines which follow the bridging sequence on knowledge and change. The Later Mohists have fully detached the logical demonstrations of the Sophists from the criticism of assimilations and differentiations more characteristic of Chinese philosophy; the Sophists themselves, from whom so little remains, may well have done so earlier. Certainly the Later Mohists are 'rational', but are they 'rationalists'? One no longer hesitates to accord this title when one perceives that this school, which like all others in China is primarily concerned with philosophy of life, is trying to establish its basic ethical concepts as logically necessary. A very striking feature of the *Canons* is a use of *hsien* 'beforehand' which approaches our 'a priori'. A passing reference to the circle as 'known beforehand'[13] is explained when one notices scattered definitions interlocking in a system which, all measurements from the centre being alike, builds up the definition of the circle from the term *jo* 'like', which does not need to be defined because it is the basis of the whole theory of naming (that the same name is given to objects which are alike).[14] We meet also a reference to 'desiring beforehand'.

"Anything which the sage desires or dislikes beforehand on behalf of men, men necessarily learn about from him by means of its *ch'ing* (close to Aristotelian 'essence', but the essential not to being *X* but to being named '*X*').[15] Anything from which desire and dislike are born in the conditions which they encounter, men do not necessarily learn about from him by means of its *ch'ing*".[16]

This too becomes comprehensible when we notice another system of interlocking definitions starting from the pair 'desire' and 'dislike'. These do not have to be defined since the purpose is to show that benevolence and the right are what the wisest man desires 'beforehand', but their different senses are distinguished in the sequence on ambiguous terms, including an irrelevant sense 'about to' of the *yü* generally translatable as 'desire'.

A 84   *(Canon) Desire.* Immediate; having weighed up. Be about to. *Dislike.* Immediate; having weighed up.

From these derive 'benefit' and 'harm' (but for the former 'desire', not being retrospective, is replaced by 'be pleased with').

A 26   *(Canon)* Benefit is what one is pleased to have got.

A 27   *(Canon)* Harm is what one dislikes having got.

The 'on behalf of' of desire 'on behalf of men' is defined in terms of the weighing of desires.

A 75   *(Canon)* To do on behalf of is to give the most weight in relation to the desires, in the light of all that one knows.

The ethical definitions depend also on definitions of the words 'love' and 'total' in the combination 'love of the total' (universal love), lost to us with the document defining words in the formulations of the ten Mohist doctrines. Judging by Mohist usage, the definition of 'love' would have been something like 'desiring benefit and disliking harm to, on his own behalf'. For the pair 'unit/total' (*t'i/chien*), used both of 'individual/class' and 'part/whole', we do have the definition of 'unit':

A 2   *(Canon)* A unit is a part in a total.

The central moral concepts, for Mohists as for Confucians, are benevolence *(jen)* and the right *(yi)*.

A 7   *(Canon)* Benevolence is love of units [loving individuals, in contrast with 'love of the total', the universal love which is not a moral virtue but a principle behind the virtues].

A 8   *(Canon)* The right is the beneficial.

The system, which has further ramifications, is evidently designed to show that benevolence and the right are necessarily, by definition, what the sage desires 'beforehand' on behalf of men. We are even told that "If there were no men at all in the world, what our master Mo-tzu said would still stand."[17] The account of 'desiring beforehand' recognised, however, that men can have no necessary knowledge of how to act in "the conditions they encounter", and continues:

"The loving which involves benefiting is born of thinking. Yesterday's thinking is not today's thinking, yesterday's love of man is not today's love of man. The love of man involved in love of Huo is born from thinking about Huo's benefit, not from thinking about Tsang's benefit; but the love of man involved in loving Tsang is the love of man involved in loving Huo."[18]

For ethical choice in particular situations *Expounding the Canons* therefore develops a procedure for weighing up benefits and harms, for which (as for the criticism of similarities and differences) no logical necessity is claimed.

By the time of the Later Mohists the logical acrobatics of the Sophists, always alien to Confucian and Legalist common sense, had provoked a principled anti-rationalist reaction from the Taoist Chuang-tzu. We can trace a continuing debate over the value of reason, with Chuang-tzu attacking the fourth-century Sophist Hui Shih and in turn becoming the target of the Later Mohists.[19] For Hui Shih, as for all the Sophists except Kung-sun Lung, we have little but sophisms mockingly reported without their explanations, notably a list in the last chapter of *Chuang-tzu* itself.[20] They appear to be mostly spatio-temporal paradoxes, such as "The south has no limit yet does have a limit", and "Simultaneously with being at noon the sun declines, simultaneously with being alive a thing dies". The list ends with the dictum "Love the myriad things indiscriminately, heaven and earth are one unit"; Hui Shih's purpose, like Zeno's, was perhaps to show that since all division leads to contradiction everything is one, and therefore we should love others as much as ourselves.[21] Although we lack his proofs, some of his conversations with Chuang-tzu show his style of argument, which is that of Kung-sun Lung and the Later Mohists.

"Chuang-tzu and Hui Shih were strolling on the bridge above the Hao river.

'Out swim the minnows, so free and easy', said Chuang-tzu. 'That's how fish are happy'.

'You are not a fish. Whence do you know that the fish are happy?'

'You aren't me, whence do you know that I don't know the fish are happy?'

'We'll grant that not being you I don't know about you. You'll grant that you are not a fish, and that completes the case that you don't know the fish are happy.'

'Let's go back to where we started. When you said *'Whence* do you know that the fish are happy?', you asked me the question already knowing that I knew. I knew it from up above the Hao.' "[22]

Hui Shih plays the logical game according to the rules, Chuang-tzu kicks over the board. But in his final stroke of wit he is not merely taking advantage of the accident that Hui Shih said "Whence (*an*) do you know . . . ?" instead of, for example, "By what means (*ho-yi*) . . . ?" For Chuang-tzu all knowing is from a standpoint, which is the whole concrete situation in which one stands.

We learn from a story of Chuang-tzu passing Hui Shih's grave[23] that, much as he enjoyed making fun of the Sophist, he remembered him as his only worthy opponent in debate. We may indeed see him as drawing the full consequences of Hui Shih's presumed case that one cannot make spatio-temporal distinctions without contradiction; it would take only one more step to recognise that all *pien*, as the arguing out of alternatives, starts from the drawing of distinctions, and so to abandon the proof that 'heaven and earth are one unit' for immersion in the undifferentiating experience of things. Chuang-tzu once takes up Hui Shih's observation that at the moment of death a thing is simultaneously alive, and draws the conclusion that both 'It is alive' and 'It is dead' may be simultaneously admissible. He is criticising the distinguishing of fixed alternatives, 'this' for what fits one's naming and 'that' for all outside its scope.

"Hence it is said 'That comes out from this, this too depends on that', the opinion that that and this come to life simultaneously. However, 'Simultaneously with being alive something dies', and simultaneously with dying it is alive: the admissible is simultaneously inadmissible, the inadmissible simultaneously admissible."[24]

There is much subtle, elliptical argument showing through the poetry of Chuang-tzu, which is becoming more intelligible as we learn more of the technical terminology of disputation; Chuang-tzu's complex sensibility includes a genuine taste for logic, missing in later Taoists, including the later writers in the book *Chuang-tzu*.[25] But the purpose is always to discredit *pien*, to show that by distinguishing alternatives, fixing them by names, arguing over which name fits and which course of action is right or wrong or beneficial or harmful, we become imprisoned in the viewpoint from which what fits our arbitrary choice of a name is 'this', and so obscure our vision of the whole. As soon as, for example, I lay down a distinction between waking and dreaming, it is impossible for me to know whether I am awake or dreaming.[26] Every statement which is admissible is also inadmissible, even 'The myriad things and I are one' (his variation on Hui Shih's 'Heaven and earth are one unit'), since as soon as I say it there are two, the one and my words about it.[27] The kind of language which Chuang-tzu approves is that which spontaneously shifts viewpoints, makes only fluid distinctions, does not tie words to fixed meanings, guides in a direction without committing to any one statement, discourse which he compares to a type of vessel designed to tip over if filled to the brim[28]—that language, poetic rather than logical, in which he himself writes.

Confucians and Mohists formulate in words a supposedly right way to behave and to order the Empire, as the 'Way (*tao*) of the ancients' or the 'Way of the sage kings'; for Chuang-tzu on the contrary the Way is the direction in which I find myself moving when submerged in the whole, when I recognise the fluidity of all distinctions (even between the direction and the whole), and simply mirror from moment to moment from my own viewpoint and surrender to spontaneity.

"The utmost man uses the heart like a mirror; he does not escort things as they go or welcome them as they come, he responds and does not store."[29]

The model for the sage is the craftsman, as in Chuang-tzu's story of a cook carving an ox,[30] and the many stories of his school about swimmers, anglers, painters, cicada-catchers. The craftsman does not analyse, he stills thought and emotion, concentrates attention on the object and responds, trusting to his knack. The crucial point is the total concentration of attention, as a hunchback catching cicadas on a sticky rod explains to Confucius.

"I settle my body like a rooted tree-stump, I hold my arm like the branch of a withered tree; out of all the vastness of heaven and earth, the multitude of the myriad things, it is only the wings of a cicada that I know. I don't let my gaze wander or waver, I would not take all the myriad things in exchange for the wings of a cicada. How could I help but succeed?"[31]

Chuang-tzu's metaphor of the mirror is further developed in writings of his school.

"When the sage is still, it is not that he is still because he says 'It is good to be still'; he is still because none of the myriad things is sufficient to disturb his heart. If water is still, its clarity lights up the hairs of beard and eyebrows, its evenness is plumb with the carpenter's level; the greatest of craftsmen take their standard from it. If mere water clarifies when it is still, how much more the stillness of the quintessential-and-daimonic, the heart of the sage! It is the reflector of heaven and earth, the mirror of the myriad things.

"Emptiness and stillness, calm and indifference, quiescence, doing nothing, are the even level of heaven and earth, the utmost reach of the Way and the Power; therefore emperor, king or sage finds rest in them. At rest he empties, emptying he is filled, and what fills him sorts itself out. Emptying he is still, in stillness he is moved, and when he moves he succeeds."[32]

A Westerner is tempted to assume that Taoists share his own 'reality/appearance' dichotomy, and credit the sage with an intuitive knowledge of ultimate reality for which reason is inadequate. It is easy to overlook that even when Chuang-tzu suggests that life is a dream from which we shall awake[33] he is once again showing only that the commonly rejected alternative is as admissible as the commonly accepted; Chinese epistemology in general is 'naive realism', acknowledging the reality of things as we perceive them, and even though Chuang-tzu rejects 'real/unreal' with all other dichotomies, he too never looks for a reality hidden behind the veil of illusion. The sage, like the craftsman, concentrates attention on the object, but he has no special source of information. Like everyone else, he thinks about things, he makes momentary and relative differentiations, but he does not trap himself in fixed distinctions and try to prove himself right. It is thinking about how to deal with things, instead of trusting to one's spontaneous reaction in full awareness of them, which Chuang-tzu forbids.

Taoism, which recommends the stilling of the passions that disturb or distract attention, and the undeliberated reaction in perfect clarity of vision from one's momentary viewpoint, is quite unlike Western Romanticism, which has a similar preference for spontaneity but exalts the subjective vision in heightened emotion. It therefore seems inadequate to class Taoism as 'irrationalism'. There is a difference in kind from what we commonly recognise as irrationalism, the principled refusal to take account of facts which conflict with one's values or desires, as with the Nazi who does not merely ignore facts incompatible with the genuineness of the *Protocols of the Elders of Zion*, but scorns one's appeal to them as barren intellectualism. Even a rationalist will concede to Chuang-tzu that spontaneity as well as reason has a function in adjusting intelligently to external conditions, that for example a tightrope walker cannot afford to pause and analyse his movements as he makes them (there was a *New Yorker* cartoon of a ski jumper seeing just ahead of him one of those office table notices, 'Think!'); what the rationalist would deny is that the tightrope walker can be our model in dealing with the fundamental issues of life. I therefore prefer to class as 'anti-rationalism' doctrines such as Chuang-tzu's which belittle the value of reason in adjusting to external conditions, as 'irrationalism' those which entitle us to ignore those conditions[34]. Admittedly Chuang-tzu, in his shifting usage for 'know', sometimes derides the knowledge of one verbally formulated alternative, and exalts ignorance; but he always has other words such as *ming* 'be clear about' for the sort of awareness which he prefers. Nothing could be more alien to him, or to the Chinese tradition in general, than Nietzsche's truly irrationalist question: "Granted we want truth, *why not rather* untruth? And uncertainty? Even ignorance?"[35]

If rationalism is no more than a brief episode in the Chinese tradition, and anti-rationalism is limited to philosophical Taoism and its descendant Ch'an Buddhism, how shall we categorise mainstream thinking? So far we have been getting along on such approximations as 'synthesising' and 'common sense'. We may approach the question obliquely by considering the Yin-Yang schematising of Chinese cosmology, which we follow Needham in calling 'correlative thinking'.[36] This has often impressed Westerners as peculiarly Chinese, and the book by Granet which remains the best introduction to it is in fact called *La pensée chinoise*.[37] It organises the cosmos by a scheme of correlated pairs starting from Yang and Yin (heaven/earth, light/darkness, male/female, ruler/subject . . .), branching into correlated sets of fours or fives starting from the *Wu Hsing* 'Five Processes'[38] (Four Directions, Four Seasons, Five Colours, Five Notes . . .), and is the basis of court calendars and of proto-sciences such as medicine, divination, musicology, alchemy, geomancy. In the chain of pairs A and B (and correspondingly in the larger sets), A1 compares with B1 as A2 with B2, and A1 connects with A2 as B1 with B2. Thus in the course of expounding its cosmogony *Huai-nan-tzu* (c. 140 B.C.) explains the ignition of tinder by the concave mirror (the 'Yang *sui*') by contrasting it with a parallel phenomenon, the dew collecting at night on the 'square *chu*', said to be another kind of mirror.

"Therefore when the Yang *sui* sees the sun it ignites and makes fire, when the square *chu* sees the moon it moistens and makes water".[39]

Examining the whole scheme we see that Yang compares with Yin as sun with moon, round with square, and fire with water; therefore the connexions between Yang *sui*, sun and fire compare similarly with those between square *chu*, moon and water. To a modern such thinking may be more alien than anything in *Lao-tzu* or the "White Horse"; it is not merely that the explanation is obscure or fallacious, for us it is not an explanation at all. But far from being peculiarly Chinese, this mode of thinking is common to proto-science everywhere, shared by Europe (with its Four Elements, Four Humours, and Pythagorean numerology) right down to the Renaissance. Moreover the philosophers from Confucius to Ham Fei (died 233 B.C.) never engage in this schematising; except for Hsün-tzu in the third century B.C. they do not mention even the *Book of Changes*, and even Hsün-tzu does not yet include it in the Confucian Classics.[40] The entry of correlative schematising into the philosophical literature is at the final eclectic stage of the classical period, in the syncretistic philosophical encyclopedia *Lü-shih Ch'un-ch'iu*.[41] Previously we meet it only in historical and other non-philosophical sources, as the lore of physicians, musicmasters, and diviners. The philosophical schools conspicuously neglect the sciences, with the single exception of the Later Mohists, who ignore the Yin and Yang, mention the Five Processes only to say "The Five Processes have no constant ascendancies",[42] and offer only the purely causal explanations for which they claim *pi* 'necessity'.

We may contrast with the *Huai-nan-tzu* explanation of the burning mirror an account in the *Canons* of another peculiarity of the concave mirror, the inversion of the image if you stand outside the centre of curvature (which the Mohist fails to distinguish from the conjugal focus).

> B 23   *(Canon)* When the mirror is concave the shadow is at one time smaller and inverted, at another time larger and upright. Explained by: outside or inside the centre.
>
> *(Explanation) Inside the centre.* If the man looking at himself is near the centre, everything mirrored is larger and the shadow too is larger; if he is far from the centre, everything mirrored is smaller and the shadow too is smaller; and it is necessarily upright. This is because the light opens out from the centre, skirts the upright object and prolongs its straight course.
>
> *Outside the centre.* If the man looking at himself is near the centre, everything mirrored is larger and the shadow too is larger; if he is far from the centre everything mirrored is smaller and the shadow too is smaller; but it is necessarily inverted. This is because the light converges at the centre, [. . . ?] and prolongs its straight course.

In the West we find the same contrast between philosophy and proto-science, but much sharper. On the one hand syllogistic logic (absent in China except for a brief flowering in the seventh century A.D. of the Buddhist logic imported from India[43]) goes back to Aristotle; on the other, nearly two thousand years later Kepler, discoverer of the first three modern laws of nature, is still trying to organise his cosmos by correlating the distances between the planets with the five regular solids, and sun, stars, and planets with the three persons of the Trinity.

But although correlative cosmos-building, whether Chinese or Western, belongs to the proto-sciences, it would seem that the correlative thinking of which it is an exotic offshoot is basic to all thinking and to the operation of language itself. This already follows from Roman Jakobson's description of words as related 'paradigmatically' (on the dimension 'similarity/contrast') as members of sets from which we select them, 'syntagmatically' (on the dimension 'contiguity/remoteness') as elements in the phrases and sentences in which we combine them.[44]

Thought begins by correlating concepts like the words in parallel sentences: A 1 : B 1 : : A 2 : B 2 (A 1 compares with B 1 as A 2 with B 2, A 1 connects with A 2 as B 1 with B 2).

We begin to analyse when doubt arises as to a correlation, such as 'White man : black man : : good : evil'; we demand a causal connexion and fail to find one between moral qualities and colour of skin. On this account it becomes easier to understand why in both China and the West the correlating which constructs our first skeleton of a cosmos is extended throughout cosmology and the proto-sciences. In both civilizations there has always been plenty of causal thinking, and whole episodes, such as the Later Mohist, when its superiority to correlative schematising is clearly seen; but piecemeal causal explanations do not add up to a cosmology. Until the Scientific Revolution in seventeenth-century Europe discovered an alternative, the mathematisation of laws of nature tested by controlled experiment, the choice was between a cosmos organised by correlation and no cosmos at all.

That much or most of the thinking of ancient China is correlation guided and tested by analysis, as is our own as long it remains on the common sense level, is clearly exhibited by the strong tendency to parallelism in Chinese style, apparent even in the Mohist account of the concave mirror. We noticed that the Later Mohists distinguish from logical demonstration a whole discipline devoted to analysing similarities and differences, in particular to the testing of formal parallelism. As characteristic of ordinary Chinese argument we may take this example from the Legalist *Book of Lord Shang* (c. 240 B.C.).

"T'ang and Wu rose to kingship without following antiquity, Yin and Hsia fell to ruin without change of conventions. Consequently, rejection of antiquity is not necessarily to be condemned, and comformity to convention does not deserve to be made much of."[45]

Here the parallelism reflects a chain of oppositions in which the ratio 'X's rise to kingship : X's rejection of antiquity : : Y's fall to ruin : Y's conformity to convention' transfers approval and disapproval from rise and fall to innovation and conformity. But the argument has none of the artificiality for us of the *Huai-nan-tzu* explanation of the burning mirror, in the first place because the connexions between the pairs are acceptable as causal, as they tend to be in the political and other practical situations which discipline correlation by quickly fulfilling or disappointing expectations. Moreover the inference has been tightened by analysis; only two cases having been given of rise to kingship following rejection of antiquity, the conclusion is not that the rejection is good but that it "is not necessarily to be condemned".

Most Chinese thinkers, however much they may reason, do not share the Later Mohist and Western hope of establishing an independent realm of reason by a perfect system of definitions of the concepts from which it starts, leaving argument from analogy as loose thinking outside its borders. This, however, has nothing to do with being rationalists or anti-rationalists, for much modern philosophy in effect abandons this hope except in logic and mathematics—Ryle's undermining of arguments by exposing category mistakes, Kuhn's insistence that all scientific hypotheses are paradigm-dependent, Derrida's attempt to deconstruct the chain of oppositions underlying the logocentric tradition of the West. In a sense which we need no longer treat as pejorative, the correlative undercurrent of thought is 'pre-logical', although requiring logic to test its adequacy for problem-solving. An old correlation is fixed by habit, a new one appears in an unanticipated flash of insight. Kuhn describes the paradigm-shift as a "relatively sudden and unstructured event like the gestalt switch", after which scientists "often speak of 'the scales falling from the eyes' or of the 'lightning flash' that 'inundates' a previously obscure problem, enabling its components to be seen in a new way that for the first time permits its solution"; there are even times when "the relevant illumination comes in sleep".[46] That it is acceptable to speak of the creative thinking even of scientists in this way may help us to understand why Chinese thought in which we can trace no logical steps is not (as our own 'appearance/reality' dichotomy tempts us to suppose) assuming some mystical access to reality beyond the reach of reason. It implies that there are opposite ways of correcting correlative thinking, by rational criticism and by unseating conventional oppositions to restore its fluidity, both of them employed in the Chinese tradition. Granted that fixed chains of oppositions imprison thought, as is very obvious in the case of Yin-Yang schematism, how does one loosen them? We see from Derrida as from Chuang-tzu and Lao-tzu that language which deconstructs oppositions has to take the direction of poetry. The rationalist, who recognises his own kind only in the Sophists and Later

Mohists, is not bound to exclude even the texts most alien to him, *Lao-tzu*, the *Changes*, from the domain of philosophy. *Lao-tzu* is a poem which sets out to break the habit of thinking in dichotomies, something/ nothing, knowledge/ignorance, male/female, above/below, before/ behind. These differ from the oppositions which Derrida finds at the back of Western logocentrism (reality/appearance, nature/culture, life/ death, good/evil) in that the latter tradition strives to abolish B in favour of A; as has long been a commonplace, China tends to complementary Yin-Yang polarities, the West to conflicting opposites.[47] However, China does regularly assume the relative superiority of A to B. The reversals by which *Lao-tzu* presents B as superior to A are strikingly similar to the move by which Derrida reverses, for example, our habitual preference for speech over writing.[48] It is not that *Lao-tzu* wishes us to prefer nothing to something and female to male; the move, like Derrida's, is a step to undermining the oppositions.

The divination system of the *Changes*, for a rationalist surely the most repellent book in early Chinese literature, may likewise be seen as a technique for recovering the fluidity of correlative thinking. The sixty-four hexagrams, with multitudinous correlations for each line, trigram, and hexagram as a whole, seem at first sight to present a cosmology much more complicated, artificial, and confused than the neat standard system with Five Processes corresponding to Four Seasons, Five Colours, and so forth. Since the two systems share little except the binary distinction of Yin and Yang from which they start, one may wonder how the Chinese succeed in reconciling them. Needham, charitable as he is to Chinese proto-science, treats the *Changes* as a disaster in its history.[49] In so far as the system of the *Changes* was allowed to intrude into explanation by the more coherent system, one may agree with him. But the Five Process system is designed for the proto-sciences and for action in regularly recurring situations, such as the changes of ritual throughout the Four Seasons; the *Changes* on the other hand is intended for divination in particular situations (those in which artificial classifications are most restrictive and free correlation is indispensable), with the sixty-four hexagrams representing every mathematically possible se- quence of six successive choices between two alternatives. Western enthusiasts for the Wilhelm-Baynes *I Ching* generally assume that the divination could not be successful unless there really is an a-causal principle in nature (Jung's 'synchronicity')[50] by which the fall of the yarrow sticks which selects the Yin or Yang lines responds to the pattern of the diviner's situation. But it is possible to argue that they may not be misguided even though the fall of the sticks, or of the coins which replace them, is the result of pure chance. If the hexagrams thrown up by chance carried unambiguous instructions they would of course, except by a lucky accident, be grossly misleading; but since they offer only enigmatic auspices and almost unlimited latitude to correlate with a variety of images, the diviner's interpretation in the light of his personal situation becomes a meditation on his circumstances opened up to new perspectives. The effect will be to break down preconceptions and give binary thinking a fresh start.

To relate Chinese divination to creative thinking in the sciences may seem fanciful. But in fact the "Great Appendix" of the *Changes* includes the invention of tools among the four purposes of the system;[51] it also presents a legendary history of the major inventions, identifying the hexagrams which inspired them.

"They hollowed out wood to make boats, shaved wood to make oars. The advantage of boat and oars was to cross to the inaccessible and deliver over distances to the advantage of the whole world. Evidently they took it from Huan ䷺."[52]

So the idea of the boat first came to an ancient sage contemplating the trigram correlatable, among many other things, with wood (☴), on top of the trigram correlatable with water, (☵), with its attached auspice "Advantageous for crossing a great river". If one reads this not as fabulous history but as an illustration of how an original thought comes into one's head, it does not look silly at all.

It is remarkable that no account of the standard cosmological correlations ever achieved canonical status in China, while the *Changes* were eventually admitted among the Confucian classics, and *Lao-tzu* became the most influential of all the unorthodox books. It is as though Chinese civilization has been careful to preserve a certain latitude in the organisation of its cosmos, in order that throughout its long history originality and creativity should never die out. Perhaps we have here an answer to a question which Needham's great history of Chinese science helps us to put more clearly. How is it that China, which never came within sight of our seventeenth-century Scientific Revolution, has been so extraordinarily fertile in basic inventions, until late in the Middle Ages perhaps the most fertile of all?

We sum up with some highly debatable generalisations.

(1) The mainstream of Chinese thinking (as of pre-Socratic thinking in Greece[53]) is correlative, on the one hand guided and tested by analysis as in our own commonsense thinking, on the other restored to fluidity by the poetry of *Lao-tzu* and diagrams of the *Changes*.

(2) There is a brief episode of rationalism, in which the Sophists and Later Mohists exalt analytic reason and detach it from correlation, and also a minority tradition of anti-rationalism preferring spontaneity to reason in the conduct of life, as philosophical Taoism and Ch'an Buddhism. 'Irrationalism', as the principled refusal to acknowledge objective fact, seems to be unrepresented in the tradition.

(3) As in the pre-modern West, correlative cosmology is an extension of correlative thinking to the proto-sciences, in the absence of the mathematised and experimentally testable laws which were finally in the West to provide an alternative means of organising knowledge of nature.

NOTES

1. The three tests appear in various forms in the introductions of the three anti-fatalist chapters, *Mo-tzu*, chs. 35–37, trans. Mei, 183, 189, 194 : ch. 35, trans. Watson (1), 118.
2. *Mencius* 6A/1–5. Analogical argument in *Mencius* is analysed in Lau (2), 235–63.
3. Cf. pp. 109–16 below.
4. p. 109 below.
5. (G 4), 126–66
6. Hansen, 140–71. Hansen's detailed application of his proposal to the "White Horse" is very complicated; I have suggested a much simpler analysis of the argument starting from Hansen's premises in (G 4), 196–210.
7. (G 1), 73–238. The numbering of the *Canons* here follows (G 1), in which *Mo-tzu* chs. 40–45 are translated complete.
8. (G 1), 235f.

9. (G 1), 184f.
10. *Canon* B 35.
11. *Canon* A 83.
12. I formerly thought this understanding of the sentence syntactically unnatural, and emended the text in (G 1), 299; but have since noticed the same syntax in *Expounding the Canons* 8 as edited (G 1), 252.
13. *Canon* A 93.
14. (G 1), 56–58.
15. For *ch'ing* cf. (G 1), 179–82.
16. *Expounding the Canons*, 2.
17. Ut sup. n. 16.
18. Ut sup. n. 16.
19. For dialogues between Hui Shih and Chuang-tzu, cf. (G 2), 46f., 82f., 100–102, 122–24. Chuang-tzu's anti-rationalist theses are criticised in *Canons* B 35, 48, 68, 71, 72, 79, 82.
20. *Chuang-tzu*, ch. 33, trans. (G 2), 283–85, trans. Watson (2), 374–77.
21. The argument of Reding, 274–385, that the theses of Hui Shih are merely remarks about government and other commonsense themes quoted out of context is a reminder of how little we have to go on in interpreting them. I think however that there is enough evidence (as in the Mohist reference to the south as limited or limitless, and Chuang-tzu's to being both alive and dead at the moment of death, quoted on pp. 101–102 above and p. 106 below) to assure us of the orthodox reading of the theses as spatio-temporal paradoxes.
22. *Chuang-tzu*, ch. 17, trans. (G 2), 123, trans. Watson (2), 188f.
23. *Chuang-tzu*, ch. 24, trans. (G 2), 124, trans. Watson (2), 269.
24. *Chuang-tzu*, ch. 2, trans. (G 2), 52, trans. Watson (2), 39f.
25. For the composition of *Chuang-tzu*, in which only the seven *Inner Chapters* and some passages from the *Mixed Chapters* are likely to be the writing of Chuang-tzu himself, cf. (G 2), and (G 4), 283–321.
26. *Chuang-tzu*, ch. 2, trans. (G 2), 61, trans. Watson (2), 49.
27. *Chuang-tzu*, ch. 2, trans. (G 2), 56f, trans. Watson (2), 43.
28. *Chuang-tzu*, ch. 27, trans. (G 2), 106f., trans. Watson (2), 303–305.
29. *Chuang-tzu*, ch. 7, trans. (G 2), 98, trans. Watson (2), 97.
30. *Chuang-tzu*, ch. 3, trans. (G 2), 63f., trans. Watson (2), 50f.
31. *Chuang-tzu*, ch. 19, trans. (G 2), 138, trans. Watson (2), 200.
32. *Chuang-tzu*, ch. 13, trans. (G 2), 259, trans. Watson (2), 142.
33. *Chuang-tzu*, ch. 2, trans. (G 2), 59f., trans. Watson (2), 47f.
34. I have developed this distinction between anti-rationalism and irrationalism in (G 3), 156–227, taking Sade, Nietzsche (in one of his aspects) and Hitler as exemplars of irrationalism, and Chuang-tzu, three modernisms (Futurism, Dada, and Surrealism) and Bataille as exemplars of anti-rationalism.
35. Nietzsche, 15.

36. Needham, v. 2, 279–303.
37. Marcel Granet, *La pensée chinoise* (Paris, 1934).
38. 'Five Phases' is coming to replace as equivalent for *Wu Hsing* the 'Five Elements', still used by Needham (Major, op. cit.). For pre-Han usages I prefer 'Five Processes' (G5, 74–76).
39. *Huai-nan-tzu* ch. 3, trans. (G 5), 30–32. There is not yet a complete translation of *Huai-nan-tzu*.
40. (G 5), 9. The *Changes* is mentioned in the standard text of *Analects* 7/17, but there is a variant reading preferred for example by Lau (1), 88.
41. The correlations appear in the introductory calendrical sections of *Lü-shih ch'un-ch'iu* chs. 1–12, and in the account of dynasties succeeding each other by the conquest cycle of the Five Processes in ch. 13/2. The full text is available in the German translation of Wilhelm.
42. *Canon* B 43.
43. Harbsmeier, op. cit.
44. Jakobson, in particular "Two Aspects of Language", 239–59. Cf. pp. 62–63 above.
45. *Shang-tzu* ch. 1, trans. Duyvendak, 173.
46. Kuhn, 122f.
47. For a recent essay in using Chinese polarities to deconstruct the Western tradition, cf. Hall and Ames, 11–25, and passim.
48. Derrida, 1–94.
49. Needham, v. 2, 305–345.
50. Jung, preface to Wilhelm-Baynes, xxiv.
51. "Great Appendix" A 9, trans. Wilhelm-Baynes, 314.
52. "Great Appendix" B 2, trans. Wilhelm-Baynes, 332.
53. Cf. Lloyd, op. cit.

REFERENCES

Derrida, Jacques. *Of Grammatology*. Trans. G. C. Spivak. Baltimore: Johns Hopkins University Press, 1976.

Duyvendak, J. J. L. *The Book of Lord Shang*. London, 1928.

Graham, A. C. (G 1) *Later Mohist Logic, Ethics and Science*. London: School of Oriental and African Studies; Hong Kong: Chinese University Press, 1978. (Abbreviated *LML*.)

———. (G 2) *Chuang-tzu: The Inner Chapters, and Other Writings from the Book 'Chuang-tzu'*. London, 1981. (Abbreviated *CIC*.)

———. (G 3) *Reason and Spontaneity*. London: Curzon Press, 1985. (Abbreviated *R & S*.)

———. (G 4) *Studies in Chinese Philosophy and Philosophical Literature*. Singapore:

Institute of East Asian Philosophies, National University of 1986. (Abbreviated *SCP.*)

———. (G 5) *Yin-Yang and the Nature of Correlative Thinking.* Singapore: Institute of East Asian Philosophies, National University of Singapore, 1986.

———. (G 6) *Disputers of the Tao: Philosophical Argument in Ancient China.* La Salle, Illinois: Open Court, 1989.

Granet, Marcel. *La pensée chinoise.* Paris: Albin Michel, 1934.

Hall, David and Roger Ames. *Thinking through Confucius.* Albany, NY: SUNY Press, 1987.

Hansen, Chad. *Language and Logic in Ancient China.* Ann Arbor: University of Michigan Press, 1983.

Harbsmeier, Christoph. "Language and Logic in Ancient China". Forthcoming.

Jakobson, Roman. *Selected Writings.* Vol. 2. The Hague and Paris: Mouton, 1971.

Kuhn, Thomas S. *The Structure of Scientific Revolutions.* Chicago: University of Chicago Press, 1970.

Lau, D. C. (1) *Confucius, the Analects.* Penguin Classics, 1979.

———. (2) *Mencius.* Penguin Classics, 1970.

Lloyd, G. E. R. *Polarity and Analogy.* Cambridge: Cambridge University Press, 1966.

Major, John. "A Note on the Translation of Two Technical Terms in Chinese Science", *Early China* 2 (1976): 1–3.

Mei, Yi-pao. *The Ethical and Political Works of Motse.* London, 1929.

Needham, Joseph. *Science and Civilisation in China.* Cambridge: Cambridge University Press, 1954.

Nietzsche, Friedrich. *Beyond Good and Evil.* Trans. R. J. Hollingdale. Penguin Classics, 1973.

Reding, Jean-Paul. *Les fondements philosophiques de la rhétorique chez les sophistes grecs et chez les sophistes chinois.* Berne: Peter Lang, 1985.

Ryle, Gilbert. *The Concept of Mind.* London: Hutchinson's University Library, 1949.

Watson, Burton. (1) *Mo Tzu: Basic Writings.* New York, 1963.

———. (2) *The Complete Works of Chuang Tzu.* New York, 1968.

Wilhelm, Richard. *Frühling und Herbst des Lü Bu We* [*Lü-shih ch'un-ch'iu*]. Jena, 1928.

(Wilhelm-Baynes). *The I Ching or Book of Changes.* The Richard Wilhelm translation rendered into English by Cary F. Baynes. London, 1951.

A Chinese Approach to Philosophy of Value: *Ho-kuan-tzu*

In the West non-philosophical thinking easily accepts that the changes in a person's tastes, inclinations, and values are to a great extent involuntary and unconsidered, and often so gradual that they come about without him noticing them; and that if he is now more knowledgeable, clear-thinking, experienced, insightful into other people, his values are now finer, more discriminating, profounder, *better*. Since in the course of this maturation changes of valuation are not a simple matter of inference from additions to his propositional knowledge, and in any case such impressions seem to have more to do with aesthetic than with moral judgments, there has never been much place for this line of thought in Western moral philosophy, except for such as Nietzsche who draw no line between morals and aesthetics.[1] I have argued, however, that precisely because spontaneous shifts of inclination follow increased awareness not by inference but by causation, the value of an inclination in greater awareness is implied by the value of awareness itself (which will be that which one ascribes to knowledge and to truth), and that the implication can be formulated as a quasi-syllogism.[2] A point of interest in the Chinese tradition is that, various as it is, it seems everywhere to start from the assumption, quite foreign to at least the Kantian tradition in the West although familiar to common sense, that the ultimate springs of action are in spontaneous preference the value of which depends on the wisdom of the agent.[3] This shows up especially at the rationalist extreme, in the Later Mohists, and at the anti-rationalist, in the Taoist Chuang-tzu. The Later Mohist ethic resembles Western Utilitarianism in building a system on actual desires and dislikes, whether immediate or modified by the weighing of circumstance; it differs, however, in deriving the moral virtues from the desires and dislikes not of anyone but of the sage, who for the Mohist is indeed the person who thinks most rationally about his circumstances but, like the rest of us, simply *does* desire or dislike.[4] Chuang-tzu shares the same presupposition, refined to its essence by the dismissal of rationally deliberated action for the pure spontaneous reaction—not, however, anybody's reaction, but that of the sage who reflects his situation with the luminous clarity of a mirror.[5] This difference in starting-point has far-reaching consequences for the philosophy of value. Thus, although Chinese schools agree in seeking a constant Way behind change and multiplicity, the Later Mohists seem to be unique in trying, like Western philosophers, to find it in unalterably valid propositional knowledge. By the third and second centuries B.C. it is commonly identified as the Way on which one finds oneself when viewing comprehensively, and the objection to rival philosophers is that, although there may be something to learn from them, their vision is too narrow.[6] One is reminded of Nietzsche's perspectivism, according to which each of us acts on spontaneous drives channelled through different perspectives, but the wider perspective is better than the narrower. The Chinese share the same visual metaphor, with the restricted vision described in *Chuang-tzu* by such images, later to become clichés, as the 'frog in a well' and 'using a tube to peer at the breadth of the sky'.[7]

In a general history of philosophical argument in the classical age (500–200 B.C.), *Disputers of the Tao*, I traced this underlying assumption from Confucius onward, and have elsewhere noted it in the neo-Confucianism of Chu Hsi (A.D. 1130–1200).[8] It is shared by *Ho-kuan-tzu*, a text which has only recently attracted attention and which got only a few mentions in *Disputers of the Tao*; as a further illustration it is especially useful because its thought is almost equally remote from Chu Hsi, from the Mohists, and even (despite its traditional classification under the Taoist school) from Chuang-tzu. It professes to be the work of a mysterious and otherwise unknown thinker passing under the pseudonym Ho-kuan-tzu ("Master of the Pheasant Cap"), supposedly the teacher of the Chao general P'ang Hsuan who defeated the rival state of Yen in 242 B.C. The book was formerly neglected because of the lack of firm evidence of its existence before about A.D. 500, but is now dated with some confidence to the period 230–200 B.C., just before, during, and just after the temporary unification of China by the Ch'in dynasty (221–209 B.C.[9] Its main theme is the one behind the many, and comparison with contemporary documents in which the theme is less obtrusive has revealed that at the very end of the classical age there was a brief period when the One actually replaced the *Tao* "Way" as the central metaphysical concept. In approaching its philosophy of the One, we shall be concerned especially with the manner in which it relates the Way which heaven and earth *do* follow to the Way which man should follow.

The unification of the empire under the Ch'in and the succeeding Han dynasty encouraged the search for a unified ideology, mingling, within the framework of Yin-Yang cosmology, different tendencies of the classical schools, Confucian moralism, Legalist politics, and the Taoism of *Lao-tzu* (c. 250 B.C.) and of *Chuang-tzu*, the writings of Chuang-tzu (c. 320 B.C.) and his followers. By the late second century B.C. this syncretism generally centered on the doctrine of *Lao-tzu*, for which the ultimate source was the *Tao* or Way. But in the earlier experiments in syncretism, in the *Lü Spring and Autumn* (c. 240 B.C.) as well as in *Ho-kuan-tzu*, the Way is still the path of the cosmos and of man, as it had been for earlier philosophers other than the Taoists, and for the ultimate source from which all paths diverge the preferred term is the One or the Supreme One. Thus the *Lü Spring and Autumn* only once mentions the Way as the source of things, and immediately adds: "The 'Way' is the utmost quintessence, which cannot be deemed a shape, cannot be deemed a name; forcing a name on it one calls it the 'Supreme One'."[10]

The Taoists themselves do occasionally speak of the One, but treat the concept with a certain reserve. Continuing the universal quest of Chinese philosophy for the Way, which is primarily the way to order the empire and to conduct social and personal life, they take the radically new step of dismissing all the competing doctrines of Confucians, Mohists, and others as consequences of an initial error, the posing of alternatives and the formulation of one of them as the Way to be followed by man. Man separates himself from the cosmos by distinguishing, naming, and trying to discover a verbalisable way of his own; but by suspending distinctions he can return to spontaneity and find himself moving on the same path as heaven and earth. You are on the Way only if you withdraw to the starting-point from which all paths diverge. What is this ultimate source to be called? Since it is reached by ceasing to distinguish and name, no name can be adequate to it, but the Way being the goal of the quest 'Way' will be the most convenient, even if the natural metaphor is 'gate' rather than 'way'. In ceasing to distinguish we unify, and *Lao-tzu* and *Chuang-tzu* have no reservations about describing the sage as *treating* everything as one. But to call the whole in which all distinctions lapse the 'One' would be to distinguish it from the many. Chuang-tzu, having tried out the formulation "The myriad things and I are one", at once raises the question: "Now that we are one, can I still say something? Already having called us one, did I succeed in not saying something? One and the saying make two, two and one make three . . ."[11]

Ho-kuan-tzu is not one of the Chinese texts rich in the analytic thinking we expect of philosophy in the West. It proceeds by blank assertion, presenting its own variation on the traditional structure of universe and society by correlating the usual pairs (Yin/Yang, heaven/earth, life/death, generation/completion . . .) as dividing from the One and further subdividing into fours or fives; in improvising its own arrangements of other than current pairs (similar/different, figure/pattern, shape/name, clairvoyance/illumination . . .) it aims to persuade, not by logical proofs, but by the harmony of a scheme in which everything may be seen to fit. In spite of its later classification as Taoist, and frequent echoes of *Lao-tzu* and *Chuang-tzu,* it does not question the necessity of distinguishing and naming. It has a quite different philosophy in which the Way is multiple, the divergent paths of heaven, earth and man, which, however, compose an order unified by the One from which they derive. Since the starting-point of a path is itself on the path this does not quite forbid it to speak of the Way as the source of things, but on the single occasion when it does so it says explicitly that the appropriate metaphor is the gate: "The Way is what sagehood makes serve it, what arrival at the utmost grasps. Arriving by it at that which no picture can contain nor name pick out, at that of which the mouth cannot convey the idea nor description establish the appearance, it is the gate which is the image of what the Way is like. Worthy and inadequate,

124

foolish and wise, issue from it; it lets them out and in without differentiating between them" ([ch. 18] C, 21B/5–9).

Things as they follow the Way of heaven and earth, which is neutral to all human values, rise and fall according to their *shih* 'positional advantage/disadvantage' within the *li* 'patterns'.[12]

"What gets the Way to security earth can secure, what gets the Way to danger earth cannot secure . . . What gets the Way to survival heaven can preserve, what gets the Way to destruction heaven cannot preserve. Security and danger are from positional advantage, survival and destruction are from pattern" ([ch. 18] C, 21A/8f, 21B/1f).

Positional advantage or disadvantage is present everywhere, sometimes in the nature of the thing, as in the conquest cycle of the 'Five Processes', by which metal cuts wood, wood digs soil, soil dams water, water quenches fire, and fire melts metal.

"Things have their natures, therefore metal and wood, water and fire, are controllers of each other before yet being put to use. No doubt you have seen a door bar? Stand it up, and even a woman will by leaning on it get it upright; lay it on the ground, and anyone irrespective of his nature is able to lift it from the middle; if he grasps it by the tip even a picked man cannot get it clear of the earth. That the bar is different in weight even for a single person is because positional advantage causes it to be so. To judge by the door bar, wherever there is a thing positional advantage is present" ([ch. 14] C, 9A/2–8 trans. Neugebauer, 213–17).

The Way treats life and death, survival and ruin, as interchangeable, it lets them alternate in turn. The sage on the other hand grades things but treats them "equally", by the same standards, justly. The Way has the course laid down by the sages inside it.

"The Way is the opener-out of things, not the equaliser of things. Therefore sagehood is the Way, but the Way is not sagehood. The Way is the interchanger of things, the sage is the grader of things. This is why there is a Way of the former kings but there are not former kings of the Way" ([ch. 18] C, 21B/9–22A/3).

The sage therefore puts man before heaven and earth.

"P'ang asked Ho-kuan-tzu, 'In the way of the sage what is to be put first?'

'Put man first.'

'In the way of Man what is to be put first?'

'Put arms first.'

'Why put man first instead of heaven?'

'Heaven is too lofty to be easily known, its blessings cannot be pleaded for nor its disasters escaped; to take-it-as-standard would be cruelty. Earth is broad and big, deep and thick, it benefits much but awes little; to take earth as standard would be abasement. The seasons call up and cast down and there is no oneness in their alternations; to take the seasons as standard would be inconsistency. These three cannot make transformations stand nor implant customs, therefore the sage does not take them as standard'" ([ch. 7] A, 13A/1–7, trans. Neugebauer 68f.).

(By 'arms', Ho-kuan-tzu later explains, he means the ceremonial and the right, loyalty and trustworthiness).

The sage is even described as "the one who gathers in and scatters the blossoming quintessences in order to console earth and lay blame on heaven" ([ch. 10] B, 22B/1), which the commentator Lu Tien (A.D. 1042–1102) compares to Zen blasphemies against the Buddha.

Ho-kuan-tzu is exceptional among ancient Chinese philosophical texts in explicitly distinguishing the heaven and earth of philosophy from the sky (which is *ch'i* 'air, breath') and the soil.

"What we call 'heaven' is not this azure *ch'i*, what we call 'earth' is not this conglomerated soil" ([ch. 8] B, 1B/9f trans. Neugebauer 9f.).

"What we call 'heaven' is the pattern in things as it is in itself,[14] what we call 'earth' is that which being constant does not depart from it" ([ch. 1] A, 1A/9f.).

The conception of the Way followed by heaven and earth as morally neutral and distinct from the Way of Man was widely current in the time of *Ho-kuan-tzu*, shared by both the Confucian Hsün-tzu and the Legalist Han Fei. How are these divergent paths related? A Westerner tends to think of Chinese attempts to unify the Way as vitiated by a confusion common in his own tradition, a failure to distinguish fact from value, physical laws of nature from moral laws. I formerly agreed but now think differently. For Chinese thought, action, however deeply considered, starts from preferences which mature with increasing knowledge but at bottom are spontaneous, "so of themselves" (*tzu jan*). The Way of the wise man or of the fool is the direction in which he finds himself moved by what he knows about the things which act on him; and the reaction of the man who knows more is the better, because knowledge is better than ignorance. For Chuang-tzu, the sage reflects his situation with the clarity of a mirror and trusts to knack and impulse; for Confucians, in responding to other things with pleasure or anger, sadness or joy, we have to guide the reaction by rules, but rules which prescribe what we would spontaneously prefer if we knew as much as the sages do ("From 70", says Confucius, "I followed what the heart desires without transgressing rule"[15]). The spontaneity of ultimate preferences, changing in relative weight with greater or lesser awareness, is one of the unspoken presuppositions a Westerner has to make explicit in interpreting Chinese thinkers. To do so may shake his own very questionable presupposition that as rational Ego he somehow detaches himself from his own spontaneity, as though to watch unmoved even his own emotions, and only afterwards starts his ratiocination. For *Ho-kuan-tzu* the motions of the sage start from the *ch'i*, the cosmic breath out of which things condense and which continues in its original purity to flow through and activate them; he does not follow the same path as heaven (*t'ien*), but like the stars on their courses he moves as heaven does, he 'heavens' (*t'ien* used verbally), taking like other things the direction set by positional advantage or disadvantage, a direction better than the fool's simply because it is wiser.

"What lets things go and leaves all to positional advantage is heaven. Let things go and leave all to positional advantage. Hence no one is capable of taking charge who does not *heaven*" ([ch. 4] A, 9A/7f.).

Under the sage ruler every other positional advantage of strong over weak will be outweighed by that of the throne inside the pattern of a perfectly ordered realm, so that his equalising Way preserves us from what in human terms are the cruelty of heaven and abasement of earth. As for his knowledge, it depends not on a piecemeal scrutinising of things but on a grasp of their patterning by the One.

"Of getting the Way to generation and never having perished, the sun, moon and stars are examples; of getting the Way to destruction and never having been preservable, a stray leaf touched by the frost or morning dew meeting the sunshine are examples. Hence the sage takes his direction by positional advantage and does not search for it by scrutinising. Positional advantage is the focussing and settling in oneself, scrutinising is the scattering and going out to other things. Of things springing from things in all their profusion, which does not issue forth from the One as its source, to be exchanged for another when it reaches the One? Therefore fix judgments by the One, and observe alterations in the things" ([ch. 18] C, 22B/4–10).

Understanding how things are related to the One is a matter of correlating the similar and the different, and perceiving that all things fall into "kinds" (*lei*)[16] and that behind difference there is always similarity. The One divides into the Yin and the Yang, the passive and the active *ch'i*, which by a further binary division become the Five Processes, wood, fire, metal, and water arranged around soil at the centre; sets of four or five correlate with the Five Processes, pairs with the Yin and Yang.

"Hence the Ways of East and West or North and South diverge, but as quarters they are peers; Yin and Yang are dissimilar *ch'i*, but as harmonious they are similar; sour and salt or sweet and bitter tastes are opposites, but as appetising they even out; the Five Colours are dissimilar in hue, but as beautiful they are equal; the Five Notes are dissimilarly tuned, but the delight in them is one. . . . Hence it is the similar which is called the One, the differing which is called the Way, one-or-other prevailing which is called positional advantage, being fortunate or unfortunate which is called victory and defeat" ([ch. 5] A, 14B/10–15A/5, 15A/10–15B/1).

Nothing could be further from Taoism than to define the Way as 'the differing', the composite of differing trends leading to success or failure, depending on positional advantage or disadvantage. The same is implied by a definition elsewhere in the book: "The interchanging but separate one calls the Way" ([ch. 17] C, 14B/9). Among the dissimilar trends is that of the sage, whose spontaneous motivations are superior to other men's because of fuller awareness of the world around him. But for *Ho-kuan-tzu*, unlike *Chuang-tzu*, the sage does not simply react spontaneously, he takes as standard the wiser course on which he finds himself, and lays it down for man as law. As ruler he covenants with his ministers to reward or punish according to whether the "shape" of their work fits the "names" of their titles and of his decrees, as in Legalist theory.[17] Some enterprises succeed, some fail, depending on the right choice of time, but for the Way as neutral one is interchangeable with another. The operation is conceived as starting, not as for us post-Kantian Westerners from the decision of a rational Ego detaching itself from and objectivising spontaneous inclination, but from the spontaneous flow of the ruler's *ch'i*, the vitalising and energising fluids which issue from the One.

"There being the One there is the *ch'i*, then the idea, then the picture, then the name, then the shape, then the work, then the covenant. The covenant being decided the time is born, the time being set the thing is born.

"Therefore superimpositions of *ch'i* make the time, of covenants the project, of projects the achievement, of achievements gain and loss, of gains and losses fortune and misfortune, and of the myriad things victory and defeat. All of them spring from the *ch'i*, interchange along the Way, are covenanted for through the work, adjust to the time, correspond to the name, and are made complete by law" ([ch. 5] A, 12B/1–10).

As for the intelligence which makes the sage's reactions wiser than other men's, it is discussed in terms of a pair of concepts which has always resisted English translation, *shen* and *ming*, used both nominally of the spirits and verbally of the kind of intelligence possessed by the spirits and attained by the sage.[18] In *Ho-kuan-tzu* they are the active and passive sides of the unifying intelligence which exceeds a piecemeal acquaintance with things by grouping them in kinds; as rough equivalents we choose "clairvoyance" and "illumination". (Granted that *shen* is not necessarily the supposedly supernormal insight nowadays tested in laboratories by guessing what is on the back of cards, "clairvoyance" does suggest the daimonic aura of the Chinese word.) Both synthesise, do not analyse; the word *pien* "argumentation",[19] used of distinguishing contradictories and giving your reasons for one or other, is absent from the vocabulary of *Ho-kuan-tzu*.

"Clairvoyance and illumination are the means of joining together as of a kind. Therefore the clairvoyant and illumined tie the straps of them tightly, and in the generation and completion of kind after kind the use of the One is unlimited" ([ch. 11] B, 26A/1–3).

The clairvoyance of spirits and sages is the insight and power radiating out from them to see into and act on other things, their illumination is the luminous clarity with which they open themselves to reflect other things and be moved by them. In one passage even the law imposed by the sage on the empire is described as clairvoyant and illumined.

"As being here one calls law near, as issuing to transform the other one calls it far. From the near it attains, so is called "clairvoyant"; from the far it returns, so is called "illumined." The illumination is here, its radiance shows up the other; its work is shaped here, its achievement completes the other. What transforms the other from here is law. The generator of law is myself, the completer of law is the other. The generator of law is something which is present every day and never flags. One for whom the generating and completing are in himself is called the sage. Only the sage fathoms the Way as it is in itself, it is only the Way that he takes as standard" ([ch. 5] A, 12B/1–13A/9).

Law, clairvoyance, and illumination are interrelated concepts. Things other than man follow the Way unconsciously; man becomes intelligent in becoming conscious of it as law, and with full knowledge of his surroundings his *ch'i* spontaneously turns in the direction which the sage will lay down as man's Way. We may think of the Way of the sage as the course on which the sage finds himself moving as he and the things around him assume a pattern. The pattern radiating out from him to make other things intelligible is "clairvoyance", as other things presenting themselves to him in their unity is "illumination", as detached from him and formulated is law. Intelligence in recognising the pattern outside reacts to complete it, by that qualitative jump to an ideal social order which transforms and perfects. As Hall and Ames point out in their study of Confucius,[20] the pattern is not an order independent of how one acts on it; the sage is himself an agent in its interactions, extending order from the cycles of the cosmos to human society.

That the sage does not merely mirror the Way as law but generates it, does not simply reflect other things but acts on them and transforms them, is in the whole logic of this position. Every spontaneous shift of the intelligent man's *ch'i* as his situation changes will be opening up a new path as his most informed course of action, which in its turn will change other things for the better. The Way of the sage is as much outcome as origin, interdependent with the insight into and understanding of it.

" 'The Way, the Way!

It protects and is protected by clairvoyance and illumination.'

'How do they protect each other?' P'ang said.

'Worth generates sagehood, sagehood the Way, the Way law, law clairvoyance, clairvoyance illumination. Clairvoyance and illumination adjust it at the tips, the tips draw it from the roots, therefore they protect each other'" ([ch. 14] C, 10A/2–7) trans. Neugebauer 220).

Rephrasing in our own terms, intelligence advancing from "worth" to "sagehood" recognises the patterned courses of the spontaneous in oneself and other things as the Way, then formulates it as law, then issues as clairvoyance into the patterned and returns as illumination. Intelligence in discovering the path which spontaneously shifts with its own operations is itself "generating" the Way. The Way branches out from its root in the One to its tips in action, where it is "adjusted" to circumstance by intelligence.

Even in the Way of heaven and earth *Ho-kuan-tzu* sometimes speaks of things has having laws which they follow by taking the One as standard. Here, as Needham notices,[21] law has a metaphorical extension as in our own "laws of nature", with clairvoyant heaven occupying the same place as the divine lawgiver in the formation of the Western concept.

"When the handle of the Dipper points east, south, west, north, it is spring, summer, autumn, winter. With the handle of the Dipper revolving above the work is set below; with the handle of the Dipper pointing in one direction, it is brought to completion throughout the four borders. This is the employment of law by the Way. Therefore to illumine requires more than sun and moon, achievement requires more than the four seasons; the One serves as standard to them to complete their vocations, so none is not on the Way. When the standard of the One is set, the myriad things all come as its dependents' ([ch. 5] A, 13A/9–13B/7).

These laws or standards are "decreed", by the Decree of Heaven which is destiny.

"Therefore the generator of law is Decree, generation by law is also Decree. The Decree is the so of itself. What Decree establishes, the worthy do not necessarily win, the inadequate do not necessarily lose" ([ch. 5] A, 13B/10–14A/2).

Heaven being "the pattern in things as it is in itself", the Decree is simply the "so of itself". It may be noticed that when it uses personifying language *Ho-kuan-tzu* sometimes fails to sustain the structural parallelism with Way, law, and human ruler, for example in that reference to the motion of the Dipper as "employment of law by the Way".

The author of *Ho-kuan-tzu* was an enthusiastic designer of ideal political systems, with marked changes of mind which may be related to the rapid changes of events before and after the Ch'in reunification.[22] One ideal regime set in the era of the otherwise unknown sage emperor Ch'eng-chiu (ch. 9) is predominantly Legalist, with a background in Yin-Yang cosmology; since it uses the titles of the state of Ch'u, it is likely to be earlier than the fall of Ch'u to Ch'in in 223 B.C. A second, the Utopia of the "Nine Majesties" (chs. 10, 11) roots community more deeply in cosmology, shifts the emphasis from reward and punishment to the harmonising of desires, and may be taken to reflect the discrediting of Legalism by the tyranny of the Ch'in dynasty (221–209 B.C.). The next chapters (chs. 12, 13) treat the whole history of government as a decline from an original pacific community without ruler and subject, and relate closely to texts from the time of civil war in the Ch'in-Han interregnum which proclaim a total disillusionment with all organised government (the Primitivist and "Robber Chih" chapters of *Chuang-tzu*).[23] But as long as his confidence lasts, the writer is always trying to relate government to a cosmic order unified by the One.

"Heaven is one, law its sameness; before or after, to left or right, law is as it was from past to present, therefore there is nothing which does not recognise it as constant. Heaven is sincere, trustworthy, illumined, accordant and one; it does not for the sake of the myriad fathers [the ancestors of the myriad kinds of thing] substitute any for the One, therefore none is able to contend with it for priority. A substitute for the One is not the One, therefore it cannot be reduced or increased. Ch'eng-chiu grasped the One, therefore everything looked up to and was organised by him" ([ch. 9] B, 7B/1–7, trans. Neugebauer 139–41).

In the systems of Ch'eng-chiu and of the Nine Majesties, the operations of government (reward and punishment, peace and war, ceremony and music, measures, the calendar) harmonise with the cosmic cycles through the correlations of numbered sets. The following introduces a calendar for reports from different levels of the hierarchy.

"Heaven employs the Four Seasons, earth employs the Five Processes; the Son of Heaven holds on to the One and uses it to reside at the centre. He attunes by the Five Notes, adjusts by the Six Pitch-tubes, sequences by measure and number, governs by punishment and bounty. From root to tip succession is from Chia to Yi [calendrical terms]. Heaven starts from New Year, earth from the new moons, the Four Seasons from the calendar . . ." ([ch. 9] B, 10B/1–5, trans Neugebauer 164f.).

In the system of classifications, already before *Ho-kuan-tzu* laid out in detail in the calendrical chapters of the *Lü Spring and Autumn*, all differences lead back to similarity, and "it is the similar which is called the One".[24] Without attempting a comparison with the One of neo-Platonism, there is a general difference which deserves attention. Hansen has contrasted a Western tendency to build the cosmos up from discrete particulars with a Chinese to conceive it as a variously divisible and sub-divisible mass, which he connects with the grammar of the noun in Indo-European languages and in Chinese.[25] The West has always had some trouble explaining how isolated individuals can be unified, unless by a hierarchy of Platonic forms on some other plane than commonsense reality, a problem which does not arise in Chinese thought because things are seen as only relatively similar or different, with names assigned on the basis of relative similarity. The teaching of *Ho-kuan-tzu*, as the first developed Chinese philosophy of the One, is highly relevant to Hansen's still controversial proposal. It is immediately obvious that *Ho-kuan-tzu* does treat the cosmos as a variously divisible whole. When asked whether Ch'eng-chiu's system can be valid for all times and places, Ho-kuan-tzu says:

"It's simply that what is from the past we ourselves cause to continue, what is multiple we ourselves cause to be multiple. . . . When proceeding to measure and number them, in the One they are not reduced nor in the myriad made more numerous; they are the same like trees in a forest, an accumulation like grains in the granary; what is laid out in pecks will not be missing in the pints. Lands distributed and people divided are after all still simply one" ([ch. 9] B, 15A/7f, 16A/4–7, trans. Neugebauer, 208f.).

In the system of the Nine Majesties, based not on detailed regulations but on harmonising of desires, the same point is repeated.

"The multiple we ourselves make multiple, therefore it can be sought through a single schema" ([ch. 10] B, 21B/3f.).

The cosmos presents itself for division as a whole in which 'figures' (*wen*) stand out from their background, and 'patterns' (*li*) ramify throughout. Figures belong especially to heaven (as the heavenly bodies showing up against the sky), patterns to earth. In one passage figures and patterns are related as the members and joints of a universal organism.

"The layout of the members and placing of the joints, for a myriad ages never changing, are from the positions of heaven and earth; the dividing of things and sequencing of names, so that figure and pattern are clear and distinct, is equalising by the clairvoyant sages. . . . Therefore figure is what they use to divide things, pattern is what they use to sequence names" ([ch. 11] B, 24A/3f, 24B/3f.).

For *Ho-kuan-tzu*, then, the characteristic type of classification is not the grouping of individual oxen or horses which can be counted in only one way, but the dividing up of an organic whole in accordance with the figures and patterns. The figures and patterns are objective, belong to heaven and earth; the dividing and naming of the figures, and the linking of names to convey the patterns, are the work of the sage. The sage "equalises" things, meaning, as we have seen,[26] not that he treats them all the same but on the contrary that he judges them by the same law, secures them from the injustice of morally neutral heaven and earth. He is already prescribing in imposing the classification itself, which regularly distinguishes superior A from inferior B: "Yang/Yin, heaven/earth, light/darkness, male/female, ruler/subject . . .". Dividing and naming begin then from the sage's reaction for or against, as clairvoyant and illumined he contemplates the figures and patterns of the world. For *Ho-kuan-tzu* there can be no such thing as a purely objective description of the world, any more than for Confucius, who proposed the "correction of names" as the first duty of government.[27]

NOTES

1. Cf. ch. 2 above.
2. Cf. pp. 22–23 above.
3. Cf. my *Disputers of the Tao (DT)* (La Salle, Illinois: Open Court, 1989), Appendix 1 and passim.

4. Cf. pp. 103–4 above, and *DT* 144–46.
5. Cf. p. 107 above, and *DT* 191–93.
6. *DT* 378, 398, cf. 206f., 236, 376–81.
7. *Chuang-tzu* ch. 17, trans. A. C. Graham, *Chuang-tzu: The Inner Chapters (CIC)*, (London: George Allen & Unwin, 1981), 145, 155. Burton Watson, *The Complete Works of Chuang Tzu* (New York: Columbia University Press, 1968).
8. Cf. my *Studies in Chinese Philosophy and Philosophical Literature*, (SCP) (Albany NY: State University of New York Press, 1990), 414–35.
9. Cf. my "A Neglected Pre-Han Philosophical Text: *Ho-kuan-tzu*", *Bulletin of the School of Oriental and African Studies*, University of London, v.52/3 (1989): 497–532. Of the nineteen chapters, seven are translated in Klaus Karl Neugebauer, *Hoh-kuan tsï: Eine Untersuchung der dialogischen Kapitel (mit Übersetzung und Annotationen)* (Frankfurt am Mein: Peter Lang, 1986). References to *Ho-kuan-tzu* are to the Chinese text in the Taoist Patrology edition, and to Neugebauer's translation where available.
10. *Lü-shih ch'un-ch'iu* ch. 5/2 ("Great Music") trans. R. Wilhelm, *Frühling und Herbst des Lü Bu We* (Jena: Diederichs, 1928).
11. *Chuang-tzu* ch. 2, trans. Graham, 56, Watson, 43.
12. For *shih*, often used of the ruler's power cf. *DT*, 278–82, 494. For *li*, cf. *DT*, 286, 487f., also pp. 60–61 above.
13. For *ch'i*, cf. *DT*, 101–104, 477, also pp. 60–61 above.
14. More literally, 'the *ch'ing* of the pattern of things'. For *ch'ing* and its relation to Aristotelian essence, cf. DT 98f., 478f., also p. 103 above.
15. *Analects*, 2/4.
16. For *lei* cf. *DT*, 148, 417, 487.
17. Cf. *DT*, 283–85, 485.
18. For *shen* and *ming* cf. *DT*, 101, 489 (*ming*), 494 (*shen, shen ming*), there translated "daimonic and clear-seeing".
19. For *pien*, cf. *DT*, 36, 491.
20. David L. Hall and Roger T. Ames, *Thinking through Confucius* (Albany: SUNY Press, 1987).
21. Joseph Needham, *Science and Civilisation in China*, vol. 2, (Cambridge University Press, 1962), 547.
22. Cf. "A Neglected Pre-Han Philosophical Text" (as in 7 above) Part 5, "The Three Utopias".
23. For the dating of the Primitivist chapters (*Chuang-tzu*, chs. 8-11/28) and "Robber Chih" (ch. 29), cf. *SCP*, 305–308.
24. Cf. p. 123 above.
25. Chad Hansen, *Language and Logic in Ancient China* (Ann Arbor: University of Michigan Press, 1983), 30–54. But cf. pp. 73–74 above and *DT*, 401f.
26. Cf. pp. 125–28 above.
27. *Analects*, 13/3.

China, Europe, and the Origins of Modern Science: Needham's *The Grand Titration*

Why China lost its former lead and fell behind Europe is almost the first question that a layman asks about Chinese civilization, a question from which sinologists tend to shrink into their separate compartments, afraid of being caught up in inconclusive generalizations. Recently it has appeared in the context of a relatively new discipline, the history of science, presented in a more exact form that gives it a new claim on our attention. We now know that the supposed stagnation of China and the rest of Asia was illusory, their changes being slow only in relation to the accelerating development of Europe since the Renaissance, a transformation for which the only precedent is the discovery of agriculture and the transition from nomadic to settled life during the Neolithic Age. The crucial event in this process was the "Scientific Revolution" in the seventeenth century, the refining of methods of stating hypotheses in mathematical terms and testing them by controlled experiment. This was the "discovery of how to discover," the takeoff for an accelerating accumulation of knowledge, and its application to technology generated the Industrial Revolution. It seems then that we have only to ask, "Why was there a Scientific Revolution in Europe about 1600?" and "Why was there no Scientific Revolution in China or India?"—questions that look as though they are two sides of one coin.[1]

It is the second question that interests inquirers into Chinese science. I intend shortly to suggest that although the positive question is real and important there is something wrong with the negative question, but whether it is conceptually confused or not, there is no doubt that important social and cultural differences between China and the West have been brought to light by those who insist on asking it. The search for an answer has provided much of the impetus for Dr. Joseph Needham's great *Science and Civilisation in China,* and in eight papers now assembled in one volume[2] he returns to the theme again and again. In these papers, each of which displays in miniature his nearly superhuman capacity for organizing his vast store of material in the service of a lucidly argued case, the development of his thought on this problem can be followed over twenty years. *On Science and Social Change* (1944) already asks, "Why did modern science not arise in China?" and gives a fairly straightforward Marxist answer influenced by the early Wittfogel: the bourgeoisie provided the setting of free and equal debate within which science can develop, but the growth of the bourgeoisie that accompanied the decay of European feudalism was not possible inside Asiatic bureaucratism. In this essay he does not yet make great claims for Chinese technology, being aware of few additions to the traditional list of Chinese inventions (gunpowder, printing, paper, the compass). His later researches revealed more and more inventions first attested in China, which he delights in listing in article after article (the mechanical clock, the driving belt, the crank, efficient equine harness, the wheelbarrow, segmental arch bridges. . . .). The more recent papers recognize the technological superiority of China over most of history as a second problem; he is inclined to find the explanation in the absence of the mass chattel slavery that is commonly thought to have discouraged technological progress in Greece and Rome. By the time of *Science and Society in East and West* (1964) he gives equal weight to the questions "Why modern science had not developed in Chinese civilization (or Indian) but only in Europe" and "Why, between the first century B.C. and the fifteenth century A.D., Chinese civilization was much *more* efficient than occidental in applying human natural knowledge to practical human needs." Unsympathetic to the "internalist" approach to the history of science dominant for the last thirty years, he repeats his sociological explanation but in a much more developed and refined form, for which he acknowledges a debt to Jean Chesneaux and André Haudricourt. Although primarily interested in social and economic factors, he considers with sympathy the possibility that the genesis of modern science required the concepts of linear time and of a divine legislator, in *Time and Eastern Man* and *Human Law and the Laws of Nature*.

The researchers embodied in *Science and Civilisation in China* have dispelled much of the haze which surrounded this issue. It is now clear that for most of its history the West showed no special bent toward technology. The three inventions which according to Francis Bacon had changed the face of the world, "those three which were unknown to the ancients, and of which the origin though recent is obscure and inglorious, namely, printing, gunpowder and the magnet" (that is, the magnetic compass), all reached Europe from China. Nor is it true that the West already had science while China only had technology. The systems based on the yin and yang and the Five Processes which underlie Chinese alchemy, medicine, and geomancy, do not seem to be different in kind from medieval science, and if we prefer to speak of "proto-science" we must apply the name to both. The greater rationality of modern science is already present in Greek logic, geometry, and philosophy, but for two thousand years it gave no technological advantage for those who had it over those who had not. It is still no doubt common to lump together Greek logic and the modern science to which it contributed under some such heading as "the generalized conception of scientific explanation and of mathematical proof" or the "rational conception of the cosmos as an orderly whole working by laws discoverable in thought."[3] This kind of description, which rouses Needham to polemic, illustrates, it may be suggested, the mistake of looking for distinguishing features of a "Western civilization" conceived as a unity nearly three thousand years old which includes Greece and excludes Israel, instead of tracing the connections of a "Western tradition" which is a stage, starting as far back as one chooses to make the cut, in one of the diverging and converging lines of development that go back to Egypt and Babylon (in which, for example, Christendom and Islam diverge out of the late Roman civilization on which Greece and Israel have converged). Indeed if we wish to find the best historical perspective for looking forward toward the Scientific Revolution, there is much to be said for choosing a viewpoint not in Greece but in the Islamic culture that from A.D. 750 reached from Spain to Turkestan. This was the first civilization in history that was in varying degrees the heir of all the great civilizations of the Old World. It was in most cases the channel by which Chinese inventions reached the West, but it was also the meeting place of Indian numerals, zero and algebra and Greek geometry, and of the Hellenistic and Chinese influences which ran together in the alchemy which is one of the ancestors of chemistry. A pool in which older discoveries could mix and interact, Greek, Indian, Chinese (scarcely ever Roman), was an important preliminary of the "discovery of how to discover." From about A.D. 1000 Christendom set out on the enterprise of translating the corpus of Arabic learning into Latin (including the Arabic translations of Aristotle, Euclid, Galen, Ptolemy). When the Arabic sciences passed into decline, of the three great cultures on the edges of Islam (China, India, and Christendom) it was the last that inherited its great synthesis.

The vague old question, "Why did China fall behind?" has therefore clarified and concentrated in recent decades; we might even dramatize it as "Why was Galileo born in Europe and not in China?"

First of all it is essential to define the differences between ancient and medieval science on the one hand, and modern science on the other. I make an important distinction between the two. When we say that modern science developed only in Western Europe at the time of Galileo in the late Renaissance, we mean surely that there and then alone there developed the fundamental bases of the structure of the natural sciences as we have them today, namely the application of mathematical hypotheses to Nature, the full understanding and use of the experimental method, the distinction between primary and secondary qualities, the geometrisation of space, and the acceptance of the mechanical model of reality. Hypotheses of primitive or medieval type distinguish themselves quite clearly from those of modern type. Their intrinsic and essential vagueness always made them incapable of proof or disproof, and they were prone to combine in fanciful systems of gnostic correlation. In so far as numerical figures entered into them, numbers were manipulated in forms of "numerology" or number-mysticism constructed a priori, not employed as the stuff of quantitative measurements compared a posteriori. We know the primitive and medieval Western scientific theories, the four Aristotelian elements, the four Galenical humours, the doctrines of pneumatic physiology and pathology, the sympathies and antipathies of Alexandrian protochemistry, the *tria prima* of the alchemists, and the natural philosophies of the Kabbala. We tend to know less well the corresponding theories of other civilizations, for instance the Chinese theory of the two fundamental forces yin and yang, or that of the Five Processes, or the elaborate system of symbolic correlations. In the West Leonardo da Vinci, with all his brilliant inventive genius, still inhabited this world; Galileo broke through its walls. This is why it has been said that Chinese science and technology remained until late times essentially Vincian, and that the Galilean breakthrough occurred only in the West. That is the first of our starting points.[4]

Among earlier contributions to the problem, Needham quotes the charming letter of Einstein to J. E. Switzer printed by Derek Price:

> Development of Western Science is based on two great achievements, the invention of the formal logical system (in Euclidean geometry) by the Greek philosophers, and the discovery of the possibility to find out causal relationship by systematic experiment (Renaissance). In my opinion one has not to be astonished that the Chinese sages have not made these steps. The astonishing thing is that these discoveries were made at all.[5]

Needham takes this as a slight on Chinese civilization and springs to its defense. But Einstein does not seem to be saying anything about Chinese limitations. He seems rather to be advising Switzer not to think that a discovery was always obvious because it is now familiar, to recover the fresh eye by which it is seen to depend on a nearly miraculous conjunction of improbable circumstances. For 1400 years between Ptolemy and Copernicus the West remained satisfied with the geocentric theory although the heliocentric theory had already been proposed and the evidence tying the motions of at least the inner planets to the sun was still available, and it forgot Hero of Alexandria's steam engine for even longer; who are we to be surprised if other civilizations failed to notice things which in retrospect seem to have been just around the corner? One does not ask why an event did *not* happen unless there was reason to expect it, and nothing in the conditions even of Europe in the sixteenth century justifies thinking of the Scientific Revolution as an event due at a certain point of maturation, as though civilization were an organism with stages which it passes through unless its development is arrested. In the absence of grounds for expectation I explain why a house did catch fire (because someone left a cigarette burning), do not go through all the other houses in turn explaining why they did not catch fire (no one was smoking, the wiring was sound, there were no bombs, no lightning). The difference follows from the fact that like effects may have unlike causes; if the event does happen we can select from the possible causes, if it does not we may not be able to enumerate all the unrealized possibilities.

If the Western development after 1600 began from a single though complex discovery, that of the means to accelerate discovery, we are concerned with an event like the invention of the wheel or of metallurgy, which we are not surprised to find diffusing from a single center where conditions for the invention are not visibly better than in many other places. We may of course find places lacking necessary conditions of an invention (the Polynesians did not invent skis because they have no snow), but for the most part it is conditions at the place of discovery that interest us. It would be pointless to ask why the Swiss did not invent skis for themselves before getting them from Norway in the nineteenth century, still more so to run over the list of maritime countries asking of each why its swimmers did not discover the crawl before its dissemination from the Pacific. But these considerations would not stop us from asking the positive question, looking for conditions favorable to the inventions in Norway and Polynesia.

The positive and negative questions are inseparable only as long as we are thinking of the difference between China and the West as one of degree. "Why is China backward?" and "Why is the West ahead?" really are two ways of putting the same vague question. We tend to suppose that this is still so when we sharpen the issue to the occurrence or nonoccurrence of the Scientific Revolution. But the questions remain two sides of the same coin only if we think of the event as having a single cause which is both necessary and sufficient, as in the more elementary kind of Marxist explanation ("Why did modern science emerge in Europe?—Because the bourgeoisie had broken free of the bonds of feudalism. What prevented it in China?—The shackling of the bourgeoisie by Asian bureaucratism"). But if Needham ever inclined to such a simplification certainly he does not now:

Whatever the individual prepossessions of Western historians of science all are necessitated to admit that from the fifteenth century A.D. onwards a complex of changes occurred; the Renaissance cannot be thought of without the Reformation, the Reformation cannot be thought of without the rise of modern science, and none of them can be thought of without the rise of capitalism, capitalist society and the decline and the disappearance of feudalism. We seem to be in the presence of a kind of organic whole, a packet of change, the analysis of which has hardly yet begun. In the end it will probably be found that all the schools, whether the Weberians or the Marxists or the believers in intellectual factors alone, will have their contributions to make.[6]

Clearly the analysis of this complex of events would not explain or need to explain why the Scientific Revolution did not occur in China. It will hardly be suggested that the spontaneous emergence of modern science in China would have required the equivalents of any of these events except, arguably, the rise of capitalism.

When we ask the negative question, we assume that there are necessary conditions for a Scientific Revolution which were present in Europe but absent in China. This assumption might conceivably turn out to be correct; but if not, how are we to enumerate all the situations in which the event could have taken place, and prove that none existed in China, and why should we wish to do so? As Einstein perceived, we are not bound to ask why a civilization did *not* do something as improbable as exploring the possibilities of mathematizing its generalizations about nature and testing them by controlled experiment—a prospect less obvious, one would think, than that of a Swiss getting the idea of skis. Here it may be objected that the simple inventions we are using as analogies may be misleading us. There are scarcely any relevant preconditions, for example, of the invention of the boomerang, and scarcely any peoples on earth of whom one would wish to explain why they never got around to inventing it. But we would expect the birth of modern science to have a much more varied complex of preconditions, not the concomitant events considered in the last paragraph, but such heterogeneous factors as the meeting of Greek logic and geometry with Indian numerals and algebra, capitalism, the Judeo-Christian sense of linear time and of a cosmic legislator. However, it is precisely when factors are interrelated that it is most difficult to show that any one of them is a necessary condition. If *X* is ill and *Y* is a nurse and they meet in a London hospital it does not follow that they could not have met earlier when they were both in New York because *X* was well and *Y* was not yet a nurse. The combination of the mathematization of hypotheses and experimental methods certainly requires some mathematics and some tradition of experiment, which is enough to explain why it did not happen among Australian aboriginals; but may it not be that where these and a few other conditions are satisfied the result could follow from any number of complicated, improbable, but quite different conjunctions of circumstances?

The trouble is that explanations of China's failure to attain modern science are generally no more than proofs that she was not following the route by which we arrived at it. We are shown that one of the interlocking factors in sixteenth-century Europe was missing in China, a kind of explanation which is liable to reduce itself to the vacuous observation that conditions in sixteenth-century Europe differed from those of any other place or time. The "why not?" question could be fruitfully asked only if it should prove possible to detach the factors from their historical situation and show that they are necessary as snow is necessary to the invention of skis. We have no particular reason to expect this can be done. The problem can be seen in Needham's simplest version of his sociological argument, in the early essay *On Science and Social Change* (1944):

> As we have already seen above, the rise of the merchant class to power, with their slogan of democracy, was the indispensable accompaniment and *sine qua non* of the rise of modern science in the West. But in China the scholar-gentry and their bureaucratic feudal system always effectively prevented the rise to power or seizure of the State by the merchant class, as happened elsewhere.[7]

But the rise of the merchant class would be a *sine qua non* of the rise of modern science outside Europe only if there are necessary conditions that the merchant class alone can fulfill. Are such conditions implicit in the connections that Marxists find between science and the rise of capitalism? We may instance the arguments that competing capitalists are attracted by the profitability of technical innovations, irrelevant to landowners whose income is rent; that science flourishes only in an atmosphere of free and equal debate, provided by the merchant class "with their slogan of democracy"; that the fusion of mathematics and experiment could happen only when the theoretical discoveries of Greek slaveowners were circulating among people not ashamed to work with their hands. Of course all these points are relevant to the positive question of how the Scientific Revolution came about. The close connections between science and middle-class attitudes and interests are plain enough; in English society at least science has hardly lived down its vulgar origins yet. But if we try to detach necessary conditions (a social force with a vested interest in technological advance, an atmosphere of free debate, people who could use both their minds and their hands), conditions that become vaguer the further one tries to detach them from the historical situation, it becomes less and less clear that they could be fulfilled only by the merchant class. In any case the conditions favorable to scientific advance in a merchant class have little to do with whether or not it has won political power. Galileo after all lived at a time when the medieval fight for republican institutions in the Italian cities had long ago been lost. Asian bureaucratism did not inhibit the growth of a flourishing bourgeois culture in late imperial China: why should the political impotence of the merchant class be more of an obstacle to science than to the novel, which was already emerging in the sixteenth century? In Europe the Scientific Revolution did not wait for the seventeenth-century political struggle in England, but the novel did.

In the very interesting paper *Human Law and the Laws of Nature* (1951), Needham suggests that the concept of a divine legislator, absent in China, may have been necessary for the genesis of the idea of "laws of nature," and also for Western confidence that the secrets of a cosmos ordered by a rational being will be intelligible to rational beings. We no longer think of the phrase "laws of nature" as anything but a metaphor, but "the problem is whether the recognition of such statistical regularities and their mathematical expression could have been reached by any other road than that which Western science actually travelled."[8] Here of course we are at the crux of the matter. As with most if not all answers to the negative question we can think of alternative routes; and the trouble is not that they are plausible but that we can neither estimate their plausibility nor set limits to their proliferation. On the issue of cosmic rationality one can come to closer grips with Needham by doubting the relevance of a divine legislator to cosmic rationality even in Europe. Since Zeus gave laws only to gods and men, the Greeks should have had rather less grounds for faith in a rational universe than the Chinese, whose Heaven, however impersonally conceived, commands nature as well as man by its *ming* 'decree.' Nothing discourages Christians from stressing the incomprehensibility of a transcendent God rather than the rationality of his works, depending on how much of the Greek they have in them. But on the issue of laws of nature we are again trapped in the kind of debate in which one side suggests that there was no possibility but the one actualized and the other side produces speculative alternatives. The neo-Confucian cosmos was rational in the sense that it reinterpreted the heaven that one obeys and the Way that one walks as *li*, the pattern or layout of things, within which, wherever we discern a local arrangement, we can infer (*t'ui*) from one case to another. The neo-Confucians identified *li* with the decree of heaven and might conceivably have built a legislative metaphor on this basis, but it is difficult to see why they would need it. They were interested in laying down general principles, moral, political, and also natural, which they presented as *li;* if they had ever reached the point of formulating principles in mathematical terms and testing them by experiment, the concept of the myriad *li* which go back to one *li* would surely have provided a sufficient theoretical framework. Needham, always meticulous in collecting the relevant facts, admits that the use of the term "law" did not really catch on until after Galileo, who had spoken instead of "proportions," "ratios," "principles."[9]

This is not to deny the importance of a divine legislator in the European development. Indeed the significance of God as designer of the clockwork is clear in seventeenth- and eighteenth-century science, which inclined even after diverging from official religion to deism rather than to atheism. If there is a personal Creator, the universe is not simply there (as for Aristotle) and has not simply grown (as for the Chinese) but has been designed and constructed, so that the way to understand it is to take it to pieces like a man-made instrument and see how it works. This implies that nature is comprehensible in a special way, narrower than its rationality for the Greeks or the universality of *li* in neo-Confucianism. Indeed the kind of rationality that seems to be guaranteed by a divine order is partly repudiated by modern science. It denies that there are reasons for coincidences; if asked how some rare conjunction can be explained except as a warning omen, or how to account for a cruel accident without imputing injustice to God, it absolutely refuses explanation. What it requires is the treatment of a hypothesis about nature after the analogy of an instruction how to build a model, which justifies itself only when tried out, and can be tried out only if it includes exact measurements. The existence of the divine artisan authorizes the universalization of the viewpoint of the artisan, whose practice, as Needham notices elsewhere,[10] united mathematics and experiment long before 1600 but took a long time to make an impression on theory because the thinking classes do not soil their hands.

Would the absence of a Creator in Chinese thought prevent such a development? In China we find only the idea of impersonal *shen* 'the daimonic, the clairvoyant' as the power behind the *tsao-hua*, 'the productive process', the process of nature by which things develop, and of a 'maker of things' who is a consciously poetic personification. But it is interesting to notice how easily Chinese writers fall into this kind of language when admiring constructed models of nature such as automatic toys[11] and armillary spheres. The artificial man in a well-known story in *Lieh-tzu*,[12] who seems human until taken to pieces, excites the comment: "Can man's skill then share the achievement of the author of the productive process?" The *Chin shu*, after describing how the rotation of an armillary sphere made by Chang Heng about A.D. 140 fitted the rotation of the heavens like two halves of a tally, quotes the panegyric: "His mathematics comprehended heaven and earth, his workmanship equaled the 'productive process,' his high talent and glorious art exactly coincided with the Daimonic."[13] The use of such language rouses one's curiosity as to whether it occurred to anyone that man can infer how nature itself works from how his own constructions work. There is in fact a remarkable example in the comment of Chang Chan (c. A.D. 370) on the *Lieh-tzu* passage:

> Recently there have been people who say that human sentience is generated through a mechanism. Why? The achievements of the "productive process" are extremely subtle, therefore the myriad varieties are all fostered and their

activities are boundless. Man's arts are crude and clumsy, and all they can do is reproduce[14] already developed shapes in a rough way. But if human skill were perfected, it would hardly fall short of the "productive process."

Chang Chan rejects the idea and asks: "How can it mean that a thing does not have a daimonic master?" The interest of the passage is its suggestion of a conceptual framework suitable to the development of modern science. Given an inquirer who sets out in earnest to show that something in nature works in the same way as its artificial model (such as the heart working like a pump) he would find himself drawn into measurement and experiment.

Time and Eastern Man (1964), a particularly brilliant examination of the Chinese sense of time ranging from historiography to clocks, is included in the volume for the sake of its discussion of the common claim that the cyclic time of Greece and India turned attention from the future while Christian eschatology encouraged a hope secularized in the doctrine of progress. Needham argues that much Chinese thought about time conceives it as linear rather than cyclic, so that the problem has nothing to do with the failure to achieve modern science. The supposed links between the Scientific Revolution and conceptions of time are in any case so tenuous and involve so many imponderables that he offers only tentative suggestions.[15] I must confess to a personal inability to understand why the Hindu is supposed to be paralyzed by the knowledge that no human achievement can outlast a kalpa of 4,000,000,000 years, while the Christian, cramped inside a time scheme of a few thousand years from Creation to Judgment, works hopefully at sciences that have nothing to do with his salvation in the knowledge that the Last Day may already have dawned.

With regard to internal factors in the development of science, Needham shows that practical experiment without the refinement of experimental methods is common to China and medieval Europe, and that in mathematics China was strong in algebra but weak in geometry. He estimates that in the thirteenth and fourteenth centuries Chinese algebra was the most advanced in the world.[16] But the mathematics of modern science required from the beginning the entire Arabic inheritance, not only the decimal place-value system and algebra but the geometry of the Greeks. All this passed to Europe with the Arabic-Latin translations but did not reach China, although here there is a fascinating example of a historical near-miss; the Mongols brought Muslim astronomers with Arabic books, and there is evidence of a translation of Euclid in the imperial library in 1273,[17] but this knowledge never attracted attention or passed into general circulation. The mathematics developed in Europe after 1550 was an application of algebra to geometry, and Derek Price has examined an earlier nodal point in the history of science (uncovered by the researches of Neugebauer and others) at which Greek geometry had already proved itself essential.[18] The crucial discipline in the development of scientific procedures was astronomy, which even at the stage of the most primitive calendar-making combines mathematization with testing (of course by observation and not by experiment); and the most important advance in mathematization before the sixteenth century was the application of geometry to astronomy by the Hellenistic school that culminated in Ptolemy (c. A.D. 140). Behind this was the meeting of two independent traditions, Greek geometry and Babylonian astronomical observations and arithmetical computations, in Hellenized Mesopotamia after 300 B.C. (The Greeks had been weak in arithmetic as well as in astronomy.) This event, which we now see to have such decisive significance, bore no further fruit for nearly a millennium and a half, until the renewed application of geometry to astronomy by Copernicus and Kepler in the sixteenth century, followed almost at once by fusion with experimental methods. In China, as Nathan Sivin shows,[19] mathematical astronomy made a false start in arithmetical systems of simple interrelated time cycles, and interest in them soon waned as the hope was lost of reconciling them with observation. Post-Han astronomy is no longer a system, but a collection of algebraic techniques—many of them resembling the methods of Babylonian astronomy in the Hellenistic period—developed with reference only to apparent motions.[20] Needham quotes a letter in which J. D. Bernal identifies the absence of an adequate geometry to apply to astronomy as the basic weakness of Chinese science.[21] Needham is not much impressed, being more interested in external than in internal factors. We may notice, however, that this is an example which shows up particularly clearly what is involved in comparing the Chinese and Western traditions. We can examine the route by which the West arrived at the Scientific Revolution and show that China was not taking this route. But unless we wish to entangle ourselves in a demonstration that modern science could only have begun in the field of astronomy, could never have made its takeoff with laws statable in terms of traditional Chinese mathematics, only afterwards refining its geometry to deal with astronomy, we are not even talking about the negative question which is supposed to be so important, "Why was there no Scientific Revolution in China?" The question may also be raised whether Ptolemy or even Copernicus and Kepler were in principle any nearer to modern science than the Chinese and the Maya, or indeed than the first astronomer, whoever he may have been, who allowed observation to outweigh numerological considerations of symmetry in his calculations of the month and the year. Astronomy seems to have been a mathematized discipline in which numerology was at war with observation from its very beginnings up to Kepler himself; the importance to it of geometry was merely as a model for demonstration and a tool to carry it beyond a certain point of development.

A general consideration which will occur to anyone comparing Chinese and Western thought is the much greater intellectual stringency of the latter. Granted that it is arbitrary to include Greek logic itself under the heading of scientific explanation, the importance of Greek rationality in the ancestry of modern science is not in doubt. The quality of Chinese argumentation varies with the extent of division and controversy, and it never returned to the height that it attained in the third century B.C. at the very end of the period of the competing Hundred Schools. Needham quotes the observation of H. O. H. Strange that the Greek philosopher debates with equals by logical disputation, the Chinese advises a prince with the support of historical precedents.[22] (Is it perhaps symptomatic of Needham's commitment to China that he uses the quotation not to criticize Chinese thought but to rebut the curious claim that only Europe has a sense of history?) It may be noticed that here the difference is one of degree, so that for once the positive and negative questions do come together; to the extent that the logical prowess of the West was a precondition of the Scientific Revolution, the relative weakness of China explains its failure. However, people who ask why China never advanced from proto-science to science are hoping for rather more than a vague consideration which suggests that Europe would have a better chance than China. Is it possible to find some difference in kind between traditional Chinese thinking and that required by the Scientific Revolution?

The transient first impression of a fundamental strangeness, a difference in kind, does not survive a prolonged study of Chinese thought. The Chinese weigh practical advantages and disadvantages, perceive and utilize analogies, appeal to precedents, concentrate their insights in aphorisms, fascinate themselves with numerical symmetries, and sometimes reason analytically, very much as we do; if we find their thought difficult it is because of unnoticed differences in underlying concepts and in the implicit questions behind their inquiries. What we do miss, as Nathan Sivin observes, is "the notion of rigorous demonstration, of proof."[23] This concept of proof, it may be necessary to insist, is narrower than any vague idea of "Reason" that could be supposed to characterize Western thought in general. Even in the West it requires quite a special temperament to appreciate the full value of the geometrical proofs we learn as schoolchildren, demonstrations that are far in excess of the ordinary demands of common sense. Intelligent people who do not share this temperament often positively mistrust and dislike it, whether from the point of view of religious faith, romantic intuition, or Anglo-Saxon empiricism. Nor is the concern for rigorous proof equivalent to an interest in logic for its own sake. The fathers of the Scientific Revolution were interested in demonstration, not the logical forms of demonstration, and their recognition that deduction cannot lead to new knowledge compelled them to work outside the forms established as necessary by logicians. Their contempt for logic as a discipline in fact made the period from the fifteenth to the early nineteenth century a veritable Dark Age in its history, which supposed, as befits a Dark Age, that the edifice was completed by Aristotle, and forgot the advances of Stoics, Arabs, and scholastics which research is now rediscovering.[24]

It is therefore hardly profitable to make the vague accusation that Chinese thinkers lack our respect for reason, or to stress that even the later Mohists, who did study certain types of valid and invalid argument, never abstracted necessary forms like the Greek and Indian syllogism. What matters is that most Chinese thinkers (like ourselves, in most of our thinking outside the exact sciences) exchange arguments of varying and indefinite weight without seeing any point in putting premises and conclusion in the same form, filling in all steps however obvious, and pressing every line of thought to its logical end. In particular the Chinese never developed geometrical proofs like those of Euclid, which served as the model for the demonstrations in physics of Archimedes and of Galileo and Newton. But although the ideal of rigorous demonstration has had lasting effect only in the Greek, Arabic, and Western cultures, it certainly emerged at least once in China, among the sophists and Mohists of 350–200 B.C. We may instance Mohist Canon B73, the refutation of an objection to the Mohist doctrine of universal love, which illustrates the meticulousness with which later Mohists try to put premises and conclusions in the same forms, make all logical steps explicit, and delimit what they claim to prove (in this case, merely that a position cannot be "treated as certain" or "is free from difficulty").

As for the Chinese language, Needham is content to expose the fallacy that the script, mistakenly supposed to be not logographic but ideographic, would inhibit abstract thought, and to point out that the exposition of twentieth-century science in Chinese has presented only the problem common to all languages of evolving a technical terminology.[25] I have myself argued elsewhere that claims that Chinese thought is hampered by confusions over distinctions marked by Indo-European number and case always break down when a concrete instance is offered, but also that the discovery of logic as an independent discipline (a dispensable luxury for the Scientific Revolution, as we have seen) may be easier in an inflected than in an isolating language.[26] Logically the advantage of an inflected language is that the changing word forms illuminate the organization of the sentence, an advantage which has nothing to do with the supposed utility of the distinctions marked, which may be quite irrational (as with gender). The structure of an isolating language is invisible without the aid of modern linguistics and offers no foothold for an exploration of grammar or logic; it allows any degree of exactness or inexactness, so that the vagueness or precision of Chinese thinking must always be attributed to extralinguistic factors. The sharpening philosophical controversies of the fourth and third centuries B.C. involved a clarification of terminology and tightening of syntax in some ways comparable with the effects of science on contemporary Chinese. In the language of late Mohist dialectics, vocabulary is regularized (a fact obscured by great graphic variety due to imperfect adaptation of graphs to later usage), there are virtually no synonyms among particles, idiom is avoided, syntactic consistency is observed even at the cost of sentences so extraordinary that they have generally been taken to be corrupt.[27] Given the extra-linguistic conditions for the development of modern science, the Chinese language would presumably have adapted itself much as seventeenth-century English allowed itself to be reformed by the Royal Society.

An important point of Needham's, further developed in *Science and Civilisation in China*,[28] is that medieval science or proto-science with its Galenic humors in Europe and yin and yang and Five Processes in China is culture-bound, but from the point that science is mathematized and experimentally testable it acquires the cultural universality of mathematics and logic. There is nothing in our culture that carries so openly the marks of its Oriental origin as the numerals that we still call "Arabic" in contrast with "Roman," or the concepts which still bear Arabic names— algebra, zero, zenith, nadir, chemistry—but since they belong to culture-free disciplines we do not feel them to be alien at all. There is no reason to assume that the world will keep for long its feeling that modern science is specifically Western. The geographical region where modern science began remains important only as long as it keeps the initial advantage of having been the discoverer, but afterwards presumably will concern historians alone, like the origin of agriculture in the Middle East and, within the already industrialized world, the origin of industrialism in England. To think of the modernization of Asia and Africa as their "Westernization" in any but a short-term sense is to forget that the Industrial Revolution disrupts and transforms all preceding cultures in West and East alike, and at the same time throws their resources into a common pool. It is possible to wonder whether we ourselves will necessarily be classed as belonging to a "Western civilization" by historians of the not so far future. They may find it more convenient to treat the West as the first of the great agrarian civilizations to lose its identity after the Industrial Revolution. If we knew more about the tribes that first settled on the banks of the Nile we might find cultural continuities comparable to those between medieval Europe and ourselves, but we should not be tempted to regard the revolutionary change to agriculture as a mere episode in an Egyptian tradition. Such assumptions of a surviving homogeneous culture as that a Westerner, whatever his overt beliefs, has a sensibility rooted in Christian symbolism that allows only a superficial conversion to Vedantism or Buddhism, and a coherent artistic heritage from the Renaissance that admits Oriental influences only at the level of the picturesque, no longer seem self-evident as they did even a generation ago. The whole European and Middle Eastern conception of religion as the pursuit of moral improvement in the service of a personal and transcendent God seems to come less and less naturally to the spiritually hungry even when they are professing Christians, which suggests as profound a break in a cultural succession as it would be possible to conceive. However we may judge the alien contributions during the last century and a half to every aspect of our culture outside the immediate reach of science, from Schopenhauer's debt to the Upanishads to the Black American and now African and Indian elements in popular music, it is already obvious that more is involved than the mere exoticism of eighteenth-century chinoiserie. The Japanese woodblock for the Impressionists and Japanese architecture for Frank Lloyd Wright, Chinese poetry for the Imagists and African sculpture for Picasso, were active influences at crucial moments in the development of major modern styles.

It is not altogether easy to break the habit of thinking of history as blindly groping toward a goal that the West alone was clever enough to reach, and Needham himself sometimes has the air of making allowances for the Chinese and offering compensations. But the only conscious goal that anyone has been able to find in the social processes that led to modern science is capitalist profit. Accidents such as Greek geometry encountering the Babylonian astronomy which it was to transform or China (which had the astronomy) developing algebra instead of geometry, are hardly to the credit or discredit of a civilization. When we consider how slowly both the West and China have responded to alien discoveries as long as they were confident of their own cultural superiority (the Indian numerals adduced by the Syrian bishop Sebokht in 662 as proof that the Greeks do not know everything, but their use in Europe unattested until 976, after which they only very slowly superseded Roman numerals; Euclid unnoticed in China until the Jesuit translation of 1607 although apparently available from Muslim astronomers as early as 1273),[29] we can see a direct connection between the superiority of the West about 1600 and its abject inferiority about 1000, which forced it to borrow the Arabic sciences wholesale and thus become the possessor of the all-important combination of Greek and Indian mathematics. Is it necessary to say more than that one set of conditions for the genesis of modern science came together in sixteenth-century Europe, and that since it spread too fast to allow independent occurrence elsewhere this is the only set of conditions of which we can ever know? The tremendous dynamic of the Scientific Revolution distinguishes it in this respect from the only comparable episode in history, the Neolithic invention of agriculture and the ensuing urban revolution in the Middle East. Agriculture continued to spread through the millennia between the natural barriers of the Atlantic and Pacific, so that there could be time and space for its independent discovery elsewhere. But the few centuries of the spread of modern science, although long in terms of its own accelerated time scale, are short in relation to the slow rise and fall of agrarian civilizations.

Nathan Sivin begins his book on Chinese alchemy with the observation that to ask of Chinese science, "Why did it not spontaneously evolve into modern science?" is a question best postponed until more is known. But he does not doubt its importance:

> This question, to be sure, is crucially important, for much of China's convulsive experience of the past century or so, and indeed much of her predictably convulsive experience of decades to come, are part of a world upheaval in which intellectual, social and economic consequences of the Scientific Revolution are gradually asserting themselves.[30]

But here we are concerned with something different, the factors in Chinese society and culture favorable or unfavorable to the assimilation of industrial civilization in all its aspects, and the problem of origins is left behind. If we imagine sixteenth-century Europe invaded from outside by electronics and plastics, air travel, nuclear energy and napalm, television and pop music, its struggle to adapt would not be eased by being itself on the verge of the discovery of quantitative physical science. Whatever China's problems, absence of conditions in which mathematization could combine with experimental methods is no longer one of them. That tradition of centralized bureaucracy which according to Wittfogel and Needham inhibited the growth of the merchant class and therefore of science, may have turned to China's advantage, since as soon as science is visibly a means to power a state's fear of more modern states becomes a stronger motive for importing it than commercial profit. The un-Chinese concept of a divine legislator or watchmaker has long ago lost its utility. Needham himself has often emphasized that a tendency toward organic rather than mechanistic thinking, although it conflicted with the presuppositions with which modern science began, may facilitate the assimilation of twentieth-century science. Here one is again reminded of the difficulty of throwing off the assumptions of the old vague question, "Why did China fall behind?," even when the issue has narrowed to the presence or absence of certain conditions immediately preceding Galileo. If the historians of science are right in so concentrating the issue, the setting of the Scientific Revolution in Europe becomes a matter of particular conditions, some persistent (such as the habit of philosophical and theological logic-chopping) and others transient, and we can no longer assume that outside them Western civilization in 1600 was any less remote than China from a civilization already revolutionized by modern science. An English sinologist reading such a book as E. M. W. Tillyard's *Elizabethan World Picture,* which uncovers the hierarchic order and systematic correspondences of the cosmos presupposed by Shakespeare, may be startled to find our national poet thinking like a Chinese—but that is to say no more than that he thought as a member of an agrarian, pre-industrial civilization. It is irrelevant that the conflict between traditional culture and the Scientific Revolution has been so much weaker in the West than elsewhere (with the remarkable exception of Japan). The civilization that first advances from proto-science to science will have only the problem of adapting to the Scientific Revolution itself; all others must adapt also to the alien civilization from which it reaches them, which is less and less like themselves or any other agrarian civilization, including the Europe of the past.[31]

NOTES

1. A suspicion of generalizations about nature that depend solely on authority or a priori deduction or are presented in untestable "protoscientific" forms, a recognition that the final appeal is to observation and experiment, are preconditions of modern science, but have appeared more than once in the histories of Greece, Christendom, and China without leading to a Scientific Revolution. In China the later Mohists in their writings on the sciences (c. 300 B.C.) confine themselves to strictly testable explanations in optics, mechanics, and economics, ignore such proto-sciences as medicine, and reject the proto-scientific theory of the ascendancies of the Five Processes (Mohist Canon, B16–B31, B43). In medieval Christendom experimental method was developed by Grosseteste (c. 1170–1253), only to drop from sight during the fourteenth century (A. C. Crombie, *Medieval and Early Modern Science*, New York, 1959, II, 1–35, 103–211). The Scientific Revolution required not only the recognition in principle of the importance of empirical testability, but the refining of the techniques of mathematization, observation, and experiment in at least one crucial discipline. Historically the event followed the supersession of the qualitative physics of Aristotle by a quantitative and therefore strictly testable physics initially inspired in part by the sixteenth-century revival of the Pythagorean faith in number as the key to the secrets of the cosmos. See Alexandre Koyré, *Metaphysics and Measurement* (Cambridge, Mass., 1968).

2. *The Grand Titration: Science and Society in East and West* (London, 1969). Abbreviations: *GT, The Grand Titration; SCC, Science and Civilisation in China* (7 vols. projected, Cambridge, England, 1954). Needham has also discussed the problem of the origin of scientific method in *SCC*, III, 150–68.

   I do not hesitate to apply the adjective "great" to Needham's work, although like other sinologists I am aware that his linguistic understanding is below the highest available standards. The best qualifications in both sinology and science are unlikely to meet in one person whose native language is not Chinese or Japanese, and it is lucky that there is someone who has come so near to combining them.

3. *GT*, pp. 42, 43.

4. *GT*, pp. 14, 15.

5. Derek J. de Solla Price, *Science since Babylon* (New Haven, 1961), p. 15, n. 10. The version quoted by Needham (*GT*, p. 43) unobtrusively smooths Einstein's English.

6. *GT*, p. 40.
7. *GT*, p. 150.
8. *GT*, p. 330.
9. *GT*, p. 307. For a fuller treatment of laws of nature written in 1956, see *SCC*, II, 518–84.
10. *SCC*, III, 158.
11. For the kind of toy automata that presumably inspired the *Lieh-tzu* story of the artificial man, and for parallels in other cultures, see *SCC*, IV. 2, 156–65.
12. A. C. Graham, *The Book of Lieh-tzu* (London: John Murray, 1960), p. 111.
13. The context (*Chin shu*, Pai-na ed. 11, p. 3b) is translated in *SCC*, III, 359.
14. Mistranslated at this point in my *The Book of Lieh-tzu*, p. 111.
15. *GT*, p. 292.
16. *GT*, p. 44. For the Sung algebra see *SCC*, III, 38–53.
17. *SCC*, III, 105.
18. Price, *Science since Babylon*, pp. 1–22; Otto Neugebauer, *The Exact Sciences in Antiquity* (New York, 1969).
19. N. Sivin, "Cosmos and Computation in Early Chinese Mathematical Astronomy," *T'oung Pao* (Leiden), 1969, 55: 1–73.
20. Ibid., pp. 67, 68, 70–73.
21. *GT*, p. 42.
22. *GT*, p. 243.
23. Review of *John Fryer*, in *Technology Review*, January 1969, 71, 3: 63.
24. William and Martha Kneale, *The Development of Logic* (Oxford, 1962), pp. 298–378; N. Rescher, *Studies in the History of Arab Logic* (Pittsburgh, 1963).
25. *GT*, pp. 37–39.
26. *Disputers of the Tao*, 389–428.
27. A. C. Graham, *Later Mohist Logic, Ethics and Science*, Chinese University of Hong Kong Press, 1978, 111–65.
28. *GT*, pp. 15, 16; *SCC*, III, 447–51.
29. *SCC*, I, 220; III, 52, 105, 146.
30. Sivin, *Chinese Alchemy: Preliminary Studies* (Cambridge, Mass., 1968), pp. 1, 2.
31. My argument that to ask why China had no Scientific Revolution is a pseudo-question is criticised by Wen-yuan Qian, *The Great Inertia* (London: Croom Helm, 1985), 92–94, and passim.

Liberty and Equality

9

It is commonly supposed that political arguments in favour of liberty and equality depend on certain moral principles which the defender of authority and privilege rejects: "All men have the right to be free", "All men ought to be equal". The purpose of this essay is to suggest that libertarian and egalitarian arguments assume no such moral premisses, only certain logical rules which are accepted by both sides in moral debate.

The arguments of several classical documents of political philosophy share a feature which looks at first glance like a suicidal logical weakness, but which deserves closer examination. This is an implicit assumption that liberty and equality are sufficiently justified by refuting the arguments used against them; the burden of proof is always on the enemy. The first of Locke's *Two Treatises of Civil Government* refutes at length Filmer's argument that Adam's sovereignty over his family and over the rest of creation is proof that there was never a state of natural freedom. The second *Treatise*, in which Locke develops his constructive case, begins by stating flatly that men are by nature free and equal and proceeds to argue from this axiom, in spite of Locke's earlier scorn for Filmer's presumption in expecting us to take for granted his own first premiss, the sovereignty of Adam. A little later he has already slipped into using such phrases as "Man being born, as has been proved, with a title to perfect freedom", and "Every man being, as has been showed, naturally free".[1] Similarly, Rousseau's *Discours sur l'origine de l'inégalité parmi les hommes* begins by distinguishing 'physical' inequality, of age, health, strength, and intelligence, from 'moral' or 'political' inequality, of wealth, rank, and power, proceeds to an inquiry into the origin of moral inequality which discredits the grounds commonly supposed to legitimate it, and in his final paragraph reaches the conclusion: "It follows also that moral inequality, authorised only by positive right, is contrary to natural right wherever it is not in proportion with physical inequality—a distinction sufficient to decide what one should think in this connexion of the sort of inequality which reigns among all civilized peoples. . . ."

It would seem that Locke and Rousseau refute certain objections to liberty and equality but offer no arguments on the other side, so that the most one can say for them is that they expose as entirely open a question which might have once seemed closed. However, let us take a concrete instance touching the issue of 'liberty' in the sense of absence of coercion. Suppose that a father forbids his young son to play in the street, fearing that the boy will be run over. Later the street is closed to traffic but he does not lift the ban. When the boy protests, the father replies: "Yes, there is no more reason for me to forbid it; but can you suggest any reason why I should allow it?" This answer would seem nonsensical even to one who denies the right to any degree of freedom before the age of responsibility. The boy wants to play in the street and suffers by the ban. If there is a reason for the ban, well and good; if not, the father is injuring his son gratuitously.

Whatever the reasons in favour of coercion there is always at least one reason against it, the end served by the action frustrated. This consideration applies equally whether one is thinking in prudential or in moral terms. If I want to do X, which you forbid, then resistance to the ban being necessary as a means to X, I ought to resist; this is a straightforward hypothetical imperative. You may nonetheless convince me that I ought to accept the ban, for other prudential or for moral reasons; but these only outweigh the argument for resistance without refuting it, and if at any time they become irrelevant it will recover all its force. Proceeding from prudential to moral considerations, if our relation of power is reversed, and I recognise a moral obligation to accord to you what I demand for myself, then I ought to allow you whatever there is no reason to forbid. There may of course be an overwhelming case for coercion in particular instances and even for coercion in general. Conceivably I might come to believe that human nature is so radically corrupt that all natural inclinations must be suppressed; then there will always be a reason to forbid the actions to which they tend, and the burden of proof within my system will rest on anyone who claims the right to something which he happens also to want. But even in this event the case against coercion will only be outweighed, and will recover its force should I ever lose faith in the system. After my disillusionment it will be senseless to ask: "Even if there is no more reason to deny myself, is there any reason why I should do as I want?" "I want X" or "I like X" is the only kind of reason which can be required for decisions which do not touch issues of moral or prudential principle.

Thus permission is fully justified logically by refuting the grounds for prohibition. This rule, which puts the burden of proof on the defender of coercion, applies even when the forbidden is unwanted or the commanded wanted. It is always possible that the situation will change, so that an injunction which does not cause hardship now may do so in the future. The relevance of this rule depends on the particular situation, on the extent to which ends vary and change is probable, but its validity does not. In a peasant society with a fixed traditional way of life ends are few and stable; the thought of a change of occupation can come to mind only as the fear of losing one's land, the thought of a change of creed hardly even as the fear of losing one's soul. Against such a background, a man is likely to resent certain specific kinds of coercion, forced labour or military conscription, or the pressure of taxes, rent and debt compelling him to give up a good part of his crop; but the possibility of conceiving or sympathising with goals outside his experience, or anticipating changes in his own situation or needs, will be too remote to impress him with the case for risking the unknown by allowing what he and his fellow villagers at present cannot or would not do. As society becomes more complicated, social evolution more rapid, and the possibilities of thought and action more varied, there is a progressively stronger case for 'Liberty' in the abstract, absence of coercion even in fields unrelated to anyone's at present imaginable needs. But when a liberal insists on the legitimacy of all behaviour which cannot be shown to injure others, he is not necessarily appealing to some principle which the peasant would deny. The validity of the rule that one ought to permit whenever there is no reason to forbid has nothing to do with social conditions; it is simply that in the peasant's situation there are only trivial occasions for applying it.

Turning now to the question of equality, let us suppose that X defends the privileges of a hereditary ruling class on the grounds that it has a preponderant share of the country's brains, culture, moral responsibility, and political experience, and therefore deserves its preponderance of wealth and power; Y denies the claim to superiority and insists that men should be treated 'equally' irrespective of birth—that is, that some should not enjoy greater benefits or suffer greater hardships than others as a result of being born into one class, sex, or race, only as a result of differences in honesty, intelligence, and other personal qualities which Y admits to be distributed unequally. Y's practical proposals, liberal, socialist, or communist, will of course assume decisions on many sociological issues—whether we know enough of the working of society to foresee the consequences of radical alterations, whether culture depends on the continuity of a leisured minority, whether a classless society is a practical proposition. But do they also depend on a moral premiss: "All men ought to be equal"?

As a parallel case, let us suppose that X is especially careful on Friday because he thinks it unlucky, while Y denies that one day is unluckier than another and is equally careful or careless on all days of the week. Clearly Y's case does not assume as a premiss that all days ought to be treated as equal. His rejection of the grounds for supposing one day especially unlucky obliges him to treat all as equal, just as disproof of the detective's reason for singling out for suspicion one of the guests at the country house obliges him to suspect all equally. This analogy can be pressed further:

X. Be careful today; Friday is unlucky.	Be careful with that man; you can't trust Jews.
Y. It's no unluckier than any other day; you shouldn't treat it any differently.	You can trust them as much or little as anyone else; you shouldn't discriminate against them.
X. Then you think all days are equally lucky? That's nonsense; there are no two days of our lives on which we have exactly the same luck.	Then you think all men are equal? That's nonsense; no two men are exactly equal in honesty, intelligence, or anything else.

162

Y. Certainly, but that has nothing to do with the day of the week.	Certainly, but that has nothing to do with race or class or sex.
X. You're wrong; Saturday and Sunday are lucky days, because we don't have to work.	You're wrong; there's no doubt that some peoples make braver soldiers, harder workers, more honest traders, than others do.
Y. That is a matter of convention; if the weekend were shifted to Tuesday and Wednesday, you would feel the same about them.	That is a matter of upbringing; if someone born a foreigner is brought up in England, he thinks and acts like an Englishman.

Y, holding that society should be organised for the benefit of its members, is obliged to claim that they should be benefitted equally wherever he rejects the grounds for benefitting some more than others. His concern for the benefit of all is moral, but his obligation to treat all equally is not; on the contrary his rejection of the grounds for treating men unequally would impose it even if he thought solely in prudential terms, although it would then be the obligation to exploit others equally as means to his own ends. Suppose that a big criminal hates West Indians or Jews or Catholics or Communists, will not have them in his gang, and robs them in preference to anyone else. If he comes to doubt the beliefs which seemed to justify his discrimination—that the people in question are dull-witted and lazy or cunning and treacherous—then it will be plain to him that he hurts his own interests by hiring a Gentile rather than a cleverer Jew, or robbing a West Indian rather than a richer Englishman. If he still discriminates it will be for other reasons, because he has to take account of his gang's prejudices even without sharing them, or because an unpopular minority is at a relative disadvantage against attack. There are even situations in which prudential and moral calculations can both lead to the same egalitarian conclusions. An employer, let us say, pays one category of worker more than another for the same kind of work, because he thinks that the former do the work better. Should he change his mind on this point, he must equalise the wages whether he has fixed them as a minimum outlay for the maximum work or as the payment which the work deserves in the name of justice. In one case he has evidently been paying one or other category either more or less than it needs as an incentive, in the other case either more or less than its due.

It would seem then that Locke and Rousseau were right in assuming that the burden of proof lay on their opponents. Indeed, have not their opponents always implicitly accepted the burden? Even the most convinced authoritarian knows that the case for liberty and equality has a specious plausibility which is bound to mislead shallow minds unless people of judgment and responsibility can show them just why social order requires discipline and degree. He may object that the case seems plausible because it appeals to interest and not to reason. But it happens that this is not an issue around which reason can pull in one direction and interest in the other. It is from one's own and other's interests that prudential and moral reasoning starts. The authoritarian begins to talk to the point only when he tells us why he thinks that men who seek to be free and equal mistake their own interests.

What both sides overlook is that the placing of the logical advantage derives from two rules of moral and prudential thinking:

> Absence of grounds for forbidding obliges one to permit.
> Absence of grounds for discriminating obliges one to treat equally.

The grounds for forbidding and discriminating may raise questions of fact alone or of value as well as fact. If the reason given for treating a class or race as inferior is that its members do not wash, an egalitarian may try to settle the question factually by showing that they keep themselves very clean; if he fails, the dispute may come to a dead end with him denying and the other affirming the moral importance of washing. But the basic disagreements about value on which many political controversies founder are not disagreements about the value of liberty and equality themselves, as the two words are understood here. Of course one must admit the qualification that these words have other important senses with other logical implications.

Thinking according to these unformulated rules, a mediaeval philosopher who justifies submission and subordination as earned by our wickedness must conclude that unfallen man would have been free and equal, and Rousseau criticising the present grounds for submission and subordination must conclude that we should be free and equal now. But to those who follow the rules without noticing them, it seems that destructive criticism can arrive only at the point where the issue is entirely open, and that in taking the further step of justifying liberty and equality we appeal to moral standards: "All men ought to be free and equal." The logical obligation to the next step is then intelligible only on the assumption that the moral premises are valid a priori. Following a tradition which goes back to Roman Law, the seventeenth- and eighteenth-century political philosophers founded these principles in the Law of Nature, a system of eternal standards in the light of which we can criticise the imperfect and mutable laws of men. The doctrine of natural rights led in turn to the concept of a social contract to legitimise government. For it is clear that as long as men keep their natural right to liberty, even if they choose to waive it for the sake of the security provided by government, there can be no duty to obey; this duty implies that they have lost at least part of their natural right, and therefore, since a right cannot be taken by force, that they have renounced it voluntarily in exchange for security.

The language of natural rights and the social contract bred parasitic arguments which no doubt often led Locke and Rousseau very far from the problems which they were trying to solve. But it is arguable that we have lost as well as gained by discarding this language, and also that to the extent that it misled we have not yet shaken off its influence as completely as we suppose. The natural rights to liberty and equality were not mere nonsense, but distorted reflections of logical rules. We have abandoned a part of the doctrine of the Rights of Man from which there is still something to learn, but kept the part which is most deceptive, the assumption that libertarian and egalitarian arguments start from moral premises. These premises we either try to justify metaphysically, for example as recently secularised principles inherent in the Christian conception of man, or else treat frankly as imputations of value relative to time and place, for example as ideological expressions of bourgeois interests in the competitive phase of capitalism. We are still tempted to think of the choice between coercion and liberty or discrimination and equality as a single choice for the whole of a society, not as a decision to be made over again for every particular issue. The result is that the burden of proof has shifted to the wrong side, and Liberty and Equality have the air of noble, unwordly ideals which we betray whenever the ends served by coercion outweigh those which it frustrates, or the undeniable differences between individuals in every mental and physical quality compel us to treat them unequally.

NOTE

1. Op. cit. Book 2, § 87, p. 119.

The Question behind Marx's Concept of Alienation

10

In a series of notes jotted by Marx in the manuscript of the *German Ideology,* in 1845 or 1846, we find this item:

> Individuals always started, and always start, from themselves. Their relations are the relations of their real life. How does it happen that their relations assume an independent existence over against them? and that the forces of their own life overpower them? (*GI,* 658).[1]

If the account of alienation in Marx's *Economic and Philosophical Manuscripts of 1844* often seems obscure and confused, it is above all because Marx has not yet succeeded in clearly formulating the question he is trying to answer. He discovers his question in the process of answering it. Elsewhere in the *German Ideology* he poses it in a fuller form:

> How is it that personal interests always develop, against the will of individuals, into class interests, into common interests which acquire independent existence in relation to the individual persons, and in their independence assume the form of *general* interests? . . . How is it that in this process of private interests acquiring independent existence as class interests the personal behaviour of the individual is bound to undergo substantiation, alienation, and at the same time exists as a power independent of him and without him, created by intercourse, and becomes transformed into social relations, into a series of powers which determine and subordinate the individual, and which therefore appear in the imagination as 'holy' powers? (*GI,* 265)

A society appears to be a collection of individuals co-operating for common goals or forcing their wills on each other. How is it that association generates institutions which have their own mechanics (the state, classes, the market, religion), which become alien to the particular and even the common interests not only of the weaker but of the stronger, following social and economic laws which are impersonal like the laws of nature? It is not that the institutions are entities distinct from individuals; it is the actions of the individuals themselves as they co-operate or compete, and the resources and products which they treat as private property, which become systems alienated from their wills. To Marx, who has the capacity like all great thinkers to be surprised by the obvious, it is extraordinary that political economy can reduce the behaviour of individuals voluntarily competing in the market to impersonal laws like those of physics and chemistry. It appears that, to parody Rousseau, men are born as creatures that consciously pursue ends, yet everywhere they are caught in chains of cause and effect forged by themselves. Society cannot be an association for mutual benefit until all institutionalised groups dissolve into individuals voluntarily co-operating and taking their common fate into their own hands.

Marx borrowed the concept of alienation from Hegel's *Phenomenology of Mind* and developed it in his writings of 1843 to 1846. It is in his Paris manuscripts (*Economic and Philosophic Manuscripts of 1844*) that the abstract noun 'alienation' (*Entfremdung, Entaüsserung*)[2] especially catches the eye. However, as I hope to show shortly, it is in the *German Ideology* (written in collaboration with Engels in 1845 or 1846), where Marx becomes suspicious of the abstract noun and prefers more concrete expressions with the adjective 'alien' (*fremd*), that he first fully clarifies both his question and his answer. Hegel had presented social evolution as man's progress towards the final resolution of his divided consciousness of himself as individual and as social being, by which, whether he chooses one standpoint or the other, he is alienated from himself. Marx, as he tells us in the *Critique of the Hegelian Dialectic* in the Paris manuscripts, much admired Hegel's studies of the divided consciousness, in particular those of "the 'Unhappy Consciousness', the 'Honest Consciousness', the struggle of the 'Noble and Base Consciousness' " (*EPM*, 150). But Hegel considers man only in his role of thinker, not as a *"corporeal*, living, real, sensuous, objective being full of natural vigour" (*EPM*, 156). Men are not simply thinking but acting against their individual interests when they behave as members of existing societies. Hegel's analysis of evolving self-consciousness, valuable as it is, exhibits only one aspect of man's development towards the realisation of all the potentialities of his 'essence' (*Wesen*). Instead of subjectively exploring the growth of self-consciousness and illustrating it with historical examples, we must study objectively the history of the social, political, and economic institutions through which the behaviour of individuals becomes independent of their wills.

The Left Hegelians of the 1840s had found new and revolutionary uses for Hegel's concept, first in the criticism of religion by Bruno Bauer (and by Feuerbach, who seems however to avoid the *word* 'alienation'), later in the criticism of capitalism by Moses Hess and by Marx himself. It provided them with a tool to develop their perception that human liberation requires something more than the overthrow of priests and kings. They transform the Hegelian analysis of the divided consciousness into a revolutionary criticism by admitting only the self-alienation of the individual as citizen, not of the citizen as individual. The state appears as an alien power imposing its laws on men, yet it exists only in the political activities of individuals who in their role as citizen behave in ways alien to their own ends. Similarly religion, although a creation of the human imagination, has somehow become independent of human wills, so that it seems to impose itself on us as an external authority. Moses Hess extended the same principle to money, which is no more than metal or paper to which we ascribe a social significance, yet operates as an economic power independent of the wills of capitalist and worker alike. State, religion, money, all dominate us as alien powers, yet do not exist except in our own social activities, in which therefore we are alienated from ourselves; we can become free only by co-operating to reclaim these powers for our own. According to Hess (in *Über das Geldwesen*, 1843, 1844) "what God is for the theoretical, money is for the practical life of the inverted world: the alienated capacities of man, the vital activity he has bartered away." The same comparison of religious and economic alienation recurs in Marx's writings of 1843 and 1844 (and even, in *Capital*): "Just as in religion the spontaneous activity of the human imagination, of the human brain and the human heart, operates independently of the individual—that is, operates on him as an alien, divine or diabolical activity—in the same way the worker's activity is not his spontaneous activity" (*EPM*, 73. Cf. *EW*, 39, *EPM*, 70, 103. Cf. 72).

On the Jewish Question (1843) presents Marx's first original conclusions about "man as he has been corrupted, lost to himself, alienated, subjected to the rule of inhuman conditions and elements, by the whole organisation of our society" (*EW*, 20). In this essay he is still like Hegel thinking in political rather than in economic terms, of the split between civil society and the state (which is "the alienated political power of the people", *EW*, 28), "the division of man into the public person and the private person" (*EW*, 15). But he also recognises that within civil society itself each individual makes his living "by subordinating his products and his own activity to the domination of an alien entity, and by attributing to them the significance of an alien entity, namely money" (*EW*, 39). "Money is the alienated essence of man's work and existence; this essence dominates him and he worships it" (*EW*, 37). Marx cannot yet analyse the operations of this medium of exchange which, invented to serve the ends of its users, rules them by its own impersonal laws; his education has been in philosophy, history, and jurisprudence, and in 1843 he is only just beginning to study economics. He has nothing so far to say about the exploitation of the worker, only about the self-alienation of the bourgeois in the sterile processes of money-making. "What is the worldly cult of the Jew? Huckstering. What is his worldly god? Money" (*EW*, 34). The Jew will attain his true emancipation only when he "turns against the supreme practical expression of human self-estrangement" (*EW*, 34). The extraordinary revulsion with which Marx speaks of money (without yet knowing anything about economics) and of the Jew (although he recognises that the worldly cult of the Jew now pervades the Gentile world also) suggests that his anti-capitalism has deeper personal roots in a horror of being sucked into the commercial life of his own kin than in sympathy with the proletariat.

The proletariat makes its entry into Marx's thought in the introduction to the *Critique of Hegel's Philosophy of Right*, written in 1843, 1844. Its earliest significance for Marx is that, unlike the slave and peasant classes of the past, it is an unarticulated mass of individuals in which all the institutions through which man becomes alien to himself have already dissolved, "a class which is the dissolution of all classes . . . a sphere of society which claims no traditional status but only a human status" (*EW*, 58). Only the revolutionary proletariat can re-make society, "no longer assuming certain conditions external to man, which are none the less created by human society, but organising all the conditions of human life on the basis of human freedom" (*EW*, 58). In the memorable words which a few years later will startle readers of the *Communist Manifesto* (1848), "The proletarian is without property; his relation to his wife and children has no longer anything in common with the bourgeois family relations; modern industrial labour, modern subjection to capital, the same in England as in France, in America as in Germany, has stripped him of every trace of national character. Law, morality, religion, are to him so many bourgeois prejudices, behind which lurk in ambush just as many bourgeois interests." (*CM*, 63)

In the Paris manuscripts of 1844, the first-fruits of his study of economics, Marx discovers that the life of a Jewish huckster is far from being "the supreme practical expression of human self-estrangement". The perfect example of the sacrifice of individual ends to impersonal social forces is the sterile labour subject to mechanical routines by which the worker earns his bread, the hours of drudgery subtracted from his real life, imposed on him by the laws of the market in which others buy his labour and sell the goods which he himself produces. This is the theme of the chapter on *Estranged Labour* in the Paris manuscripts. To see it in its right perspective it is necessary to estimate how far Marx has succeeded in detaching himself from the subjectivism which he criticises in Hegel and moving towards the objectivism of the *German Ideology*. In the Paris manuscripts Marx has much to say about the 'essence' of Man, in particular about his essential need for free productive activity. Does he, like Hegel, still find his starting-point in man himself, not of course in man's self-consciousness, but in the activities by which we realise ourselves as fully human? If so, it should not much matter whether our potentialities are stunted by natural conditions, by submission to another's will or by social mechanisms independent of the wills of all. Hegel's 'alienation' will then have degenerated into little more than a rhetorical way of describing any kind of enforced, sterile, or frustrated activity. Or has Marx arrived at the point of grounding his argument in the laws of political economy? In that case the drudgery, and having to take orders from a boss, will be incidentals, the painful consequences of being trapped in the operations of an impersonal system. A conception of the human essence will no longer be indispensable to the argument. Even without identifying any needs as specifically human Marx would be entitled to equate the alien with the inhuman, the alienation of individuals with their dehumanisation, since he conceives it as the sacrifice of their wills to laws which are inhuman like physical laws, independent of their needs whatever they may happen to be.

Some expositors of Marx's theory choose the first alternative, for example Richard Schacht, who tells us that Marx "tends to regard the submission of labour to the direction of another man as the necessary and sufficient condition of its alienation from the worker".[2] But it is the "inhuman power" of the market, which Schacht treats as an inessential appearing at a late stage in the argument, which is the argument's true starting-point. The first of the Paris manuscripts begins with a chapter on *Wages of Labour*, which discusses the principle of political economy that labour is itself a commodity to be bought and sold. "The worker's existence is thus brought under the same conditions as any other commodity. The worker has become a commodity, and it is a bit of luck for him if he can find a buyer" (*EPM*, 22). The *Estranged Labour* chapter, which concludes the first manuscript, starts with the sentence, "We have proceeded from the premises of political economy" (*EPM*, 67), and later declares that "it is as a result of the movement of private property that we have obtained the concept of alienated labour (of alienated life) from political economy" (*EPM*, 80). Throughout the chapter, therefore, it is under the impersonal pressures of the market as analysed in political economy that the product of labour "confronts it as something alien, as a power independent of the producer" (*EPM*, 69); that the worker is self-estranged in a drudgery of which the "alien character emerges clearly in the fact that as soon as no physical or other compulsion exists labour is shunned like the plague" (*EPM*, 72); that the individual, denied activity except as a means of subsistence, is estranged from his nature as a man, since "free conscious activity is man's species character" (*EPM*, 75, "Life itself appears only as a means to life"). When Marx does come to consider, among the other miseries of alienation, the worker's subjection to another person, the capitalist, he finds it necessary to argue at some length that this is the way that "in real life the concept of estranged, alienated labour must express and present itself" (*EPM*, 78).

In discovering the alienation of the worker Marx has not forgotten that of the capitalist. "Finally (and this applies also to the capitalist) all is under the sway of inhuman power" (*EPM*, 126). The point of making money is presumably to get some fun out of it, but the capitalist who enjoys himself too much is at a disadvantage as a competitor in the market. "He does not by any means return to the unnatural simplicity of need; but his pleasure is only a side-issue—recuperation—something subordinated to production; at the same time it is a calculated and therefore itself an *economical* pleasure" (*EPM*, 128). The system, evolving according to its own laws, compels everyone in varying degrees to act against his own will, but also puts some in the key positions from which they can impose their wills on others. According to the *Holy Family* (written with Engels in 1845), "the possessing class and the proletarian class express the same human alienation. But the former is satisfied with its situation, feels itself well established in it, recognises this self-alienation as its own power, and thus has the appearance of a human existence. The latter feels itself crushed by this self-alienation, sees in it its own impotence and the reality of an inhuman situation" (*SW*, 236).

Is labour already alienated in pre-capitalist economies, in which it is servile but not yet a market commodity? The much briefer observations on feudalism in the Paris manuscripts confirm that subjection to another person is *not* a sufficient condition of alienation. Feudal service is alienated in so far as it is shaped by institutions deriving from private property in land. But it differs from wage-labour in being also a bond between persons, and in this respect is not alienated at all, since the control is that of a human will, the lord's. It allows some scope for a cultural development of individuals in direct, though servile, relation with each other and with the land.

In the same way, feudal landed property gives its name to its lord, as does a kingdom to its king. His family history, the history of his house, etc.—all this individualises the estate for him and makes it literally his house, personifies it. Similarly those working on the estate have not the position of *day-labourers*, but they are in part themselves his property, as are serfs, and in part they are bound to him by ties of respect, allegiance and duty. His relation to them is therefore directly political, and has likewise a human, *intimate* side. Customs, character, etc. vary from one estate to another and seem to be one with the land to which they belong; later, on the other hand, a man is bound to his land, not by his character or his individuality, but only by his purse strings. (*EPM*, 62)

However, Marx refuses to "join in the sentimental tears wept over this by romanticism". In feudalism there is already some alienation, not because of the direct subjection of serf to lord, but because the land is private property (although not yet a market commodity), and therefore imposes its institutions on men of every status. "The domination of the land as an alien power over men is already inherent in feudal landed property. The serf is the adjunct of the land. Likewise the lord of an entailed estate, the first-born son, belongs to the land. It inherits him" (*EPM*, 61).

By 1845 it has become plain to Marx that the concept of the human essence, the postulation of certain potentialities as essential to Man as a species, is both a dispensable and a vulnerable part of the theory of alienation. The egoist Max Stirner, in his *Self and its Selfdom* (1844), had derided all proposals that the individual should sacrifice his actual interests to realise a phantom 'essence of Man'. Marx and his collaborator Engels devote more than half of the *German Ideology* (1845 or 1846) to answering the challenge of Stirner, but on this point they allow the egoist to have his way. The theory of alienation assumes its final form in the long *Feuerbach* chapter, which is perhaps the most lucid, compact, flexible, many-sided, finely articulated statement of his total position which Marx ever achieved.

In this book Marx finally rids himself of the habit of thinking in terms of man's unfolding essence rather than of individuals in historical situations. It now seems to him that this intellectual vice has encouraged the Left Hegelian delusion of mistaking a revolution inside one's head for a revolution in the real world outside. In the *Theses on Feuerbach* (1845) he had noted that "human essence is no abstraction inherent in each single individual. In its reality it is the ensemble of the social relations" (*GI*, 646). The *German Ideology* displays an almost obsessive concern to leave no possibility of doubt that 'Man', tribes, estates, classes are always collections of living individuals with historically changing social relations. The argument of the *Feuerbach* chapter starts with the announcement that "the premises from which we begin" are "the real individuals, their activity and the material conditions under which they live" (*GI*, 31). Marx is now quite ostentatious in his refusal to define the essence of man: "Men can be distinguished from animals by consciousness, by religion, or anything else you like". He does proceed to say that "they themselves begin to distinguish themselves from animals as soon as they begin to produce their means of subsistence", but he is no longer interested (as in the Paris manuscripts) in claiming that it is man's nature as a producer that is alienated by wage-labour. The only nature which concerns him is that of individuals, which is historically determined by modes of production: "the nature of individuals thus depends on the material conditions determining their production" (*GI*, 32).

From this starting-point Marx proceeds to his first sketch of the history of social development. From time to time he notes how, from social relations between individuals, the state, the class, the market, emerge as powers independent of individuals and 'alien' to them. Once he refers to the process as "this *'alienation'* (to use a term which will be comprehensible to the philosophers)" (*GI*, 46). At a later stage he observes that when the Left Hegelians theorise about 'Man' they are conceiving individuals who do not yet exist, individuals whose natures have developed inside a society which allows them to fulfil all their potentialities:

> The individuals who are no longer subject to the division of labour have been conceived by the philosophers as an ideal, under the name 'Man'. They have conceived the whole process which we have outlined as the evolutionary process of 'Man', so that at every historical stage 'Man' was substituted for the individuals and shown as the motive force of history. The whole process was thus conceived as a process of the self-alienation of 'Man', and this was essentially due to the fact that the average individual of the later stage was always foisted on to the earlier stage, and the consciousness of a later age on to the individuals of an earlier. (*GI*, 84)

It is this passage, and one in the *Communist Manifesto* of 1848 deriding the True Socialists (the followers of Moses Hess) for conceiving the economic functions of money as "Alienation of Humanity", (*CM*, 913) which used to be taken as proof of Marx's abandonment of the doctrine of alienation. But all through his historical outline Marx has himself been referring to the 'alien' (*fremd*), and the statement that 'self-alienation (*Selbstent-fremdung*) of Man' is a wrong conception of 'the whole process' merely confirms that the emergence of the alien is seen as the guiding principle throughout the process. Marx's objection is that the alienation of individuals is misconceived as the alienation of Man. From now on he will consider only the alienation of individuals acting against their wills, of resources and products valued in detachment from human needs, under the compulsion of impersonal systems: "Private property alienates the individuality not only of people but also of things" (*GI*, 248).

"Hence instead of the task of presenting actual individuals in their actual alienation and in the empirical conditions of this alienation, we are here presented with the mere idea of alienation" (*GI*, 304).

There is, however, an important terminological difference between the Paris manuscripts and the *German Ideology* which is in the first place grammatical. Marx used to employ the verb 'alienate' and noun 'alienation' much more freely than the adjective 'alien', now he confines himself almost entirely to the adjective. Later, in the *Grundrisse* (1857, 1858), he will again be using the verb and noun without inhibition, but with the same care to establish what is 'alien' by expanded constructions with the adjective.[4] This reluctance to use the abstract noun has often been mistaken for abandonment of the concept. But its true significance can be discerned in the passage where it first appears:

> The social power, i.e. the multiplied productive force, which arises through the co-operation of different individuals as it is determined by the division of labour, appears to these individuals, since their co-operation is not voluntary but has come about naturally, not as their own united power, but as an *alien* (my italics) force existing outside them. . . . This *'alienation'* (to use a term which will be comprehensible to the philosophers) can of course only be abolished given two *practical* premises. . . . (*GI*, 46)

This passage is not comparable with the one in which Marx rejects outright the concept of "the self-alienation of 'Man'" (*GI*, 84). He is himself using the abstract noun, but only after clarifying his position by means of the adjective, and rather apologetically, because 'alienation' is a form over-used and misused by philosophers. Elsewhere he uses it only when contrasting Max Stirner's theory of alienation with his own (*GI*, 248, 265, 304 quoted above).

What worries Marx is apparently that by verbalising and then nominalising 'alien' we allow the word to assume a dangerous independent life, so that it is no longer plain what is being alienated from what, and what kind of act or state is envisaged. He sees that the way to escape this danger is to revert regularly to expanded constructions with the adjective. Richard Schacht, applying the tools of analytic philosophy in his *Alienation*, has shown how slippery the abstract noun becomes both in the Paris manuscripts (which however, as we have noticed, he misunderstands) and in the usage of contemporary sociologists, psychologists, and existentialist philosophers. (But he makes his task too easy by refusing to recognise the concept except through the verb or abstract noun). A particular danger of verbalising and nominalising too freely is that we lose sight of whether the word is being used technically or idiomatically. The analogy with the legal alienation of property may or may not be relevant, the 'alienation of man from man' may or may not mean more than becoming unfriendly, the 'self-alienation of man' (for someone combining Marx with psychology) may or may not have a suggestion of losing one's mind and passing into the care of an alienist. Marx was no analytic philosopher, but he knew well that abstractions are constantly wrestling themselves out of our control (and indeed in the Paris manuscripts treated this as one of the processes of alienation, *EPM*, 142–74). He criticises Stirner for "the arbitrary way in which he presents or does not present any relation as a relation of alienation (for everything can be made to fit in the above equations)" (*GI*, 303 f.).

Among the sources for Marx's thought the *German Ideology* is especially illuminating because of its terminological freedom. He has thrown off the Hegelian abstractions of the Paris manuscripts, not yet evolved the characteristic Marxian vocabulary which will in due course imprison the minds of his successors. (He still distinguishes between 'classes' and 'estates', and does not even use the word 'capitalism'.) He is not proud of his debauch with the abstract noun in the Paris manuscripts, and in re-thinking his theory of the liberation of the individual he uses it as little as possible. (Contrast such excesses as *EPM*, 72, "If then the product of labour is alienation, production itself must be active alienation, the alienation of activity, the activity of alienation. In the estrangement of the object of labour is merely summarised the estrangement, the alienation, in the activity of labour itself".) The most striking proof of this temporary self-denial is that although he certainly still conceives the sale of one's labour in the market as the supreme example of "man's own deed becoming an alien power opposed to him", he never speaks directly of alien or estranged labour. In the Paris manuscripts the estrangement of labour is the basic kind of alienation (and indeed is easily misunderstood to be the source of the concept itself), and later the phrase 'alien labour' is common in the *Grundrisse*[5] and even occurs in the *Communist Manifesto,* disguised in the English translation (*CM, 75*, "the labour of others" for *fremde Arbeit*). But in 1845 and 1846 Marx is at a phase in which he distrusts technical usages which force ordinary language.

With the shift of attention from the essence of 'Man' to the changing relations between historically existing individuals, it becomes urgent to explain how there can be such things as states and classes, which seem to be more than the sum of the individuals which compose them. It is in struggling with this problem that Marx at last succeeds in putting his finger exactly on the question which he was trying to answer in the fascinating but jargon-ridden pages of the Paris manuscripts. We quoted his two formulations of the question at the head of this essay. How is it that the interactions of individuals can generate forces independent of their wills, so that "the personal behaviour of the individual is bound to undergo substantiation, alienation, and at the same time exists as a power independent of him and without him"? The state, law, class, religion, are all examples of the alien powers which emerge from the intercourse of individuals; but the most palpable instance, and the one which historically comes to predominate over all others, is the market. With the worldwide victory of capitalism "separate individuals have, with the broadening of their activity into world-historical activity, become more and more enslaved under a power alien to them (a pressure which they have conceived of as a dirty trick on the part of the so-called universal spirit, etc.), a power which has become more and more enormous, and in the last instance turns out to be the *world market*" (*GI*, 49). In the market each tries to act on his own will, yet the results are against the wills of the propertyless majority, and even (as in the trade cycle) against the will of all. It appears as a paradox that the voluntary actions of individuals can be bound, as though they were physical events, by economic laws created by their own interactions; and in fact these laws would simply evaporate if the individuals could break through the social forms which oblige them to compete, and enter into voluntary co-operation:

> Or how does it happen that trade, which after all is nothing more than the exchange of products of various individuals and countries, rules the whole world through the relation of supply and demand—a relation which, as an English economist says, hovers over the earth like the fate of the ancients, and with invisible hand allots fortune and misfortune to men, sets up empires and overthrows empires, causes nations to rise and to disappear—while with the abolition of the basis of private property, with the communistic regulation of production (and implicit in this, the destruction of the alien relation between men and what they themselves produce) the power of the relation between supply and demand is dissolved into nothing, and men get exchange, production, the mode of their mutual relation, under their own control again?" (*GI*, 47)

Voluntarily co-operating individuals can enter into "the intercourse of individuals as such" (*GI*, 84), without the mediation of state, law, religion, private property, the market; indeed in the future communist society it will be "impossible that anything should exist independently of individuals" (*GI*, 87). But historically the forms of association with which human society began have been not voluntary but natural, starting from the division of labour, "which was originally nothing but the division of labour in the sexual act, then that division of labour which develops spontaneously or 'naturally' by virtue of natural predispositions (e.g. physical strength), needs, accidents, etc., etc." (*GI*, 43). The distribution of labour involves distribution of its products and therefore private property. By the separation of crafts separate interests diverge, and the communal interest, soon embodied in the state, becomes "an interest 'alien' to them and 'independent' of them, as in its turn a particular, peculiar 'general' interest" (*GI*, 45). At the same time the division of labour imprisons each man inside his craft, on pain of losing his livelihood. This is "the first example of how, as long as man remains in natural society, that is, as long as the cleavage exists between the particular and the common interest, as long therefore as activity is not voluntarily but naturally divided, man's own deed becomes an alien power opposed to him, which enslaves him instead of being controlled by him" (*GI*, 44). In this account it is to be noticed that the alien powers arise from conflict between groups or between individual and groups, not between individuals. Marx is not interested in mere clashes between individuals, which may disturb the stability of a society but do not alter it structurally. The division of labour is the beginning, not of conflict, but of organised interests in conflict.

How does Marx conceive the connexion between social relations and what he describes so often as alien powers or forces? It is not of course that the relations themselves turn into powers, but that a system has positions of relative strength and weakness. Any alien power exerted against me will in fact be that of other individuals—rulers or priests in the case of state or religion, competitors in the case of the market, my peers or my oppressors in the case of my own class or the one above me. My own liberation will be won only when the majority unites to overthrow its living and human masters. The concepts, however, of state, religion, market, class are indeed concepts of relations; and until we locate them where they belong, inside our heads, it is in them that the power seems to reside. Our consciousness of them is like the primitive "consciousness of nature, which first appears to men as a completely alien, all-powerful and unassailable force, with which men's relations are purely animal and by which they are overawed like beasts" (*GI*, 42). (It may be noticed from several of our quotations that Marx involuntarily illustrates the spontaneous evolution into numinous concepts by the vivid, metaphorical language touched off in him by the word 'alien'.) Even when we see through the sacredness of these concepts, we may deceive ourselves that we are already liberated from the alien powers (the error of the Left Hegelians assailed in the *German Ideology*), and forget that social relations in the real world remain as they were.

In the course of historical development the growth of productive resources has less and less to do with the ends of individuals, more and more with the impersonal laws of the market, until "the productive forces appear as a world for themselves, quite independent of and divorced from the individuals, alongside the individuals; the reason for this is that the individuals, whose forces they are, exist split up and in opposition to one another, whilst on the other hand these forces are only real forces in the intercourse and association of these individuals" (*GI*, 82). To the extent that the behaviour of individuals is governed by something independent of their particular or common ends, that land or machinery is treated as something other than things utilisable for these ends, it is 'alienated':

> Private property alienates the individuality not only of people but also of things. Land has nothing to do with the rent of land, the machine has nothing to do with profit. For the landed proprietor, land has the significance only of rent of land; he leases his plots of land and receives rent; this is a feature which land can lose without, for example, losing any part of its fertility; it is a feature the extent and even the existence of which depends on social relations which are created and destroyed without the assistance of individual landed proprietors. (*GI*, 248)

However, as we have seen, Marx has become very cautious in using the verb 'alienate'. In rethinking his older conception of man as a conception of the development of individuals under changing historical conditions he evolves a new terminology, in which the words which attract attention are 'self-activity' (*Selbstbetätigung*) and 'accidental' (*zufällig*). 'Self-activity' is never defined, but it seems to be activity directed towards positive ends of one's own. Thus wage-labour, which has only the negative end of avoiding starvation, is generally treated as the loss of self-activity, but once as a "negative form of self-activity" (*GI*, 83). Self-activity develops within limits set by genetic factors, locality, the division of labour, class. The growth of trade and cultural communications, dissolution of fixed estates into fluid classes, racial intermingling, tend to break down these limits. (Marx conceives races as genetically limited and improved by cross-breeding, a theory which is both decidedly un-Marxist and perfectly congruent with the rest of his system at this stage. Cf. *GI*, 31n, 89n, 467.) The division of labour confines the worker within his craft but at first allows a personal satisfaction in his work as an end in itself, "a contented, slavish relationship" (*GI*, 67). Later the craftsmen turn into wage-labourers, and what they produce is determined by the market, losing all connexion with their positive ends and personal satisfactions ("the alien relation between men and what they themselves produce", *GI*, 47):

> The only connection which still links them with the productive forces and with their own existence . . . labour . . . has lost all semblance of self-activity and only sustains their life by stunting it. While in the earlier periods self-activity and the production of material life were separated, in that they devolved on different persons, and while, on account of the narrowness of the individuals themselves, the production of material life was considered as a subordinate mode of self-activity, they now diverge to such an extent that altogether material life appears as the end, and what produces this material life, labour (which is now the only possible but as we see negative form of self-activity), as the means. (*GI*, 83)

But the loss of craft status and of all self-activity has the consequences that the proletarian is not tied to any one mode within the division of labour, and is therefore, when the opportunity comes, "in a position to achieve a complete and no longer restricted self-activity" (*GI*, 83). The growth of production and intercourse has established the material conditions for "all-round activity and thereby the full development of all our potentialities" (*GI*, 276). With the proletarian revolution, associated individuals can voluntarily allot the tasks formerly apportioned by nature or the market, so that I can "hunt in the morning, fish in the afternoon, rear cattle in the evening, criticise after dinner, just as I have a mind, without ever becoming hunter, fisherman, shepherd or critic" (*GI*, 45).

How does Marx conceive the relation between the individual and the member of a class? We have already noticed his observation that as class interests emerge "the personal behaviour of the individual is bound to undergo substantiation alienation" (*GI*, 265). One is tempted to read into this the contemporary experience that the individual becomes self-alienated by conforming to his class at the cost of his individual needs. But Marx's position is that even in the classes which give scope to self-activity one enjoys personal freedom only to the degree that one is an "average individual" (*GI*, 92). It would seem, therefore, that it is the sum of the average behaviour of the individuals in a class which becomes a power alien to each member as an individual. The distinction which he makes between "the individual as a person and what is accidental to him", which is "not a conceptual difference but a historical fact" (*GI*, 87), concerns quite a different issue. When social forms cease to accord with the mode of production they become accidental to the individual ("e.g. the estate as something accidental to the individual in the eighteenth century, the family more or less so too", *GI*, 87). But until this contradiction emerges, to *be* a hunter or a fisherman, even to be a noble or a commoner, is inseparable from one's individuality:

> The conditions under which individuals have intercourse with each other, so long as the above-mentioned contradiction is absent, are conditions appertaining to their individuality, in no way external to them; conditions under which these definite individuals, living under definite relationships, can alone produce their material life and what is connected with it, are thus the conditions of their self-activity and are produced by this self-activity. The definite condition under which they produce thus corresponds, as long as the contradiction has not yet appeared, to the reality of their conditioned nature, their one-sided existence, the one-sidedness of which only becomes evident when the contradiction enters on the scene and thus exists for the later individuals. Then this condition appears as an accidental fetter, and the consciousness that it is a fetter is imputed to the earlier age as well. (*GI*, 87, 88)

What is new about social forms wholly pervaded by market relations is that, although for the bourgeois social role is still inseparable from individuality, for the propertyless majority *all* conditions of life become accidental.

> There appears a division within the life of each individual, insofar as it is personal and insofar as it is determined by some branch of labour and the conditions pertaining to it. (We do not mean it to be understood from this that for example the capitalist, the rentier, etc. cease to be persons; but their personality is conditioned and determined by quite definite class relationships, and the division appears only in their opposition to another class and, for themselves, only when they go bankrupt.) (*GI*, 93)

Since this accidental character becomes apparent in the rise and fall of competing individuals, "in imagination individuals seem freer" (*GI*, 93), but in fact this freedom is simply the reign of chance (*Zufall*), in which the personal liberty of the bourgeois is the "right to the undisturbed enjoyment, within certain conditions, of fortuity and chance" (*GI*, 92), while all others are "more subjected to the violence of things' (*GI*, 94).

The proletariat is "the class which no longer counts as a class in society, is not recognised as a class, and is in itself the expression of the dissolution of all classes, nationalities, etc. within present society" (*GI*, 86). In its total atomisation it has no basis of unity except common opposition to the bourgeoisie. Its unity can be achieved only, slowly and painfully, in the revolutionary struggle itself. But this atomisation has its positive side. It is important to Marx at this stage in his thought (odd as it may seem in the light of later Marxism), that the proletariat "has no longer any particular class interest to assert against the ruling class" (*GI*, 93). Its interests are those of the individuals composing it; there is no 'alien' general interest to generate a new form of the state. Moreover, the former intercourse between members of classes restricted by conventional forms has now polarised into the impersonal relations of the market and the personal relations between workers:

> Never in any earlier period have the productive forces taken on a form so indifferent to the intercourse of individuals *as* individuals, because their intercourse itself was formerly a restricted one. On the other hand, standing over against these productive forces, we have the majority of the individuals from whom these forces have been wrested away, and who, robbed thus of all real life-content, have become abstract individuals, but who are however only by this fact put into a position to enter into relations with one another *as individuals*. (*GI*, 82 f.)

The proletariat when it has learned to unite, is therefore the one social stratum which is qualified to organise the productive resources as a voluntary association of individuals, by "the intercourse of individuals as such".

In the *German Ideology* (as elsewhere) Marx does not use the word 'equality', for him a bourgeois slogan of which he was always contemptuous. The concept of equality is completely dissolved in the idea of individuals (who have shed everything accidental to their individuality, such as membership of a class) voluntarily co-operating for the sake of the unrestricted development of each. "Only in community with others has each individual the means of cultivating his gifts in all directions; only in community therefore is personal freedom possible" (*GI*, 92). Certainly there has never been a theoretical exposition of socialism or communism less open to the charge of sacrificing freedom to equality. Indeed, since Marx has not yet developed his theory of the temporary proletarian dictatorship before the state withers away (which appears in the *Communist Manifesto* in 1848) there is nothing to distinguish his position from anarchism. The long and close-knit argument of the *Feuerbach* chapter ends with the sentence: "In order therefore to assert themselves as individuals they must overthrow the State" (*GI*, 95).

When Marx took his next step, from the analysis of alienation to the service of the proletarian revolution, his theorising in collaboration with Engels, from the *Communist Manifesto* onwards, inevitably took a new direction. Marx himself seems never to have abandoned his original identification of communism with the abolition of alienation. He was a thinker who covered endless pages of manuscript, the Paris manuscripts, the *German Ideology*, the *Grundrisse*, struggling to develop his grand synthesis, but could bring himself to publish only special studies in economic theory and history, and analyses of current issues and events, in which his basic principles are only sporadically visible. However, the unpublishing Marx continues to write of alienation in the *Grundrisse* (1857–1858),[6] and the "fetishism of commodities" in *Capital*[7] is another treatment of the same idea. But if Marx supposed that in involving himself in the working-class movement he was merely turning his attention from the final goal to immediate practical issues, he was profoundly mistaken. If we look at the *German Ideology* in detachment from what we know of later Marxism, we see that its conception of the Revolution is purely theoretical, and that any attempt to introduce it into practical politics is foredoomed by the argument itself.

Marx was of course right in identifying wage-labourers as those whose ends conflict most directly with the alien forces; higher wages, shorter hours, security of employment, are won by interfering with the free play of supply and demand, which according to classical economics —fortunately in this matter no better at prophesy than Marxism itself—should be to the long-term disadvantage of the workers themselves. But the role of the proletariat in the *German Ideology* as the agency for abolishing alienation depends on it remaining an atomised mass which has no class interest which could generate new institutions, only personal ends to be achieved by co-operation. Within a couple more years the *Communist Manifesto* has acknowledged that the proletariat does have a class interest, and that its victory requires a transitional form of state, the collective dictatorship of the proletariat over other classes. This prepared the ground for what became the classic Marxist solution, a two-stage revolution in which "socialism", as ownership of the means of production by the workers' state, leads to "communism", voluntary co-operation following the withering away of the state. But the *German Ideology* had insisted that the division of labour inevitably leads to private property and to the dominance, for example, of mental over manual workers (*GI*, 43f.). It saw capitalism as preparing the abolition of the division of labour by breaking down occupational barriers, and ignored the opposite tendency to more complex technical specialisation, but did not suggest postponing the Revolution until after its disappearance. Moreover, for the *German Ideology*, state and class are alien formations which emerge side by side from the division of labour; the strongest class dominates the state, but this does not alter the fact that state and class remain alien to each other as well as to their members. In view of these considerations, groups differing in economic function and therefore in the power they exert in the economy, especially if competing for scant resources as in Russia and China, would have to develop into classes. A workers' state would have to become alien to the workers, and its ownership of the means of production would be not socialism but that collective ownership by the bureaucracy itself which Marx found in Asia and distinguished from the slave, feudal, and capitalist orders as the "Asiatic mode of production". The Asiatic mode, as Wittfogel shows,[8] became a skeleton in the cupboard for later Marxism, which resorted to treating all forms of state as no more than instruments for class rule, thus theoretically excluding the possibility of a bureaucratic deformation of socialism generating a new class; both Stalinist Russia and Maoist China denied the existence of the Asiatic mode.

In making this point we are of course being wise after the event, although Marx's rival, the anarchist Bakunin, already diagnosed socialism as a new form of state tyranny, and even seems to have frightened Marx at one time into shunning mention of the Asiatic mode of production.[9] But in retrospect we can see that before and after his involvement in the working-class movement Marx was in at the birth of two fundamentally different radicalisms directed to incompatible ends.

(1) The movement to replace alien institutions by the voluntary co-operation of individuals, dissolving the "It" in society into "I" and "You". This was the goal of anarchism, and in the 1950s it again became the most active concern of radicalism in the West. Even Fascism (which in Italy had an anarcho-syndicalist strain in its ancestry) might be seen as a deviation from it, intensifying state power but promising an end to alienation by dissolution of the "It" into not "I" and "You" but "We". It is by now clear that it is not directly related to the working-class movement, and that it can be achieved only locally and as a matter of degree; the Revolution of the *German Ideology* is only its theoretical limit.

(2) The working-class movement with socialism as its ideology. In the fully industrialised West, where Marxism belongs, socialism became in practice a quasi-scientific Utopia to serve the working-class as patriotism and royalism or republicanism serves as ideology for its employers. Through reforms imposed by elected socialist governments or conceded by conservative, it helped to bring liberal democracy plus social services. In "semi-Asiatic" Russia and "Asiatic" China, into which it unexpectedly intruded, revolution realised it as Asiatic bureaucratism plus social services. (Utopia after all is pursuable as a goal only as the society one lives in with the changes one desires.) Unfortunately by the 1980s the "Asiatic" realisation had discredited the very serviceable working-class ideology of the West.

The exposition of the first radicalism in the *German Ideology* has one striking defect, Marx's blindness to the difference in kind between small- and large-scale organisation. There may even be something wilful about it, for it was part of accepted wisdom up to the eighteenth century that direct democracy is possible only in small communities (it is common ground between Rousseau and Joseph de Maistre). In the *German Ideology,* however, workers of all advanced nations are pictured as simultaneously seizing the factories and getting together like a gathering of tribes to re-organise their lives on a voluntary basis. For those of us for whom the total abolition of alienation is worth conceiving only as a theoretical limit, this is not a basic flaw in the argument. But it implies that the intensification of alienation derives not only from the autonomy of market forces but from the increasing scale and complexity of organisation, and will continue in the centralised and planned economies of states which call "socialism" what Marx would have called the Asiatic mode of production. We know now that these can achieve a degree of alienation beyond Marx's imagination. Subjection to the mechanics of a system which frustrates its own professed ends and those of everyone trapped in it can reach such an extreme that a significant proportion of the bureaucracy itself becomes disaffected, and a police state is overthrown without violence, as we discovered with amazement when it happened to several East European states in 1989.

With this reservation, the argument of the *German Ideology* has a lasting relevance no longer possible for Marx after he became the ideologist of the nineteenth-century working-class movement. One of his great strengths, never entirely lost, is his many-sided view of capitalism. He sees it as exploitation, of course, and as the reduction of the individual to the plaything of market forces, but also as a gigantic acceleration of production and an unprecedented revolutionary transformation disrupting all traditional values and social relations; the opening pages of the *Communist Manifesto* are a hymn of praise to the dynamism of early capitalism. He is neither unjust to capitalism because of its social injustice, nor deceived by the assumption of classical economics that the "hidden hand" which continually expands trade and industry is pursuing the overall good of mankind. But from 1848 he is persuading himself that behind the hidden hand there is a truly benevolent historical necessity which will ensure the final victory of the working-class. He allows the divine providence which he denies to reappear in the guise of the Hegelian dialectic, and comes to see the progressive tendency of capitalism as a phase already past, and the future as the irresistible development of contradictions which turn it into a fetter on production and will finally destroy it. The fossilising Marxism of the first half of the twentieth century, derived from the later Marx and above all from Engels, was to console itself with "scientific" predictions of deepening crises of over-production, the elimination of competition by monopoly, and the concentration of property in fewer and fewer hands eliminating small ownership and further impoverishing the propertyless majority— predictions which deserved to fail, because motivated by wish-fulfilment fantasy always focussing on such social and economic trends as were working in its favour, to the exclusion of others running counter to them. By now it seems that the system which is a fetter on production, and is driven by its contradictions to become its own gravedigger, is not capitalism but full state socialism: capitalism itself is the Permanent Revolution, and any danger from within is rather from an uncontrollable acceleration of change. In the *German Ideology* on the other hand the good and bad sides of capitalism are inseparable, and the laws of the market drive it towards an outcome which is simultaneously the best and the worst, a plenitude of resources and the reduction of the majority to atomised individuals deprived of the use of them. Marx derides a True Socialist who "ascribes to nature itself the mental expression of a pious wish about human affairs" (*GI*, 521). Nature, including the humanly uncontrolled in social relations, is neutral, but interacts with human wills consciously exploiting its opportunities.

Here Marx makes predictions which have mostly come true; capital- ism has indeed continued its tireless multiplication of material resources, continued also to reduce the majority to atomised individuals bereft of traditional values and relationships and more and more subject to the impersonal forces of the market. The one false prediction further exposes the irrelevance of the working-class movement to his basic argument. Instead of depriving the majority, capitalism in the advanced countries of the late twentieth century floods them with consumers' goods, even turns proletarians back into small property-owners; the genuinely deprived become a minority denied self-respect in a society which judges all by material success, and without outlets for discontent which are not destructive and self-destructive. The industrial working- class, in any case too shrunken in countries which have progressed to the "post-industrial" age to have realistic hopes of winning control of the state, is content to seek improved conditions within the existing system. It is among the relatively prosperous that the self-alienation which Marx diagnosed first in the Jewish huckster came to be seen as the central social problem. The farther the worker diverges from the description of him in the *Communist Manifesto,* the better it looks as a description of post-modern man: "his relation to his wife and children has no longer anything in common with the bourgeois family relations; modern industrial labour, modern subjection to capital, the same in England as in France, in America as in Germany, has stripped him of every trace of national character. Law, morality, religion are to him so many bourgeois prejudices . . ."

For some fifty years after Marx's death his followers had to satisfy their hunger for a general theory from the writings of Engels. The significance of the "fetishism of commodities" in *Capital,* and of the stray references to alienation in Marx's known writings, was divined by Georg Lukács in his *History and Class Consciousness* (1920), but could not be fully appreciated until the publication of the Paris manuscripts and the *German Ideology* in 1932 and of the *Grundrisse* in 1939; and as long as attention centered on the Paris manuscripts the unpublishing Marx could be misconceived as the young Marx. By the 1950s and 1960s the discovery had both temporally rejuvenated Marxian theory and circulated the word "alienation" throughout sociology, psychology, philosophy, and theology. It offered a key to the contemporary experience, in capitalist and socialist countries alike, of living at the mercy of systems which impose social roles which make us traitors to ourselves, grow into vast bureaucratised structures out of reach of democratic control, hurry us by their own dynamics towards nuclear annihilation or ecological breakdown. What was once a social order with coherent values appears as the "System" (a long established name for the elusive entity which cannot be identified with any human oppressors), economic and political forces mechanically interacting to distance what you do as means farther and farther from what you want, if you any longer know what you want. We see the point when Marx says that the economy with its plethora of goods to satisfy every need functions only by continually 'creating a *new* need', by '*contriving* and ever-*calculating* subservience to inhuman, refined, unnatural and *imaginary* appetites' (*EPM,* 116), and that to give work a rational purpose by insisting on untroubled leisure to enjoy its fruits is forbidden by the market as a drag on economic success, more recently seen to be causing the British (with their tea breaks and long weekends in the country) to fall behind the Americans and the Americans behind the Japanese. Since the 1950s the first radicalism has in consequence grown at the expense of the second, with resistance to alienation as the unifying thread running through an extraordinary variety of movements. The working-class is now only one of many social cross-cuts discovering that the System denies them their own kinds of "self-activity", youth, women, gays, blacks; and the "intercourse of individuals as such" has been pursued in experiments in communal living or participatory democracy or in protest movements on issues where the mechanics of political or economic process manifestly drive it counter to the wills of all, the nuclear armament race, environmental pollution. Such movements, even when they cling to socialist slogans, in practice renounce the old socialist aim of winning state power; their only options are anarchism or the achievement of limited concessions from the power at the centre. The word "Revolution" came briefly back into fashion as not much more than a rock musician's slogan for the liberation of personal life here and now, losing its old meaning except for minute sects with no alternative to inaction except terrorist gestures. It is true that Marxism of any kind needs faith that there can be an alternative to capitalism, and the discrediting of Eastern socialism in 1989 could still come as a disillusioning blow to the Left. But for the past quarter of a century the innovative forces on the Left had been paying no more than lip service to the nationalisation of the means of production, the Soviet Union was ignored, Mao and Che Guevara were not much more than subversive icons, and the freely associating individuals discovering and doing their own thing could not have been farther from the self-sacrificing discipline of revolutionary movements. The transition is marked dramatically by the Paris events of 1968, when the workers' strike did not lead to revolution, but so many of the upper strata enjoyed their interlude of unalienated life in the streets that the state was briefly paralysed, and seemed almost in danger of the collapse we were to see in Eastern Europe in 1989.

The word 'alienation' won its wide circulation by multiplying and debasing its meanings, but in the thought of Marx the concept is both simple and of great explanatory power, and deserves revival in its original purity. We have seen that he treats behaviour as alienated to the extent that it is controlled by the mechanics of social systems, not by human wills (the subjection of one man's will to another's is *not* alienation). Capitalism imposes the illusion that free individuals are for the first time in history taking their fate into their own hands, but in fact, as long as individuals compete instead of co-operating, alien institutions emerge from their interactions to divert their actions from their own ends and subject them to the reign of chance. The self-alienated life, in which we come to want what serves the automatic processes in society instead of making society serve our respective wants, has a psychological dimension which did not interest Marx; his paradigmatic case of subjection to the alien, the worker whose labour is a market commodity, does not have to ask himself 'Is this what I *really* want or just what I think I want?'. But psychological interpretations of alienation are secondary, and the concept itself is sociological. Marx studies alienation not in isolated but in co-operating or competing individuals. If asked for a literary illustration of the experience of alienation, one might be tempted to think first of a solitary outsider like the hero of Camus's *L'étranger*. But an apter, if at first sight perverse, artistic illustration would be Luis Buñuel's mysterious film *The Exterminating Angel*, where the guests at a party, after taking their leave, decide after all to stay overnight, and in the morning find that none of them is able to leave the room. They remain trapped, fending for themselves as though on a desert island, while the police inexplicably cordon off the house, until one day they notice that each of them happens to be sitting in the same place as at the end of the party; they rise, repeat the same motions of leavetaking, and walk straight out of the house. It would be a pity to reduce this dreamlike story to a single meaning, but one source of its power is certainly the sense it evokes of individuals bound by forces generated by their own interactions, of the invisible walls within society and the trapdoors which open under our feet, of the efficacy of rituals for which no one can give a reason.

When Marx calls the proletarian life dehumanised he is not speaking rhetorically; he thinks of the alien as the mechanical, transforming us from voluntary agents into things. What is his meaning, since human behaviour after all never ceases to be purposive? His point is most easily grasped from the many places in the Paris manuscripts where he uses the language of means and ends. In free productive activity to satisfy the human need for exercise of intellectual and aesthetic faculties as well as for the product itself, the senses "relate themselves to the *thing* for the sake of the thing" and "nature has lost its mere *utility* by use becoming *human* use" (*EPM*, 107). In the market however, "the dealer in minerals sees only the mercantile value but not the beauty and the unique nature of the mineral" (*EPM*, 109). Labour sold as a commodity is "not the satisfaction of a need; it is merely a *means* to satisfy needs external to it" (*EPM*, 72). The worker "no longer feels himself to be freely active in any but his animal functions—eating, drinking, procreating, or at most in his dwelling and in dressing-up, etc."—functions human in themselves but animalised by "the abstraction which separates them from the sphere of all other human activities and turns them into sole and ultimate ends" (*EPM*, 75). For the worker, "life itself appears only as a *means to life*" (*EPM, 75*). Similarly with the wealthy, since "all is under the sway of *inhuman* power". The extravagant spender "knows wealth as mere means, as something that is good for nothing but to be annihilated", and thinks that "*gratification* is its final aim and end" (*EPM*, 126); but the mechanism of the market puts him at a disadvantage against the sober industrialist who reinvests, for whom pleasure is recuperation and "what is squandered on his pleasure must therefore amount to no more than will be replaced with profit through the reproduction of capital" (*EPM*, 128). Consequently, all ends are reduced to the pursuit of money for its own sake. "Political economy, this science of *wealth*, is therefore simultaneously the science of want, of *thrift*, of *saving* . . . of *asceticism*, and its true ideal is the *ascetic* but *extortionate* miser and the *ascetic* but *productive* slave" (*EPM*, 118). Money, being exchangeable for anything, is reinvested to accumulate the abstract power to do things instead of actually doing them; for the capitalist, "money, which appears as a means, constitutes true *power* and the sole *end* . . . an *end in itself*" (*EPM*, 125). But a chain of means to ends which are themselves means has the mechanical relation of cause and effect. Our behaviour will be mechanical, and interlock in a system alien to all of us, if it is a means, or a means to a means, detached from our positive ends.

An ends/means analysis explains why alienation can serve simultaneously as a sociological and a normative concept. Marx is not illicitly introducing presuppositions of value with which we might not agree. As long as he was using the concept of man's essence he no doubt had to assume the value of that essence; but his case in the *German Ideology* requires no more than the logic of hypothetical imperatives—whatever your ends, it is inconsistent to choose means which do not serve them, and whatever your means, you require ends for them to serve. As we argued in another chapter of liberty and equality, the value of the unalienated life follows from the logic of value judgments, not from any moral principle. This logical invulnerability makes the concept of alienation a devastating weapon in social criticism, wherever the critic can convince us that systems of means have in fact divorced themselves from ends. There is, however, a point which for Marx, committed as he is to revolutionary and total solutions, could have no interest. The logic of imperatives shows that, *where there is an option,* voluntary co-operation to realise each others' ends is better than appealing to an institution functioning by a mechanics of its own. Thus most people find it better, wherever possible, to settle civil and even criminal matters privately between themselves than call in the law, the procedures of which can take a course unpredictably diverging from their ends, if not from those of the lawyers. It does not follow, however, that a community of any size can be organised by free co-operation without fixed and enforced rules; in assuming that there is always such an option Marx is as usual ignoring the difference between small- and large-scale organisation. Since Marx always uses the word "alien" pejoratively he often gives the impression that institutions in becoming independent of human wills necessarily work *against* them. But obviously a blind submission to law or to morality works out to the advantage as well as to the disadvantage of social beings, and no one appreciates better than Marx that the dynamism of the market system does generate a gigantic expansion of productive resources. Marx's deepest objection is to the element of chance in the functioning of alien institutions. He protests against "a state of things in which relationships become independent of individuals, in which individuality is subservient to chance" (*GI,* 483), and calls on us to undertake "the task of replacing the domination of circumstances and chance over individuals by the domination of individuals over circumstances and chance" (*GI,* 482). But can control over circumstances ever be more than a matter of degree? Do we even *want* the total elimination of chance from our lives?

An ends/means analysis of Marx's alienation requires the qualification that it applies fully only to the culmination in capitalism. Spontaneous imagination and impulse crystallising in myth and custom embodying the ends of society, which belong to what I have elsewhere called the "spontaneity of ends" in contrast with the "automatism of means",[10] also subjects us to powers generated by our own activity, not inevitably, but as a consequence of failing to distinguish myth from fact, and for Marx this is at the historical origin of alienation. He sees the compulsion to treat as sacred the forces man does not recognise as his own as present throughout the history of alienation. Like the forces of nature before they are explained by science, the alien forces in society appear superhuman until individuals succeed in identifying them as the effects of their own interactions. Hence the sacredness of all institutions the functioning of which is not fully intelligible in terms of human ends. One may again look for an illustration in Buñuel's film, in which we inevitably ascribe the self-imprisonment of the characters to the Exterminating Angel of the title; it concludes with them on the point of imprisoning themselves again inside the cathedral where they give thanks for their release.

For Marx alienation belongs, with scarcity, ignorance, superstition, and oppression, to the primordial condition of mankind, from which it is at last ready to emerge. But he sees the modern world as unique in that for the first time alienation is both total and undisguised. He considers that in pre-capitalist societies social relations were still to some extent unalienated relations between persons. But a point of equal importance to him is that even in their self-estranged behaviour men formerly conceived themselves as acting against their own wills only when obeying sacred powers, which they did not recognise as products of their own interactions. We might say (although Marx himself does not quite say this) that they were always able to make sense of their lives in terms of their own wills or the will of a superior—not an institution but a person, not the state but the King, not private property but the lord of the manor, not moral conventions but God, not the laws of supply and demand but Fate. But under capitalism the mechanics of society are nakedly exposed; people find themselves acting in ways which may be rationally explicable in terms of economics, sociology, or psychology, but which serve neither their own nor any other human or superhuman purpose. Subjectively this is to experience their lives as absurd and meaningless, a metaphysical anguish which does not interest Marx. But the cure he would propose is obvious—not religion or philosophy, but action to abolish the institutions which estrange us from ourselves.

Marx without the Revolution is indeed *Hamlet* without the prince. But if we put aside his prejudice in favour of the single and final solution, Marx in 1845 and 1846 presents us with an illuminating model for our times. On the one hand there is the "alien" System—let us give it the capital letter—reaching up to the world market and to worldwide interrelations between states, constituted of means interacting causally and erratically serving or diverging from the ends of the individuals who employ them. (The possibility of it taking final leave of us as a society of computers operating beyond the reach of merely human judgment is a recent addition to our nightmares.) On the other hand there are the individuals who, to the extent that they do not mistake the means for their own ends (i.e. are not "self-alienated"), can encroach on the System where it is relatively weak, to replace its impersonal functioning by voluntary co-operation to achieve their ends directly. The System has been expanding, for better and for worse, throughout the history of the modern West, disrupting co-operation by competition, dissolving communities into individuals, accelerating production of resources by the dynamism of the market, never more than temporarily slowed by a counter-tendency for growing organisations to clog themselves by increasing bureaucratisation. According to Marx's materialist theory of history, which on this point unreserved defenders of capitalism may be delighted to accept, it is the whole secret of the unique development of the West in the last few centuries. It is moving too fast to be stopped wherever it may be taking us, the question is to what extent it can be steered. Jean-François Lyotard in *The Postmodern Condition* notes the contrast between Talcott Parsons, with his essentially optimistic conception of society as a self-regulating system, and his pessimistic successors:

"In the work of contemporary German theorists, *Systemtheorie* is technocratic, even cynical, not to say despairing: the harmony between the needs and hopes of individuals or groups and the functions guaranteed by the system is now only a secondary component of its functioning", which depends rather on "the universal law of scientific civilization: namely that the means determine the ends, or rather that the technical possibilities dictate what use is made of them."[11]

The conflicts of class interest on which later Marxism centered have, of course, a place in Marx's original scheme, but for the *German Ideology* capitalists dominate workers only as, for example, men dominate women, through positions in the structure deriving from the division of labour, and liberation is in either case completed only by the dissolution of structures through "the intercourse of individuals as such", irrespective of class or sex. An advantage of the scheme is that it has room for criticisms of capitalism other than as exploitation of the worker which have been accumulating since the Romantic period, objections to the retreat from ends to means, the materialistic neglect of spiritual values, the erosion of meaning from life, vulgarisation of taste, the superficiality of experience when things move too fast for us to look deeply into anything, the ambivalence towards selfishness (in you socially irresponsible, in us the motor of social progress) which has wedded the two words "bourgeois hypocrisy". Let us try to pin down this type of objection by a trivial example, the difficulty, in the midst of superabundance, of finding what would formerly have been recognised as a loaf of bread or a glass of beer. It is not simply that for mass marketing as commodities it is more profitable to produce these without flavour than with; producers take the offensive by advertisement to propagandise consumers into believing that they do taste the new products. Some of course remain unpersuaded, and form such associations as the Campaign for Real Ale, which in Britain had its modest place in the wide spectrum of movements (of workers, women, gays, blacks . . .) resisting the System at different points. The System then adjusts to accommodate this eccentric taste at a higher price. In general, however, consumers habituate themselves to the easily available product, and even come to prefer a bland to a distinctive flavour. It begins to seem like élitism to insist that the product has deteriorated; but the change in preferences resulted from the System diminishing awareness of flavours. However, it is far from certain that someone who insists on real ale has noticed the taste either. He may belong to circles where you win status by parading fine discriminations, which change in fashion cycles as independent of niceties of perception as changes in the weather, by the dynamics of power relations in and between groups—a further ramification of the System outside the range of Marx's sociology. But preferences in food and drink are among the most basic in our experience; if even here we do not know what we really want, there will be still less assurance that valuation of paintings will be uncorrupted by propaganda to raise their price in the art market, or our high-minded judgments on social and political issues by radical or reactionary chic. In self-alienated social life the System of causally interrelated means tends everywhere to endanger the integrity of ends, without which, however, means lose their meaning. The inability of many people to think about their own ends except in an objectivising language designed as means for manipulation by psychology, so that instead of loving and hating they have meaningful relationships and hostile or aggressive attitudes, is an extreme symptom. Another is the tendency of artists, who until lately took pride in freeing the authentic personal response from conventional values, to lose faith that there are any feelings not stimulated artificially for manipulative purposes, or that there is anything to be done except play cool games with them without being deceived by them. John Updike quotes a chilling insight of Warhol, the supreme representative of this tendency: "During the '60s, I think, people forgot what emotions were supposed to be. And I don't think they've ever remembered. Once you see emotions from a certain angle you can never think of them as real again."

Updike comments: "What remains real, it would seem, is the semiotic shell, the mass of images with which a society economically bent on keeping us stirred up appeals to our over-solicited, over-analysed, over-dramatised, over-liberated and over-the-hill emotions".[12]

Capitalism, which undermines our capacity to respond with integrity, is treacherous in the wholly accidental manner in which it now enhances, now diminishes, our awareness of the things to which we respond. In Marx's time, the System was freeing modern man from confusion between the real and the mythic images stimulating towards ends, by focussing attention on the real as means, an advantage which he never denied; in ours, without quite losing this healthily disillusioning function, it surrounds us with phantom images designed as means, as stimuli to buy, pulling post-modern man towards a worse confusion for which there is already a name, Jean Baudrillard's "hyper-reality".[13] Michael

Herr, reporting on the Vietnam war, observes that there were always some soldiers who, when conscious of a television crew nearby, faced battle as though making war movies inside their heads. "They were insane", he comments, "but the war hadn't done that to them."

> We'd all seen too many movies, stayed too long in Television City, years of media glut had made certain connections difficult. The first few times that I got fired at or saw combat deaths, nothing really happened, all the responses got locked in my head. It was the same familiar violence, only moved over to another medium; some kind of jungle play with giant helicopters and fantastic special effects, actors lying out there in canvas body bags waiting for the scene to end so they could get up again and walk it off. But that was some scene (you found out), there was no cutting it.
>
> A lot of things had to be unlearned before you could learn anything at all, and even after you knew better you couldn't avoid the ways in which things got mixed, the war itself with those parts of the war that were just like the movies, just like *The Quiet American* or *Catch 22* (a Nam standard because it said that in a war everybody thinks that everybody else is crazy), just like all that combat footage from television ("We're taking fire from the treeline!" "Where?" "There!" "*Where?*" "Over *there!*" "Over WHERE?" "Over THERE!!" Flynn heard that go on for fifteen minutes once; we made it an epiphany), your vision blurring, images jumping and falling as though they were being received by a dropped camera, hearing a hundred horrible sounds at once—screams, sobs, hysterical shouting, a throbbing inside your head that threatened to take over, quavering voices trying to get the orders out, the dulls and sharps of weapons going off . . .[14]

War is the best of reminders that there is still a difference between reality and the social construction of reality. But might we find some consolation in the thought that, since individuality itself develops through socialisation, there can be no sense in a distinction between what the individual really wants and what society trains him to want? But the socialisation which is learning to see and respond from each others' viewpoints, widening awareness and enriching feeling, is a matter of letting one's own ends be modified by others' ends, not by confusion with means. Tastes can be socially modified without losing their genuineness; a schoolboy, although already a fairly socialised being, is never in doubt as to whether he enjoys what he is eating. Since the nineteenth century the decay of religious authority in a means-orientated society has raised the arts to a dominant role in the recovery and revitalisation of ends; the great *avant-gardes*, Futurism, Dada, Surrealism, were nothing less than collective experiments for the discovery of how to live fruitfully in the twentieth century.[15] By 1960 or so this function was being threatened by an acceleration of change which shifted the focus of conformism from traditional conventions to transitory fashions; it became harder to distinguish originality from a talent for spotting the trend ahead of others, and *avant-gardes* moved from the disturbing periphery to the reassuring centre of social life, as laboratories to be watched for the orthodoxy you must conform to or be left behind, as you watch scientific laboratories for the next technological advance. However, appreciation of the arts does remain a model for the unalienated life. There is still a distinction, if we want to hold on to it, between being excited by a poem or novel, with enjoyment becoming deeper and richer or fading and turning to distaste as friends you talk with or critics you read enhance understanding and call attention to unnoticed insights or evasions (the "intercourse of individuals as such"), and being afraid to judge it except by its utility for some school of criticism the rise and fall of which belongs to the sociology of departments of English in Academia (self-alienation).

Here we may consider one of the reasons why state socialism (as a perfecting in Russia and China of "Asiatic" bureaucratism by the most modern techniques of social control) has proved to be even more alienating than capitalism. Civilization depends on a core of unalienated social life, on personal relations with kin, friends, neighbours, and with creative minds accessible through writing and other media, and on the faith that the political and economic machinery exist to be the servants and not the masters of unalienated life. A state socialism which aims at the total politicisation of life (which is less a revolt against the System than a hypertrophy of one of its tendencies, large-scale organisation sapping its impetus by reducing competition) directly attacks and destroys this core, a project fortunately less easily achieved than Orwell anticipated in his *1984*; dissident circles somehow do survive or revive. Capitalism on the other hand, which merely erodes and corrupts this core, also opens up prospects for its expansion, provided that we see clearly the System's ambivalent nature. In the advanced world the System as it grows also becomes more flexible, allowing increasing room for leisure, personal freedom, access to cultural as well as material resources, and the dissolution of barriers to intercourse between members of different classes, sexes, and races; even those media which entice us towards hyper-reality have helped to break down the old limitations to awareness from the viewpoints of outsiders to our own parish, workers, women, gays, the Third World. This flexibility has been the despair of radicals who, as their trust in the working-class diminished, hoped to mobilise for the Revolution a grand alliance of all the heterogeneous opponents of aspects of the System, from nuclear disarmers to campaigners for real ale. We have learned that the System, in spite of occasional spasms of repression in the old style, can now accommodate and tame any revolt. Especially striking is its easy acceptance in the 1960s of sexual liberation and overt hedonism. It turns out that for regular reinvestment it is no longer necessary for the capitalist to train himself by the puritan ethic to become the "ascetic but extortionate miser". His subjection to the System may be more rigorous than ever, in that he has to be at least at the ready for work throughout his waking life, but there is plenty of scope for conspicuous leisure which advertises his status, the longer the better, provided that he does not lose touch with the moment-to-moment changes of the market. Indeed it hardly needed a new hedonist ideology to persuade busy people that brief and intense pleasures are much easier to reconcile with the accelerating demands of the System than any aspirations after more lasting satisfactions. The Sexual Revolution had the characteristic double aspect of all the gifts of modern capitalism; it released the most disalienating of drives, the instinct which most potently and immediately lifts us above all calculations of means; yet the force which speeded it, without relation to human good or ill, was the competition of advertisers, writers, and entertainers needing progressively stronger stimuli to attract attention to their wares. The promise of sexuality as pure end was inseparable from its prostitution as a means of marketing.

With superabundance the opportunity for leisure grows for all classes, and the unambitious wage- or salary-earner may even be in a better position than his employer to devote it simply to those "sole and ultimate ends" of which Marx speaks, whether merely "in his dwelling and in dressing-up, etc." or in the cultivation of the arts and sciences which Marx expected to be available to him only after the Revolution. The increasing flexibility of the System is an evil only for the believers in absolute solutions: Marx's goal, the free association of individuals to develop the capacities of each, can only, but *can,* be pursued locally here and now. The collapse of socialism as a workable alternative to capitalism may tempt us to assume that we can forget Marx, that the System is an unmixed good, and that political liberty and economic equality of opportunity are all that is required for human liberation. But if we lose his concept of the unalienated life, as a goal to be pursued on whatever scale is achievable, the effect is merely to subject us blindly to the System. We recognise political freedom as itself a matter of degree, why not also Freedom from alienation? For the one as for the other, the price is eternal vigilance, to tell apart the liberating and the dehumanising aspects of almost every contemporary social or cultural development. The market mechanism, and the System in general, like any other automatism independent of human wills, has no inherent tendency to make life either better or worse; unless we try to utilise it for, when we cannot replace it by, the "intercourse of individuals as such", we are the playthings of chance. It is our good luck that it multiplies material resources, and if it denied them to the majority in Marx's time is in the West liberal with them today, but for their fruitful enjoyment it closes prospects or opens them with the same indifference.

A significant question here is what will happen if and when leisure becomes the norm and work the exception. Will there be a turn of the tide, with the System retreating to the periphery of our lives instead of continuing to encroach on the integrity of ends? Marx in the *Grundrisse* describes how with the development of machines and of the whole "automatic system of machinery", production comes more and more to depend on "neither the immediate labour performed by the worker nor the time that he works", rather on "his understanding of nature and his mastery of it" (*GR*, 142). Consequently the future promises both increased leisure (for "education in the arts, sciences, etc.") and a satisfying exercise of the mind in work. Marx holds of course that this prospect cannot be realised before the Revolution, because the capitalist profits by the worker labouring as long as possible, and his ownership of the means of production confronts the worker with "the machine as an alien force" (*GR*, 133), but this is only another self-deceiving attempt to prove that capitalism is its own gravedigger. Since all civilization hitherto has depended on most people working most of the time, a predominance of leisure over work is the most radical social transformation we can conceive, overturning all preconceptions about what for good or evil is possible or impossible for man. We have no precedent for anticipating its promise and danger except that glimpse of it during the affluence of the 1960s, which suddenly revealed how brittle our official culture has become, and how little of it is worth anything at all to a young generation which feels the burden of choosing a career lifting from its shoulders.

In Jorge Amado's novel, *Dona Flor and Her Two Husbands*, there is a delightful description of an amateur orchestra in which for a few hours every week Bahians of varied status forget their cares and call each other by their Christian names.[16] What would be the effect if, without any change in ownership of the means of production, their social life during most of the day passed in such informal associations, and the millionaire cellist Adriano and the clerk and violinist Urbano did, not their music-making, but their work or business as sparetime occupations? We may hope that money would matter little, such capacities as musicianship would matter more, and the System would shrink to a corner of their lives. But an unintended lesson of Marx is the uselessness of wish-fulfilling prophesies. Who would have guessed before the 1960s that one of the first consequences of collective experiments in the unalienated life would be the revival of astrology, witchcraft, and white and black magic?

Appendix:
The Question as Posed by Moses Hess

It is well known that Moses Hess (1812–1875), father of the True Socialists, who introduced Marx and the other Left Hegelians to socialism, and later became one of the founders of Zionism, was writing of alienation in much the same way as Marx in 1844 and 1845. Their influence at this period was reciprocal, but the idea of money as the alienated essence of man's labour seems to have originated with Hess (David McLellan, *The Young Hegelians and Karl Marx*, London, 1969, 152–58). The following extract is from his essay *Über die sozialistische*

Bewegung in Deutschland (in Moses Hess, *Philosophische und sozialistische Schriften*, Berlin, 1961), which carries the postscripted date May 1844.

But how did it come about that hitherto man has everywhere taken his creation for his creator, has behaved as the creature and servant of his own productions, has with the religious awe of godfearing creatures subjected himself to the works of his own hands and brain, as though to higher, superhuman beings or powers, and sacrificed himself in turn to his statecraft, his theology, finally to all his intellectual and material riches? How did it come about, we ask, that the development of his power only made him more powerless, and that at last he made a present of all his capacities to a single omnipotent and omnipresent god, money?

The answer is that man has never known the secret of his own creativity, his own capacities. This secret, which is none other than the secret of socialism, how was he to discern it? He has never had any choice if he is honest but to say, in defiance of all absolute philosophy, that in the conditions in which he finds himself in this antisocial world he does *not* as an isolated individual possess this creativity in himself; he is obliged to look on what he himself creates, and creation in general, from the restricted individual standpoint in which he actually finds himself, as the work of a being which is *beyond* him, and to let himself be ruled by this being which is *alien* to him, this power *hidden* from him! In any case what use is it to him that eventually in theory he mocked the powers in the beyond, since in actual life he remains subject to them until he conceives the idea of socialism and puts it into effect? But how would he even arrive at the idea that his own life, and life in general, is only a product of the *co-operation* between individuals, since he has not viewed the operations of individuals in their interrelations? How could he perceive that he, the single individual who in relation to his alienated essence saw himself powerless, unfree, oppressed, and degraded, would be a free, creative, and almighty being if he worked as *social* man, as active member of the whole human society—for up to now there has been no such thing as *socialisation?* The social essence, the human species-essence, his creative essence, were and remain for man till now a mystical being in the beyond, which confronts him in political life as the state-power, in religious as the power of Heaven, theoretically as God, practically as money-power. In vain man strove for political *or* religious, theoretical *or* practical freedom, in vain endeavoured to win his freedom on one side or the other: always his alienated essence opposed him, tyrannising in new forms . . .

NOTES

1. Abbreviations: *EPM:* Marx, *Economic and Philosophic Manuscripts of 1844*

(Moscow: Foreign Languages Publishing House, no date). *GI:* Marx and Engels, *The German Ideology* (London: Lawrence & Wishart, 1965). *CHPR:* Marx, *Critique of Hegel's 'Philosophy of Right'*, ed. Joseph O'Malley (Cambridge: Cambridge University Press, 1970). *CM:* Marx and Engels, *Manifesto of the Communist Party* ("The Communist Manifesto") (Moscow: Foreign Languages Publishing House, no date). *SW:* Marx, *Selected Writings*, ed. T. B. Bottomore and Maximilien Rubel (London: Pelican, 1963). *EW:* Marx, *Early Writings*, ed. T. B. Bottomore (London: C.A. Watts & Co., 1963) *GR:* David McLellan, *Marx's Grundrisse* (London: Macmillan, 1971). *CP:* Marx, *Capital*, vol. 1 (London: Lawrence & Wishart, 1970).

2. The English word 'alienation' has the disadvantage of confusing the senses of *Entaüsserung* ('relinquishment', a word used, for example, of alienating rights or property) and *Entfremdung* ('estrangement', used, for example, of persons becoming alienated from each other). It seems impossible in translation even to distinguish them consistently; to use 'estrangement' for the latter hides the connexion with *fremd*, only translatable as 'alien', and where this connexion is important to Marx's argument I have taken the liberty of substituting 'alienations' when quoting from translations.

3. *Alienation* (London: George Allen & Unwin, 1971), 91.

4. Cf. *GR,* 71, 81, 100, 121, 150–52. According to I. Mészáros, in *Marx's Theory of Alienation* (London: Merlin Press, 1970, 224), "the words 'Entfremdung', 'entfremdet', etc. occur on these pages *several hundred times.*"

5. Cf. *GR,* 81, 82, 98, 99, 101, 103, 104, 105, 117, 118, 137, 150.

6. For references to alienation in the later writings, cf. Mészáros, 221–27, McLellan, *GR,* 12–15.

7. Cp. 71–83. Nine direct references to alienation in *Capital* are quoted in Mészáros, 225–26.

8. Karl August Wittfogel, *Oriental Despotism* (New Haven: Yale University Press, 1957), 369.

9. Wittfogel, 387f.

10. Cf. *Reason and Spontaneity (R & S)*, 108.

11. Jean-François Lyotard, *The Postmodern Condition: A Report on Knowledge* (Manchester University Press, 1984), 11, 89 n39.

12. *Sunday Times Magazine*, Aug 27, 1989.

13. Jean Baudrillard, *Selected Writings* (Cambridge, UK: Polity Press, 1988), 143–47 and passim.

14. Michael Herr, *Dispatches* (London: Pan Books, 1978), 169f.

15. For a study of Futurism, Dada, and Surrealism from this angle, cf. *R & S,* 192–227.

16. Jorge Amado, *Dona Flor and Her Two Husbands* (New York: Avon Books, 1988), 354–60.

Poetic and Mythic Varieties of Correlative Thinking

11

'Reason' in the narrow sense is analytic thinking. To be 'rational', let us say, is both to reason and to trust in the many other operations of human intelligence only to the extent that their functions have been clarified and effectiveness tested by reason. We take the position, if only as a still useful simplification, that the others may be classed as 'correlative' in contrast with analytic thinking, and themselves analysed by the techniques of Jakobson's structural linguistics. This is Popper's "critical rationalism". There is also a 'rationalism' in the narrow sense which insists on more than mere rationality, which acknowledges the insights, the analogising, the commonsense synthesising indispensable in practical life as no more than a second-best allowable in fields not yet conquered for analytic thinking, and dismisses altogether such exotic varieties as poetic, mythic, or mystical thinking. Our position is that on the contrary all analysis has its starting-points in the pre-logical underground of thought—in concepts born from spontaneous correlations, which may be discredited if the conclusions drawn from them are contradictory or refuted by observation, but can be replaced only by a spontaneous correlative switch; and from spontaneous motivations which are to be evaluated by the degree of awareness of oneself and of the objects to which one finds oneself responding.

The correlation of similarities and contiguities is pre-linguistic, as with Pavlov's dog expecting food when it hears the bell.

A	(Similarity)	B
(Before)		(Now)
Bell ringing		Bell ringing
Food coming		———
Satisfaction		———

(Contiguity)

So the gaps in B fill from A (bell ringing before : food coming before :: bell ringing now : *food coming now* ...). There is no reason to suppose that humans in the same situation are reacting any differently even when they break out into speech, which will very probably consist of words almost without syntactic organisation.

"The bell!"

"Ah, dinner, good."

The words, selected on the paradigmatic dimension to contrast with other words (dinner not breakfast or lunch, good not bad, a bell not some other thing, with "the" contrasting with other bells), by their mere contiguity on the syntagmatic dimension combine ringing bell, dinner, and satisfaction as contiguous events. Since in contrasting with other things and events they also class instances as similar, the words already assimilate the present to past instances. However, by allowing syntactic development in sentence form, and therefore affirmation and denial, the combining of the words releases us from the purely instinctive reaction of the dog, enabling a speaker to substitute contrast for similarity and remoteness for contiguity.

"The bell!"

"No, that's the door bell."

"Oh, no dinner yet, too bad."

We may say then that correlative thinking operates at the level of the word and non-sentential combinations of words, but is criticised at the level of the sentence. It is fully explicit in the systems of correspondences in the cosmologies of some cultures and in Mediaeval and Renaissance proto-science in the West. The Chinese yin-yang scheme is basically binary, separating out from a single chain of oppositions: 'yang : yin :: light : dark :: male : female :: heaven : earth :: ruler : subject ::

moving : still . . . . '. The terms from which it starts have no other content than the oppositions themselves; to be yang not yin is nothing else but to be light not dark, or male not female, or. . . . Its structure corresponds remarkably to the scheme which Jakobson finds at the basis of language itself, with its binary oppositions, paradigms and syntagms, metaphors and metonyms.[1] That down below we are all yin-yang thinkers is nicely illustrated by a game tried out by E. H. Gombrich (inspired by Jakobson and himself reminded of yin-yang).[2] He took pairs of words and asked which is 'ping' and which is 'pong', getting a surprising approach to agreement on apparently senseless questions. Most of us it seems, when faced with the choice, will reply that ice-cream is ping and hot soup is pong, Watteau ping and Rembrandt pong, pretty girls ping and matrons pong. The rational man will however trust correlative thinking only within the tested limits of its effectiveness. He knows by experience that in speaking he correlates words without reflection and seldom goes wrong, effortlessly selecting from paradigms and combining in syntagms, only occasionally pausing to analyse his sentence and correct a grammatical error or replace a wrong word. The proto-sciences on the other hand expose correlations to full view only because they have no other means to organise a cosmos out of phenomena of which too little is known. Compared with post-Galilean science they are almost without predictive value. But at the same time a correlative cosmology has an advantage which modern science notoriously lacks. In pursuing an objectivity independent of our likes and dislikes science has an unprecedented explanatory and predictive power, by which everything is placed at our disposal as means but emptied of its value as end; we learn how the world is but not how to live in it. Correlative cosmologies on the other hand preserve the primitive unity of fact and value. The classifications as similar or contrasting on the paradigmatic dimension, contiguous or remote on the syntagmatic, interact with desires and aversions, motivated by them and in turn modified by them; and to the extent that they do guide towards reactions in fuller awareness of our environment, they will share the value which our quasi-syllogism[3] ascribes to the spontaneous reaction in greater awareness. This is an advantage to be clearly separated from the disadvantage that correlative thinking, without the analytic to test it, most certainly does not take us far towards the understanding of physical events and the invention of machines. As Bataille recognised,[4] there could be modern mythologies to orientate us subjectively towards what science presents objectively, but they would have to respect the facts as established by science. However, the similarities and contiguities picked out for correlation as relevant to social or personal needs, with full freedom to organise by metaphor and metonymy, would not be those to which science attends for the purposes of explanation and prediction. One might add that in pre-modern societies a correlative, even a mythic mythology, however inadequate by scientific standards, covers only the outskirts of a natural and social environment which may be quite adequately pictured from the perspective of the people who live in it, also that there is a lot more to be aware of in social and personal life than can be attained by science.

Whether or not we accept the claim that all thinking is at bottom binary, pairs and the fours into which they divide easily expand to threes, fives, and beyond. Sometimes this is because a binary distinction leaves out the maker of the distinction. 'Left/right', 'above/below', 'before/after' (not, however, 'I/you', 'here/there', 'now/then') imply a spatially or temporally middle or between position from which the opposition is drawn, inviting expansion of the pair to a triad. Thus Chinese thinkers, who habitually contrasted heaven and earth, from the third century B.C. speak of man "making a triad with heaven and earth";[5] around the same period the four cardinal points sometimes became five, with the addition of the centre. Kepler, still in spite of his laws of planetary motion a mediaeval cosmologist, who correlated the distances between the planets with the proportions of the five regular solids, conceived sun, planets, and stars as a triad with man living on the intermediate member, the planets, among which earth is itself located between the correlatives of the primary and secondary regular solids.[6] Let us look more closely at two conflicting sets in the European symbolism of colours.

(A) Colours of races, deriving from the binary "white: black:: good: evil".

A	B	C	D	E
1. White	Yellow	Red	Brown	Black
2. Lightest	Less light	———	Less dark	Darkest

| 3. Good | Less good | —— | Less evil | Evil |
| 4. Clever | Less clever | —— | Less stupid | Stupid |

(B) The colourful as the vivid, the vital, deriving from the binary "colourful: pale:: life: death".

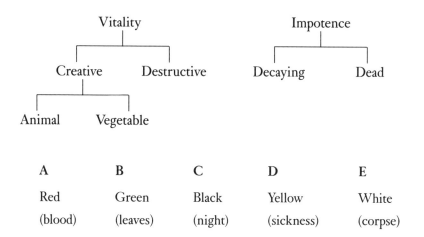

A	B	C	D	E
Red	Green	Black	Yellow	White
(blood)	(leaves)	(night)	(sickness)	(corpse)

We might derive both structures from a common "light/darkness", but in developing they contradict each other, the contradiction centering on the colour white. The white man is predisposed by them to think of other races as inferior to the degree that they recede from his own norm of colour, but also as more intensely alive. To some extent the contradiction fits in rather well with the conflict between the spontaneous and the good in the Christian doctrine of Original Sin, for which the vitality of nature is temptation. It is then reconcilable to see the black man as both the most savage and the most seductively potent. The red man, historically the latest to be discovered, has been assigned a colour which does not fit neatly into the first series. Consequently, although undoubtedly dark enough to be identified as inferior, he can draw from the second series the creative vitality of red blood to turn him into a superior kind of savage; in the Western imagination the Red Indian is indeed the main candidate for the role of the Noble Savage, with the Polynesian as his only rival among the brown races. Similarly when classifying women by the colour of their hair the fiery redhead stands outside the scale from virginally innocent blond to sultry and dangerous brunette. When doubt arises as to whether the yellow races are after all less clever than the white, this is counterbalanced by crediting them with an evil subtlety contrasting with our own honest enlightenment. The albino of course presents no difficulty. He belongs to the second series, because it is logically impossible for the whiter than the best to be better, and because his complexion is in any case against nature.

We may notice how loosely the colour classifications fit, compared with binary oppositions. Naming is by contrast within the scheme rather than by adequacy to the object. The Mongol is to the eye often whiter than the Caucasian, American Indians are red because the brown people live in Asia and Polynesia. The ease with which one classifies peoples, indeed *sees* them as they are conventionally supposed to be coloured, helps one to understand why schemes in other cultures, which to ourselves seem obviously artificial, are so resistant to conflicting observation. We may add that our more complex second structure lacks the firm lines of the first, leaving scope to expand it and make it looser still. The single association we have bracketed after each colour does not of course exhaust its significance, which is multiple, indefinite, and variable between individuals even in Western culture; thus red (bloodshed, fire) threatens to burst out of its allotted place to join black in the compartment for destructive vitality. It may be noticed that other cultures seem sometimes to be applying some approximation to the second structure where we prefer the first; thus for the Chinese the colour for mourning the dead is not black but white, and the Hawaiians call the white man *Haole* ('breathless, lifeless').

From Kepler we have travelled to a level of the mind half way back to Pavlov's dog, tracing a structural affinity between all three. "Black" becomes a pure metonym for "Evil", reducing to identity a connexion which even the most ardent racialist would not consciously maintain to be causal. There could be no clearer reminder that we cannot trust correlative thinking without rational tests. This does not however discredit as irrational correlative thinking as such. The thinking which leads to "Darkness : ignorance :: light : knowledge" does not change its nature in proceeding to "Black man : ignorance :: white man :

knowledge". It is when the syntagmatic relations are formulated in propositions and tested that the former turns out to be rational and the latter irrational; analysis confirms that there is a causal connexion between darkness and ignorance of one's surroundings but not between a black skin and low intelligence. In the former case there is nothing irrational even about the rhetorical use of light and darkness as metonyms of knowledge and ignorance.

An activity in which correlative thinking breaks away from such systems is creation and appreciation in the arts. Even those who identify the correlative with pre-scientific thinking still acknowledge its relevance to Beauty if not to Truth. Indeed, as science progresses artists seem to become more rather than less inclined to the primitivism for which they are excused. Baudelaire's *Les correspondances* is a sonnet about correlative thinking itself, Rimbaud's on the colours of the vowels is explicitly an exercise in it; and both verses were founding documents of the Symbolist movement from which modernism in poetry began. Yeats's prolonged maturation as a poet is a demonstration that a fine mind can, not deteriorate, but flourish on the degenerate systems of occultism. The function of correlative thinking in the arts is not, however, a mere matter of weaving beautiful patterns disconnected from things as they are. Remote as it is from scientific thinking, it may be seen as itself a criticism of correlative system-building, a revision of fossillised chains of oppositions in the light of closer scrutiny of the object. It takes another course than the scientific by retaining that "Between" where the observer interacts with the rest, not excluding the subjective response, not abjuring metaphor and metonym, but far from reverting to primitivism it re-patterns experience by a style of thinking more fluid, intricate, and finely discriminating than any other. It tells its own kind of truth by revealing how one does spontaneously, therefore genuinely, react in the fullest awareness of a concrete situation. However, its structure does not cease to be that which we have been analysing, a point we may illustrate from Conrad's story *Heart of Darkness*. We pick out from its texture a minor strand which relates aptly to previous illustrations leading back to "yang/yin", "Light/darkness".

Conrad's story dissolves conceptual schemes by starting from an opposition between concrete scenes, "River Thames/River Congo", and letting the chain take its own course whether in accord with or against the conflicting oppositions "white : black :: good : evil", "colourful : pale :: life : death", integrating with both in an intricate new pattern.

A	B
Thames	Congo
Gloom	Sun
City	Jungle
Civilized	Savage
Artificial	True
Progress	The primaeval
Clarity	Mystery
White	Black

This reordering chain allows comparison between A and B to suggest a deeper similarity between Europe and Africa underlying the manifest contrasts (a city is like as well as unlike a jungle). The "light/darkness" opposition introduced in the title of the story settles into place only when A and B intermingle.

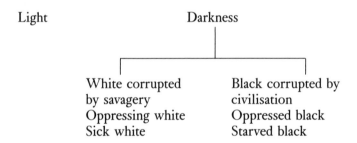

Light   Darkness

White corrupted   Black corrupted by
by savagery   civilisation
Oppressing white   Oppressed black
Sick white   Starved black

The simple "black/white" of the races adjusts in the course of the story to the complex "bronze/ivory", the bronze skins of the tribe at the end of the journey allying them with both sun and night (with the foremost tribesmen painted red), and the hairless head of the sick Kurtz become ivory, the dead matter from a living animal in pursuit of which he has lost his soul. As for the "Between", it is the narrator beginning his story in the calm evening light in a boat between river and sea, from a viewpoint which embraces a further opposition detaching moral from physical complexion ("African : European :: ancient Briton : Roman").

A	B	*Between*
Audience	Kurtz	Narrator
England	Unnamed destination	Mouth of Thames
Dazzle	Darkness	Calm light
Day	Night	Evening

(The unnamed destination is the zero of linguistics, meaningful by contrast.)

We may see thinking in the arts as intermediate between the pre-consciousness of "white : black :: good : evil" and the full consciousness of explicit schemes of correspondences, yin-yang or Kepler's. Artists of course vary greatly in the extent to which they analyse their own effects, which like the extent to which scientists' creative thinking is correlative belongs to biography and not to the appreciation of their work. One does not, in analysing *Heart of Darkness*, care whether Conrad himself would have agreed that he was contrasting bronze bodies with the ivory head of Kurtz.

The arts can develop, clarify, and intensify awareness at any or every level, sharpening sense impressions, vivifying imagination, waking to unnoticed similarities, loosing correlation from conventional schemes, educating the incipient simulation by which we understand persons from within—analysing too, but never like philosophy and science uprooting the logical from its bedding in other kinds of thinking. They have the further advantage that they free valuation from dependence on dubiously grounded or arbitrarily chosen standards, by allowing the objects of awareness to stimulate motivations to action directly, motivations which, by the logic of our quasi-syllogism, can be judged solely by the degree of awareness. The arts since the nineteenth century have emerged as the indispensable guide to the experiences and attitudes evaluable as good in themselves, a resource unnecessarily endangered by the recent failure of nerve which tends to reduce structuralist and deconstructive techniques to tools for value-free analysis, or else puts them in the service of standards imported from liberationist politics. For those of us who deny to the religions the propositional truth with which we credit the sciences, mythic world-pictures will have to be judged by some of the same tests of awareness. It does not follow, however, that myth is wholly assimilable to the arts which are so often its vehicles. The arts teach individuals how to respond to particular situations, by evoking a heightened awareness of imaginary instances; myth teaches a community how to respond to the basic and constant in the world in which it finds itself.

This is not to deny that literary fictions may themselves grow into myths, such as the stories of Faust and of Don Juan, rebels against the divine order who come to embody the positive values of post-Renaissance individualism, through successive reworkings by genera-tions of dramatists and composers. Might one think of *Heart of Darkness* as a modern myth? It is not, however, enough that a work of fiction resembles a myth in telling a tale which can enhance awareness yet cannot be pinned down to propositional truths, and can have a lasting effect on how we feel and are moved to act in situations outside the tale. Admittedly the arts have taken over much of the function of myth in the modern world. Among readers of English, *Heart of Darkness* may be identified as one of the major influences on the dark side of twentieth-century sensibility; thus T. S. Eliot put a quotation from it under the title of *The Hollow Men,* and another at the head of the original manuscript of *The Wasteland.* A myth, however, is a tale which, like history, is independent of the words in which it is told, even if there is a scriptural version by which each telling is to be judged; it is a pattern of images, not like a literary fiction a pattern of words. The story of *Heart of Darkness* hardly exists without Conrad's words, a point well illustrated by the failed attempt to re-tell it in the film *Apocalypse Now.* A further difference is that, little as may be the factual information to discipline its fantasies, myth imagines, not purely fictitious events, but the crucial events in the formation of the community and its cosmos, the origin, the changes and sometimes the end of the universe, and of mankind, the community itself and its institutions and resources. In this too when imagining the past it resembles history, and for comparatively recent events may contain genuinely historical vestiges, such as a people's original homeland; among the various kinds of simulation by which we orientate ourselves through different viewpoints and perspectives, it is a simulation of memory. It does not, like science, describe objectively the forces independent of man's will, to put them at his disposal as means, but relates him to them subjectively, as sacred or obscene powers acting on him for good or ill. The need which it satisfies is like, not a scientist's curiosity, but a foundling's for the names of his true father and mother—the need to root oneself in community and cosmos, recover the continuity of self and other. In *Genesis,* the *Theogony,* the *Kojiki,* the heterogeneous myths told in a culture are organised in a history strung on a genealogy coming down from the origin of the world to the tribes and ruling houses of today. The genealogies so boring to the modern Bible-reader would have meant as much as the stories of divine revelation and intervention to the ancient Hebrew locating himself in his cosmos, like those in the *Popol Vuh* to the Maya: "First we shall name the genealogy of the lordship. It began, from just one root, at the origin of the root of the day and the night. Jaguar Night, first grandfather and father. Coacul and Coacutec, in the second generation. . . . Lord Cotuna, in the eleventh generation. Don Cristobal, as he was called, became lord in the presence of the Castilian people. Don Pedro de Robles is Lord Minister today".[7]

The stories, like Conrad's and like the sentences of speech, proceed without exposing to view the correlations which guide them. We shall, however, follow Lévi-Strauss (although not the detail of his methods) in searching for an underlying structure, taking as example the story of the Garden of Eden. It may be objected that we should work, like Lévi-Strauss, from the raw myths of pre-literate cultures, not from organised literary mythologies. But the myth of Eden, being so deeply rooted in our own tradition, is sufficiently comprehensible to us to forbid the totally wrong-headed interpretations of which one may be guilty when a culture is viewed from outside. We need, however, to detach the story in *Genesis* from the later theological doctrine of the Fall of Man. It is a story rather like the Prometheus myth; man has stolen something from Jehovah, is still being punished for it, but has kept what he stole. Any doctrine derived from a myth will be like the moral drawn from a work of fiction, which so often, even if stated explicitly in the story itself, seems a simplification or distortion of the complex and nuanced approvals and disapprovals which it evokes.

The Eden myth relates the man of the present, who knows and chooses between good and bad, to his origin as a still spontaneous being wholly moved by the sacred power which gave him life, the power personified as Jehovah. The contrast between origin and present activates a chain of oppositions, guided both by the initial need to distinguish the desired from the disliked and by the observed contrasts and contiguities which act back on and modify preferences, so that both origin and present come to be seen as mixing advantage and disadvantage.

Chain 1

Origin	*Present*
Child	Adult
Ignorance	Knowledge
Innocence	Sexuality
Nature	Culture
Abundance	Lack
Carelessness	Care
Ease	Labour
⋮	⋮

Imagination following this chain pictures the origin as the Garden of Eden inhabited by the first man and woman, Adam and Eve, living without reflection according to the will of Jehovah. Eden has the same relation to the chain as have yin and yang to theirs; to be in Eden is to be child not adult, ignorant not knowing, natural not cultured. . . . But if this chain inclines us to prefer ignorance (ignorance : knowledge : : carelessness : care . . .) there is another which attracts us to knowledge.

Chain 2

Master	*Servant*
The sacred	The human
Ruler	Subject
Man	Woman
Power	Weakness
Knowledge	Ignorance
⋮	⋮

Humanity, in coming to know, substitutes itself for the sacred in Chain 2, and therefore lack, care, and labour for abundance, carelessness, and ease with knowledge for ignorance in Chain 1. This primal event is imagined as the story of a disobedience; Adam and Eve disobeyed Jehovah by eating of the Tree of the Knowledge of Good and Evil, the single tree of which he denied them the fruit, and were punished by man's toil on the land and woman's pains of childbirth and subjection to her husband. The first sign of their knowledge is that they cover themselves, conscious of their bodies as arousing desire. The step from spontaneous performance to the knowledge of desires which one may have to resist is thus through sexual self-consciousness, activating a further chain guided by the male assumption that the fault is always the woman's.

Chain 3

Tempted	*Tempter*
Nature as sacred	Nature as obscene
Human	Animal
Innocence	Sexuality
Ignorance	Knowledge
Woman	Phallus
Man	Woman
⋮	⋮

The tempter who is animal and phallus arousing woman (we shall allow ourselves one Freudian symbol), yet has knowledge, is imagined as the serpent, "more subtil than any beast of the field". Nature as origin (Chain 1) and the nature which tempts us from our origin have been distinguished by identifying them respectively with Eden and the serpent. So the serpent tempts Eve to eat the forbidden fruit, Eve tempts Adam, Jehovah punishes them with the miseries of Chain 1, Eve also with the subjection to the husband of Chain 2. However, by eating of the Tree of Knowledge they have become like gods. Jehovah, fearful for his power, expels them from the garden to stop them eating of the Tree of Life and becoming immortal like himself. Humanity in stealing knowledge does take over part of the power belonging to the sacred.

The correlations spring from the desires and aversions of the males in ancient Israel, which lead them to divide their world into the liked things and the disliked and to compare and connect them, a classification which, as chains interact or adjust to observation, stimulates more complex reactions. The new valuations, judged by our quasi-syllogism, will be better to the extent that the classification has indeed brought imaginers of the myth to a fuller awareness of their world; and the myth will remain valuable to ourselves to the extent that it throws an oblique light on the world as seen from our own perspective. In principle, then, mythopoeia can assist correlative thinking in its discovery of one's world and how to live in it; but does this myth in fact do so? Rational criticism will retain the function, not of discrediting the myth as history, but of testing the awareness which it reflects. Thus the assumption in Chain 3 that it is woman whose lust inflames man rather than man who seduces woman is not confirmed by disinterested observation. Nor of course can we accept our sufferings as being literally a deserved punishment for disobedience without acknowledging a personal power above us who actually exists. This, however, belongs to theology rather than to the myth, where the disobedience is not a sin against an almighty God but the successful usurpation of one of the powers of Jehovah, who "walking in the garden in the cool of the day" is on the same level of reality or unreality as Adam and Eve. We may abstract from it as its basic message that knowledge, which once acquired is irreversible, has made humanity greater, but also abolishes spontaneous well-being and leads as necessary consequence to a life of care and toil; metaphorically we are punished for it, as shifting the metaphor we might be said to pay for it.

Interpreting the myth, any number of such messages spring to mind from the comparisons and connexions of the underlying structure. As further truths or errors embodied in the myth we might cite 'Knowledge brings power and ignorance weakness' and 'Man has a sacred right to rule over woman', but it is we ourselves who have sharpened the contrasts between our columns and the contiguities within them, and have affirmed in sentence-form. Each proposition says more than does the myth, the saying of which is just the telling of the tale; on the other hand propositions never exhaust the myth. The telling suggests an indefinite number of commonplace or profound truths and errors. In comparison with the precision of analytic thinking, the correlative thinking behind the myth is of course inherently loose, never defining the respects in which the horizontally paired are similar or contrasted and the vertically paired are contiguous or remote, or distinguishing between the subjective and the objective pressures which shape the classification. We easily concede "Child : adult :: ignorance : knowledge :: nature : culture", not so easily "Sacred : human :: ruler : subject", or even that such a correlation makes sense to us. It indeed makes no sense if one cannot conceive the sacred without postulating a personal God like the Jehovah of the myth, and denies his existence as one denies the historical existence of Adam and Eve. But just as Adam and Eve represent the childhood of man and woman, Jehovah represents the power which brought them into existence and continues to activate them until they discover how to choose, an unquestionable reality which for objective description is a constellation of physical and psychological forces. There is, however, something about objective knowledge which obstructs a subjective recognition that our choices are between directions in which we are being moved by conflicting forces from outside ourselves. The present example of mythic thinking is of especial interest for the relating of different kinds of thinking; in responding to the story of Eden we find ourselves viewing knowledge itself from a wider perspective than if we confine ourselves to analytic thinking alone. The analytic remains imprisoned in itself, seems to start from itself, forgetting its dependence on spontaneous correlation for its concepts and on spontaneous motivations for its prescriptions. It can arrive objectively at the conclusion that its own operations depend causally on preceding conditions in and outside the organism, but inhibits the subjective awareness that the boundary between self and other is indefinite and fluctuating, and that much of what one does is done—or happens—*through* oneself rather than originating in one's own decisions. When this inhibition is suspended, a judgment as sacred or obscene of the spontaneous and only partially controllable forces which elevate or degrade us has the same validity as the judgment of a voluntary act as good or bad, and there really is a sense in which "Sacred : human :: ruler : subject".

The myth tells us disparate things not all of which may be welcome to us, that knowledge is good, that it does partially supersede spontaneity and make men like gods, yet it is inherent in it to do us harm as well as benefit—and once we have it the effect is irreversible. Here again, analytic thinking can arrive at such conclusions as that we could never have learned to travel to the planets without also becoming able to invent the nuclear, chemical, and bacterial weapons which may annihilate us. Confined within its own limits, however, it can see its own progress only as an unmixed good. Even when it acknowledges the dangers, it ascribes them to human irrationality and destructiveness rather than to itself. Yet even if mankind were almost perfectly rational and moral, now that a supreme exercise of reason has invented the weaponry, it will require just one lapse of judgment in a million years for us to destroy ourselves. Our quasi-syllogism requires us to seek full awareness of the factors relevant to a particular issue, but by no means obliges us to expand awareness in general whatever the cost; the pursuit of some line of research itself presents such an issue, to be decided by whether in awareness of the possible consequences hopes outweigh fears.[8] From a modern perspective the myth may suggest to us that the greatness of modern civilization cannot be that it is certain to make us happier, rather that it has embarked on a tremendous adventure, a Faustian enterprise now irreversible like the expulsion from Eden, such that it may with equal probability lead to universal plenty or universal destruction. It is the restricted perspective of the pure analytic thinker which has allowed rationalism since the eighteenth century to indulge the thought of inevitable progress, always suspect to those intelligent in more ways than merely being logical. Is it perhaps more truly rational to think that the great revolutions in history, from hunting-and-gathering to settled agriculture, or from agrarian to industrial civilization, have indissolubly united regress with progress, and that there is never any guarantee of a Hegelian-Marxist synthesis by which the lost at one stage is recovered at the next? We may even suspect that the first imaginers of Eden stood in the same relation to the former revolution that we do to the latter. The myth may well have originated at a time when the early agriculturists had not quite lost the memory of a freer life in which you picked the fruit from the trees instead of tilling the soil.

222

A great myth, like a great poem, not only evokes awareness of disparate things, it also compels us to respond to all of them simultaneously. The Eden story excites a compound reaction from which analysis can isolate, for example, regret for the lost paradise, awe at man's newly discovered powers, hope for an unknowable future, resignation to the inevitable cost. Reactions to the myth itself are much more complex than to a formulated doctrine of the Fall of Man, which would seem, if abstracted from the myth, to have the degrading implication that a carefree childishness is man's perfect state. But the ends to which we find ourselves spontaneously drawn in the fullest awareness—the most rational, the best—emerge from just such complex reactions fully articulable only by poetry or myth. Analytic thinking can discover, clarify, and confirm the separate facts involved, but to co-ordinate reactions to them requires their simultaneous correlation, a task for which we are educated by the arts and by the mythic element in the religions.

NOTES

1. Cf. pp. 62–63 above.
2. E. H. Gombrich, *Art and Illusion* (London: Phaidon Press, 1960), 314f.
3. Cf. pp. 22–23 above.
4. Cf. ch. 12 below.
5. Cf. *DT*, 136, 213, 239f, 243.
6. Johannes Kepler, *Epitome of Copernican Astronomy*, Books 4 and 5, trans. Charles Glenn Wallis, *Great Books of the World*, vol. 16 (Chicago: University of Chicago Press, 1952), 853.
7. *Popol Vuh: The Mayan Book of the Dawn of Life*, trans. Dennis Tedlock (New York: Simon & Schuster, 1985), 225.
8. This point is obscured if the imperative in the quasi-syllogism is condensed to "Be aware", as in my original formulation of it. Cf. p. 27 n. 1 above.

Bataille as Myth-Maker and as Philosopher of Value

12

One of the standard approaches to establishing a universal foundation for values is to identify an end supposedly common to all mankind, such as pleasure for ethical hedonists and power for Nietzsche. These prove on reflection to be tautological; whatever your ends, you want the power to achieve them and are pleased if you do. To the extent that the hedonist or Nietzschean fills this empty formula with a content, we see that he is merely trying to force his own perspective on the rest of us. But in any case, if the purpose is to escape relativism, it is a mistake to assume that we have to discover ends common to all and guaranteed, if not by divine revelation or pure reason, then by factual generalisations about the nature of man. If Nietzsche escapes relativism, it is by basing his Order of Rank among values on the wider or narrower perspectives which channel conscious or unconscious drives.[1] If with increasing experience, or access to more facts, or growing sensitivity from other viewpoints, I say, "Now I *see* that I shouldn't have done it", that "seeing" need not be taken either as direct intuition into value or as the result of inference from ends to means which leaves the end still unsupported, it reports the discovery of how I do find myself reacting now that I am aware of more; viewing from a wider perspective is inseparable from seeing better how to act. We can, admittedly with less confidence than an absolutist would desire, measure our valuations against those of others by the relative scope of our perspectives, without demanding that perspectives and valuations be the same as our own.

There is, however, another proposal of a universal end which, without escaping these objections, has the virtue of saying something truly surprising which sets one thinking in new directions. Georges Bataille (1897–1962), a thinker and writer loosely associated with the Surrealists, maintained that the ultimate purpose, not only of producing commodities, but of life and its reproduction, must be their consumption without further purpose, pure destruction and self-destruction as glorious and aimless as the blazing of the sun—the goal beyond all others is death itself. In *La notion de dépense* (1933) he identified "activities which have their end in themselves" as those leading to *"loss,* which must be as great as possible for the activity to assume its full meaning", among which he lists "luxury, mourning, wars, cults, the building of sumptuary monuments, games, spectacles, the arts, sexual activity when perverse (that is, deflected from its genital goal)".[2] In this early formulation of Bataille's position we meet the usual difficulty at the start. It is a tautology that what is done for its own sake is done without regard for productive consequences. But we also do things both for their own sakes and for a further end, such as satisfying work which we would have chosen even if it paid much less; and even when we act with complete disregard for consequences, whether the result is gain or loss is accidental. For lovemaking to "have its end in itself" rather than in the gain to society or family of a new member, it is enough that one does not care whether it impregnates, or that the prospect of a child is part of the joy; there is no need, as the formulation just quoted seems to suggest, to confine oneself even against one's tastes to sodomy or flagellation. Someone is enjoying his dinner without further purpose if he is wholly absorbed in flavours without thought of calories or vitamins, he does not have to refuse all but unnutritious foods. Bataille tries to close the gap between disregard of gain and direct pursuit of loss by insisting that even in the former case one necessarily dissipates energies or things—the consumption of the commodities we produce, spending of the money we earn, exhaustion of energies in sex or in play. But there is no direct relation between preservation or loss and treatment as means or as end; energy is expended in work as in play, artwork and jewels like precision tools are carefully cleaned and guarded from damage, and industrial dynamite like fireworks is exploded in one burst.

Bataille's paradoxical claim that activities valuable in themselves aim at loss "which must be as great as possible" derives from combining the logic of value judgments with his very interesting psychological and sociological observations, and also with a Romantic identification of value with intensity in defiance of the Classical preference for the Golden Mean. Central to it is the conception of sexuality developed in *L'érotisme* (1957),[3] as straining towards an intensity which would dissolve the self in unconsciousness and disrupt the body in death. To understand how Bataille arrived at this position we have to start from his earliest book *L'anus solaire* (1927, not published until 1931), and the undated manuscripts of *L'oeil pinéal* in which he comments on it a little later.[4] The manuscripts lay down a principle which continued to underlie his work. A representation of the world which finds room for the subjective side of man must be a mythic one sharply distinguished from the scientific, springing from the desires but strictly respecting the objective facts. This principle he seems never to have abandoned, although the increasing factual content of his later work makes it easy to lose sight of it. It makes Bataille a refreshing exception among myth-makers; more usually, and not only in religion, myth-makers take their myths for objective facts and try to tack them on to the rest of objective knowledge.

> Philosophy until now, as has science, has been an expression of human subordination, and when man seeks to represent himself, no longer as a moment of a homogeneous process, of a necessitous and pitiable process—but as a new rupture inside a disrupted nature, it is no longer the leveling phraseology issuing from his understanding which can help him; he can no more recognise himself in the degrading chains of logic, but on the contrary—not only in anger but in an ecstatic torment—in the virulence of his phantasms.[5]

We require then a "mythological representation" of the world, for which there are two conditions. (1):

> Methodical knowledge can be set aside only so far as it has become an acquired faculty, since, at least in the circumstances of today, without a strict contact with the homogeneous world of practical life, the free play of intelligible images would be lost and would fatally dissipate in a region where no thought or word would be of the least consequence.

> One must then start by reducing science to a state definable as subordination, so that one disposes of it freely, like a beast of burden, for ends which are not its own.[6]

If it were freed from this subordination, "nothing could stop science from blindly emptying the world of its human content"; we must follow and respect it as far as it can take us, but our thought must cross "these external limits of another existence to their content lived mythologically".

(2) There must be no mistaking mythology for science, as in the religions which science itself has now discredited.

> The exclusion of mythology by reason is necessarily a rigorous exclusion from which there is no return and which there may be occasion to mark even more distinctly, but at the same time one must reverse the values created by this exclusion, that is to say *the fact that there is no content valid for reason in a mythological series is the condition of its significative value.*[7]

The reason for this reversal is that "when the affective violence of human intelligence is projected like a spectre", it has no representational content except that given it by the closure of science against it.

> A spectral content truly exists only from the moment when the environment which contains it defines itself by intolerance of what appears in it as a crime. As far as science is concerned, its repulsion, the strongest imaginable, is necessary to the qualification of the excluded part. Such a qualification should be compared to the affective charge of an obscene element, which is such only by reason of the prohibition pronounced against it. Until the formal exclusion takes place, a mythic statement can still be assimilated to a rational statement, it can be described as real and methodically explicated. But at the same time it loses its spectral qualification, its freedom to be false.[8]

In what sense the mythic is false worries Bataille, as can be seen by notes to the manuscript. A disjointed scrap tries out the Surrealist concept of the super-real: "Parallel of the woman loved and the real woman. Say that to introduce mythological thought is simply to introduce the infra- and super-reality of the woman loved".[9]

A longer note says that "false" is not in this usage the opposite of "true", and makes the point that all representation is, to intrude a word not in Bataille's vocabulary, "underdetermined" by the object.

> ... the falsity thus envisaged cannot be basically an attribute of being as considered by metaphysics; it is only one of the inevitable forms of representation (which ought to be studied like any other part of science); but it must not be forgotten that an approximate and *general* adequation of representation to object remains *in fact* the fundamental postulate of thought (despite all the modern efforts which aimed, but vainly, at the strictest adequation).[10]

His final point is that science, having split the pre-scientific conception of the universe in two, developing the practical side of it into "a useful instrument for man's material life", and detaching the imaginative side for elimination, has in effect liberated the mythopoeic frenzy from the bonds of religion, so that "naked and lewd, it has the universe and its laws to play with as its toys."[11]

Plainly an approach so personal risks being unintelligible without some autobiography, and Bataille later leaked some relevant details, not necessarily reliable[12]—the obscene horrors of both his parents' last years, flight from the advancing Germans in 1914, his devout Catholicism afterwards until 1920. We know of his contacts with the Surrealists in the 1920s and of a breakdown of some sort and psychoanalysis leading to *L'anus solaire* and the erotic fantasy *Histoire de l'oeil* (1928). In particular his works expose his sexual idiosyncrasy, that secret which—even if it is only an idiosyncratic degree of repression—we so often have to divine to make full sense of a thinker or writer's values. What animates his thought is the conflict between his former Christianity and a sado-masochistic sensibility focussed on coprophilia and not excited by coitus; his starting-point is the datum that the experience which for him has the highest intensity is by Christian standards evil and by most standards dirty. He values above all the eruption, the excretion, which bursts the homogeneous order of reason and morality and defiles its affected purity. In *Histoire de l'oeil* his erotic imagination evokes scenes of orgiastically polluting with bodily fluids an egg, the open eyes of a corpse, a bull's testicle, and at the sacrilegious climax the gouged eyeball of a murdered priest; one can experience the extraordinary tension of these images without perceiving, until one reads his essay *Oeil* (1929), that each

229

disguises the watching and judging eye of God. A remark of the narrator throws light on his early mythology:

> But from that time I was no longer in any doubt; I did not love what are called "pleasures of the flesh", because they always prove to be insipid; I loved only what is classed as "filthy". . . . Debauch as I know it soils not only my body and thoughts but everything I can conceive in course of it, I mean the whole starry universe which is no more than the backcloth.[13]

The interest of the mythology he developed in 1927, during his mental illness, is the startling contrast between the compulsive fantasy, not poetic frivolity but near to becoming a delusional system, and the science which his lucid intelligence strives almost successfully to reconcile with it; it is an extreme case of a single mind viewing the same phenomena from opposite directions. The mythology centres on the sun, the volcano, and the pineal gland, each imagined as an anus pouring out excrement. His diagnosis of what is wrong with man is that in the course of evolution he has, like the plants, erected himself as a phallus towards the sun which he longs to become, yet cannot relinquish the horizontal and earthbound vision of his four-footed ancestors, and has eyes which cannot bear to look at the sun directly. The pineal gland on the top of the head is a third eye which in the course of man's further evolution will some day, in an agonised and ecstatic convulsion, burst out of the skull towards the sun overhead. This last fancy obsessed Bataille at the time, although he understood its physical impossibility. "I was not mad, but admittedly conceded too much to the necessity of escaping somehow from the limits of our human experience".[14] He omitted it from *L'anus solaire*.

In the mythic cosmos of *L'anus solaire* the motion of everything is monotonous, either round and round (rotating earth, planetary systems) or else in-out or up-down in coitus (the tide in coitus with the moon, the generations of upstanding and withering plants with the sun), in an interaction compared to wheel and piston on a locomotive. Life is born from the coitus of sun and sea and goes on repeating itself by reproduction; man and woman inertly copulate, get up in the morning and lie down at night. Erupting from this dull order and scandalising it are erection, sun, the corpse and the dark, from all of which man averts his eyes. Bataille, scorning the placid fecundity of the waters and of heaven (the relation of which to sun is not clarified), sides with the sterile erotic convulsions of the earth, and declares himself the volcano, anus of the earth, throwing up excrement and spreading death and terror. The force of eruption is accumulating below in the Communist workers, who will rise and butcher the sexless bourgeois who think them as vile as man's private parts. Disasters, revolutions, and volcanoes are the revolts of earth against heaven and its fecundity. "I am Vesuvius, unclean parody of the torrid and blinding sun".[15]

Later manuscripts examine human biology, and contrast unfavourably the organism's controlled and purposeful appropriation of food, water, and air with the convulsive excreting of faeces, urine, sperm, vomit, and tears under pressures outside the agent's control. It is in the horror and attraction of these decaying substances thrown off from us by forces independent of our will that we discover the wholly other, the "sacred".[16] This word, which enters his vocabulary in 1930,[17] has for Bataille the double sense of Latin *sacer* "holy/accursed". A trace of his former Christianity has revived, although in a suitably debased form. In his detailed proposals deriving secular institutions from appropriation, which makes homogeneous with the appropriator, and sacred from excretion, the rupture with the heterogeneous, Bataille is no longer generating myth from existing science, but doing his own science from, as he was later to put it, "a viewpoint such that the results of sociology can appear as replies to the most virile concerns, not to a specialised scientific preoccupation".[18] One sees that on his account myth and science must in any case converge in the study of man himself; sociology resists a purely objective approach because of "the character necessarily contagious and *activist* of the representations which the work elucidates".[19]

L'apprenti sorcier (1938) makes a new attempt to distinguish myth from science, art, and political Utopias and to clarify its relation to reality. He now starts from the existentialist position he had developed in other directions in *Sacrifices* (1936). Reality as understood by science has no place for "I", yet that reality appears shallow compared with my own existence. Far from being dismissed as unacknowledgeable by science, "profound existence ought to be projected into the illusion which encloses it".[20] Men are diminished by "the reduction of their existence to the state of servile organ",[21] for example, to such social functions as scientist, artist, or politician. They discover "true being", the "plenitude of existence", only when they suspend calculations of utility, and explanation by science, to confront the chance configurations of circumstance with the free play of their fears and desires, opening up a prospect which is not law but "destiny". (This ontological language is alien to the approach of this book, but the argument could be restated in terms of awareness: practical life contracts awareness to the useful aspects of things and relates them by the causality which links means to end: with the intensification of awareness when freed from dependence on utility we live in a subjectively heightened reality, in which conjunctions of chance outside us open up to awareness the "destined" path for spontaneity within.) For the episodes of fullness of being which give meaning to the rest of life, people require not scientific concepts but a mythology setting them in motion by 'images of destiny' exciting hope and fear. Here Bataille takes up the formerly discarded "parallel of the woman loved and the real woman". The woman imagined when a unique conjunction of circumstance confronts with the promise and risk of an adventure into the unknown is at first an illusory image floating outside the everyday world where the real woman lives; it becomes real only when the real woman responds ("each of them having assumed the impelling figure of the other's destiny") and they act out their desires. "The sudden apparition of a woman seems to belong to the disordered world of dream; but possession throws the dream figure naked and drowned in pleasures into the strictly real world of a bedroom".[22] Within the sterile world of everyday, the accord of lovers creates a miniature world with fullness of being. "The world of lovers is constructed, like life, starting from *a chance combination giving the response awaited by an avid and potent will to be*".[23]

Myths, which "bring existence 'to its boiling-point'", have a similar function in transforming a concatenation of individuals into a "world" with fullness of being. But for fantasy to become myth, as the image of destiny for a community, requires the same two conditions as before. On the one hand, just as "the encounter with a woman would be only an aesthetic emotion without the will to possess her and make true what her apparition seemed to signify",[24] so myth needs ritual enaction ("It would be fiction if the *accord* which a *people* displays in the agitation of festivals did not make of it the vital human reality").[25] On the other, there must be a sharing: "An 'avid and potent will to be' is therefore the condition of truth; but the *isolated individual* never possesses the power to create a world (he tries it only if himself in the power of forces which make of him a madman, *alienated*); the coincidence of wills is no less necessary to the birth of human worlds than the coincidence of chance configurations."[26]

By this period Bataille's personal mythology no longer displayed its coprophiliac roots but still opposed earth with its volcanic energies to the frigidity of heaven, affirming man against God, freedom against authority, tragic ecstasy against salvation, violence against order, life intensified by precipitation towards death against reason and morality, the body against the head. In his journal *Acéphale* (1936–39), disillusioned with politics by the rise of Fascism and the authoritarian outcome of revolutionary Communism, he defends Nietzsche against his misinterpretation by Fascism, which substitutes for a gratuitous a purposeful violence in the service of the nation-state (bourgeois democracy, of course, he had always despised). He finds his image of destiny in the headless figure Acéphale, with fire and sword in its hands, "who unites in a single eruption birth and death", neither god nor man and "not me but more me than me",[27] drawn for the journal by the artist André Masson, one of the apostates from the Surrealist circle who had gravitated to Bataille. Its picture in the first number has an accompanying legend: "Acéphale is the earth. The earth under the crust of soil is incandescent fire. The man who imagines under his feet the incandescence of the earth bursts into flame. An ecstatic conflagration will destroy the fatherlands. When the human heart becomes fire and steel man will escape from his head like a condemned man from prison".[28]

But where in the disintegrated communities of the present can a myth be acted out to make it real? *L'apprenti sorcier* ends with Bataille's answer: a secret society. He did in fact found such a society, of which little has come to light except that it seems to have been an embarrassing failure for all concerned. That Acéphale was to enter reality, in the manner of which he had theorised, is shown by a mysterious manuscript, "Instructions for the 'encounter' in the forest", a detailed guide to members for a journey on an unspecified date, in the greatest secrecy, to a lightning-blasted tree trunk in an unnamed forest. "It is possible to recognise in this tree the mute presence of what has taken the name of Acéphale", for whoever has "the will to seek and to encounter a presence which would fill our life with reason to be".[29] "This ENCOUNTER to be *attempted* in the forest will occur in reality to the extent that death will show through. To go before this presence is to wish to throw off the covering by which our death is hidden from us". Acéphale, who as image of destiny is so far only a picture by a Surrealist, will become "present" to the participants in the rite if their own deaths become real to them. One may wonder how far Bataille, a cautious man clinging to the security of his librarian's job and publishing his more outrageous works pseudonymously, was ready to go in the orgiastic rites which his mythology would demand. It appears that he projected a human sacrifice—for him the supremely sacred rite—but failed to bring it off. Judging by a detail divulged by Roger Caillois, he was not himself going to wield the knife: "Would you believe it? It was easier to find a willing victim than well-meaning sacrificer".[30]

Let us return to *La notion de dépense* (1933), the text from which we started. Bataille equates activity valuable for itself with loss, waste, destruction, the inherently unproductive dissipation of energies and resources, such as "sexual activity when deflected from its genital goal", because for him the experience of highest intensity is the unproductive spending of semen and excrement. No philosophy of value claiming universality can ever have been launched from more restricted and exceptional a viewpoint. It offers us the most extreme test case since Sade for the viability of an uncompromising relativism. Shall we say simply that Bataille's vision of life is as valid or invalid as anyone else's, and that he has as much right to affirm it as another has to burn him at the stake for it? (There can be no moral basis in relativism for demanding tolerance.) Or should we respond by renouncing all formulations of an objective order, whether scientific, moral, or political, as essentially self-alienating, and prefer the voice of madness, whether in Sade, Artaud, or Bataille, as the truest voice, our only deliverer from the suffocating prison in which subjectivity and creativity languish and wither? This would not be relativism but a new absolutism; it assumes an ultimate chaos which objectivising strives to tame, and the superiority of the despairingly defiant rebel who alone remains faithful to it. Such is in any case not Bataille's own position; he is a rationaliser of the irrationality of nature and of man, a systematiser in search of a new reconciliation of the claims of objectivity and subjectivity, satisfying our criteria for an "anti-rationalism" which is not "irrationalism". But in the struggle to understand Bataille, both relativism and absolutism have to be renounced for perspectivism. In assuming his viewpoint one introduces it into one's own multi-perspectival view, by what Gadamer calls a "fusion of horizons";[31] and in this fusion, as in seeing a three-dimensional object from different angles, viewpoints are not equally valid or invalid, but informative in varying degrees. If Bataille is peculiar in the way he feels, he is not at all so in the way that his passions drive him to think; if his sociological observations or his theory of myth persuade us, they enter without obstacle our multi-perspectival awareness. As for the destructive urge in his response to the world as he is aware of it, it can enter the multi-perspectival reaction without dominating it, as that of Mephistoph-eles assumes its place in the articulated complex of conflicting tendencies with which we read *Faust*. I cannot avoid judging that to feel differently when increasing awareness has widened my horizon is a further maturation, a change for the better, and that if someone else should become aware of something which I can see he overlooked the change in him would likewise be from his own viewpoint for the better. To the extent that each of us widens his horizon by coming to see from other viewpoints, we advance towards a common fusion of horizons. Any identifiable viewpoint is only one moment in a progress towards a broader view, or regress towards a narrower, or halt for more intensive exploration of where one is—unless of course one stagnates; and the career of Bataille, who could never be accused of that, is a continual progress.

In *La notion de dépense* Bataille is well aware that there can be no resources for man to waste in luxury or play unless he first produces, no lives to sacrifice in wars and cults unless he reproduces (at the biological level, no excrement to expel unless he eats). He recognises that if intensity, which for him is the measure of value, belongs to excitements which are not merely careless of consequence but positively destructive, we face a basic dilemma; society for its survival has to set limits to its own most valuable experiences as irrational and evil, yet utility and morality have ends to serve only to the extent that it finds room for them. Primitive communities understand this better than we do; they bow down before their self-immolating forces as sacred, the source of all their values, but also check them with taboos and channel them into ritually permitted transgressions, such as killing sanctioned as war or sacrifice. Bataille sees the social bond itself as ultimately depending on the self-dissolution of individuals in a common rite of sacrifice, a shared ecstasy at its most intense when the victim is human—human sacrifice remained one of his lasting obsessions. In the modern world, which loses sight of ends in the sordid pursuit of means, the sense of the sacred has faded. But it survives in the terrified attraction to the intensity of Evil rather than the paleness of Good in the *poétes maudits* (Baudelaire, Rimbaud, Lautréamont), a tradition going back to Sade of which Surrealism is the heir and Bataille himself in some sense the theoretician. In his literary studies he accepts the terminology of Good and Evil and does not shrink from the conclusion that the highest value is in Evil, to be distinguished however from the "sordid evil" which is mere selfishness ("Evil, envisaged in the light of a disinterested attraction towards death, differs from the evil the meaning of which is egoistic interest").[32]

> Intensity can be defined as *value* (it is the single positive value), duration as *Good* (it is the general end proposed for virtue). . . . What I call *value* differs then at once from *Good* and from pleasure. Value sometimes coincides with *Good* and sometimes not. It coincides at times with *Evil*. *Value* is situated *beyond Good and Evil*. . . . The very principle of *value* implies that we go "as far as possible". In this connexion, the association with the principle of Good measures the "farthest" of the social body (the extreme point beyond which constituted society cannot advance); the association with the principle of *Evil*, the "farthest" which individuals—or minorities—attain *temporarily*; "farther", no one can go.[33]

The paradox is most acute in the message of Sade; we must both acknowledge him as the single teacher who fully illumines our nature and place in the universe, and execrate him as the denier of the necessary constraints without which man would exterminate himself. Introducing an edition of Sade's *Justine* in 1950, Bataille draws four conclusions from the proposition that sadism is "a sovereign and irreducible part of man", without which he would be devitalised. As in the last quotation, his words are sober and carefully measured; after the Nazi occupation of France he is always attentive to the dangers of evoking the carefree enthusiam for disasters, volcanoes, and revolutions of his first book, while being more conscious than ever of the destructive potentialities of man.

> In the first place the proposition assumes in men an irresistible propensity to destroy and a fundamental accord with the continual and inevitable destruction of everything that is born, grows and wants to endure.
>
> Secondly, it gives to this propensity and to this accord a sort of *divine*, or more precisely *sacred* meaning. It is the desire in us to consume and ruin, to make a conflagration of our resources, and in general the satisfaction we take in consumption, conflagration and ruin, which are characterised as divine or sacred, and which alone decide in us attitudes which are *sovereign*, that is to say gratuitous, without utility, serving only what they are, never subordinated to further consequences.
>
> Thirdly, the proposition implies that a humanity believing itself strange to these attitudes which the first stirring of reason rejects, would be enervated and reduced to a state resembling that of old maids (as does tend to happen in, although not exclusively in, our own time), if it did not behave now and then in a manner diametrically opposed to its principles.
>
> The proposition relates, fourthly, to the necessity for the man of today,— that is, of course, the normal man—to attain *self-consciousness*, to know fully, in order to limit ruinous effects, to what humanity aspires *as sovereign*, to bring about if it suits him these effects, but no longer produce them in greater measure than it wants, and to oppose them resolutely to the extent that it cannot tolerate them.[34]

(Bataille's revulsion against his inextinguishable Catholic past perhaps hid from him that this sounds less like Sade than like his reactionary *mon semblable mon frère* Joseph de Maistre.)

In the post-war writings there is a decisive shift away from death and towards life, not always maintained, but especially marked in his most ambitious and comprehensive work, *La part maudite* (1949), which treats economic production and consumption as an aspect of cosmic process. Here, in contrast with the earlier *La notion de dépense*, the emphasis is on the prodigality of life which, confined by spatial limits, can renew itself only by annihilating all that it creates. The destructiveness of nature and man is now reduced to the spending of excess product and energy unusable for growth; Bataille's thought renounces the charms of the sickbed for a heartening exuberance of health. The same shift of emphasis may be seen in such late formulations as "Eroticism is the approbation of life right through to death".[35] His new vision of the cosmos, of the evolution of life, and of human history, is of a prodigal multiplication of species, populations, and resources which can be maintained within the limits of the globe only by the constant destruction of a surplus. Death itself is no longer the end served by birth, it "incessantly leaves the room necessary for the coming of the new-born, and we are quite wrong to curse *that without which we would not be.*"[36]

It is plain that this vision is directly descended from the "mythological representation" of 1927, with the sun still at its centre.

> The source and the essence of our wealth are given in the radiance of the sun, which dispenses energy—wealth—without taking anything in return. The sun gives without ever receiving; men had the sentiment of that long before astrophysics measured this incessant prodigality; they saw the harvests ripen and ascribed the splendour which belongs to it to the deed of who gives without receiving.[37]

In the preface of the book, on guard against accusations that his approach is unscientific, Bataille restates, without using the word "myth", his delimitation of the scope of science in 1927. Man constructs an objective system of nature and finds by it the means to his ends, but himself remains a subject outside the system, his ends processes without further end which belong to the process of nature, and sharing its freedom in that they are not bound by calculations of utility. To "bring ourselves to the measure of the universe"[38] we therefore need to enlarge, without departing from its data, scientific thinking which objectivises "energy in excess translated into effervescence of life"[39] to thinking which does not detach it from the effervescence in the subject, "a thought put on the level of the play of forces contrary to common calculations",[40] "that extreme liberty of thought which matches notions to the world's liberty of impulse".[41]

> Certainly it is dangerous, in extending the frigid research of the sciences, to reach the point where its object no longer leaves us indifferent, where on the contrary it is what inflames us. In fact the boiling which I envisage, which animates the globe, is also *myself* on the boil. Hence this object of my research cannot be distinguished from the subject himself, but I must put it more precisely—*from the subject at his boiling point.*[42]

Economic man, who earns not to spend but to re-invest and gives only in exchange, is blind to the wider necessities of a General Economy for which the destruction of the surplus is as indispensable as production. He brings disaster on himself by failing to see that "beyond our immediate ends, his work in fact pursues the useless and infinite fulfilment of the universe",[43] ignoring the requirement for all organic growth that "if the system can no longer grow, or if the excess cannot be entirely absorbed into its growth, one must necessarily lose it without profit, spend it, voluntarily or not, gloriously, or else in a catastrophic manner".[44]

There are then two ways of disposing of the surplus, the glorious and the catastrophic. Bataille, who has hitherto identified the end of life with loss as such, has difficulty in finding a criterion for preferring the former; it cannot be utility, and he continues to distrust pleasure. "It is simply a matter of an agreeable loss, preferable to another which is disagreeable; it is a matter of agreeableness (*agrément*) not of utility."[45] The irresistible drive throughout nature to dissipate its excess must be guided by man, away from wars like the last and towards such losses without return as the free gift of resources by rich America to war-wrecked Europe and impoverished India.

"It is plain that a curse weighs on man's life, in so far as it lacks the force to check a vertiginous impulse. One must state without hesitation that in principle it depends on man, *on man alone,* to lift this curse".[46]

It is interesting to notice how in this new account the value once attributed to the unproductive casting off from the body of sperm as of faeces is now transferred to reproduction. Sexuality still owes its value to an expenditure of energy above the minimum required to reproduce, but the spending by the individual "is most marked in sexual reproduction, where the individuals engendered are clearly separated from those who engender them—and *give* them life as one *gives* to *others*".[47]

Here we have a total shift of ground from *La notion de dépense*, and we can no longer raise our simple objection that a thing done for itself is not necessarily a consumption which is pure loss and destruction. Bataille now holds that not all loss is valuable for itself, only

1. the spending of more energy than is required for production, or
2. the *right* kind of spending of the surplus product (of which Bataille can say only that is the "agreeable" kind).

This would be an application of what seems an acceptable principle for identifying ends. Something is done for its own sake if

1. the agent is spontaneously inclined to it more rather than equally or less than to any end that it serves, or
2. it has no further end,

leaving open the question of whether to approve or disapprove of it as an end.

But then there can no longer be any claim that pure loss is the end common to all mankind which establishes a universal foundation for values, leaving Bataille with no criterion to judge between right and wrong kinds of loss except that very unsatisfactory word "agreeable". However, such a criterion does emerge from Bataille's postulates. The gratuitous inclination to do something for its own sake springs up without calculation of utility, spontaneously (although for spontaneity Bataille usually says "liberty" or "violence"). It veers with expanding or shrinking awareness, a relation which is purely causal. Thus a lasting awareness of certain issues from other people's viewpoints demands a causal language—for example, of betraying a friend or taking a life—not 'I ought not . . . ' but 'I couldn't do that', as one might say 'I can't eat that', without denying that circumstances may *force* one to do it. One bound by the causal consequences of his awareness is thought better of than the person who has to decide against betrayal or murder by a moral choice (his moral standards being socially imposed and external to him, or his peaks of awareness hard to sustain). Bataille found disaster agreeable to his imagination in 1927, but after the war knows better what disaster is like, finds it "disagreeable", and tells us that a recurrence cannot be avoided "unless the impulse from which it starts appears plainly *in consciousness*".[48] We are now back at our quasi-syllogism: his reaction has changed *for the better* because he is aware of more. Nor is it simply that the improvement is from his private viewpoint, so that an opposite reaction might be better from mine. The advance of his awareness includes a widening of perspective to embrace the viewpoints of people in general, reducing to insignificance, for example, his private distaste for reproductive sex, and if I widen mine similarly our horizons will fuse.

What can we learn from Bataille? On the themes of science and myth, ends and means, rationality and the spontaneous, the sacred and the obscene, his influence may be perceived throughout the present book. He has seen better than anyone various implications of the non-Kantian assumption which he shares with Nietzsche and also with the Chinese,[49] that ends are not rational concepts but activities to which we find ourselves spontaneously inclined irrespective of consequences. As long as he maintains his paradoxical commitment to pure loss as the universal end, he has no need to derive their value from what Nietzsche identifies as scope of perspective, the Chinese as wisdom, myself as awareness; but as we just saw, this is required by his case once the commitment is abandoned. One such implication is that the Western philosophical mainstream is wrong in drawing a sharp line between man and nature, self and other; evolving humanity distinguished itself as rational by learning how to choose means, but the ends to which it finds itself inclining never lose the spontaneity of non-human goals. It is his sense of the vague and shifting boundaries of the self and its continuity with the spontaneity outside us which leads this atheist—or "atheologian"[50]—to the religious conclusion that the most valuable in us comes from forces outside to be classed as "sacred", and to declare in the first issue of *Acéphale* "WE ARE FIERCELY RELIGIOUS".[51] His coprophiliac sensibility awakens deep insights into that affinity of sacred and obscene long noticed by anthropologists in pre-literate cultures. When Bataille first adopted the term "sacred" in 1930 it was for what is commonly called the obscene, the horror and attraction of the substances excreted by the body in unwilled convulsions; in pondering what to call his "science of the wholly other" he rejected "hagiology" and at first picked "scatology".[52] By 1949 he is seeing the forces driving towards superabundance and the free gift of the surplus as sacred, and it might be expected that the impulse to ruin and destruction would need another term to distinguish it, for which "obscene" would do very well. It so happened, however, that his wartime experiments in meditation[53] had led to a new conception of the sacred, as the undifferentiated world subjective intimacy with which is lost when things are detached from each other as means at the disposal of a detached subject ("Only a world where beings are lost in indistinction is superfluous, serves for nothing, has nothing to do and nothing it wants to say; it alone has value in itself, not in view of some other thing, this other thing for still another and so on for ever"[54]). Significantly, he has lost his taste for blood sacrifice: "sacrifice is not killing, it is abandoning and giving".[55] However, it is precisely by relating it to the obscene that Bataille revives our failing sense of the meaning of the sacred. The more familiar dichotomy 'sacred/secular' or 'sacred/profane' contrasts the unquestionably existing realm of means with a realm of ends which has to be peopled with existing God or gods for the opposition to hold. Sacred and obscene on the other hand are both excluded from the secular or profane realm of means, and require no belief in pure any more than in impure spirits. The obscene, as a sight, word, thought, or impulse which both attracts and repels as inherently degrading, belongs to common experience and requires the sacred as its opposite. The conventional rationalist who thinks of his actions as starting from his own decisions, whether as applications of principles or as existential choices, shuns with redoubled intensity the forces which threaten to dissolve selfhood and overthrow reason, but is subjectively detached from the forces behind the goals which he rationally chooses; he knows the obscene but not the sacred. But Freud has habituated us to the thought that reason merely navigates a stream springing from subconscious depths, which requires us to distinguish forces which drag us down from those which lift us to heights of love or creativity beyond all conscious control; and if the former are obscene the latter are sacred.[56]

An important observation of Bataille is that the activities valued for themselves on which means depend for their value tend, in societies and social sectors outside the range of bourgeois values, to distinguish themselves from means very sharply, if not by their destructiveness at least by their uselessness. The bourgeois society that Bataille loathes, the world of rationally calculated means, seeks its ends not in activities but in abstract ideas, so that all activities may be reduced to means. It is on guard against useless consumption, which it tends to equate with a short-sighted indulgence in the pleasures of the moment. Bataille, however, invites us to see such indulgences as one end of a spectrum which extends to activities very far from pleasant, sacrifice, asceticism, war, not to mention that for him even luxury and eroticism owe their value to the agonising rapture of loss. The bourgeois spirit ascribes the conspicuous wasting of resources to outworn religious or feudal ideas, in contrast with the rational ideas such as the Kantian end in itself on which it would like to build its system of means. It may indeed, as in some kinds of utilitarianism, find such an end in pleasure itself, but even this conflicts with the utilitarian tendency to value even pleasure by its utility, as "recreation" to restore depleted energies, "re-creating" one for hard work. The result is, not indeed the abolition of immediately satisfying activities, the opportunities for which are widely extended by the dynamism of capitalist production, but their contraction wherever the mechanics of the system pull us into purely instrumental action, also an erosion of immediate satisfaction by the incapacity to think of anything we do other than as a means to something else. Bataille's work reminds us how very peculiar economic man is, seen in his context in history and anthropology. The astonishing habit of investing money as it is made, on which the great capitalist takeoff around the sixteenth century initially depended, required a radical break with the very sensible assumptions previously current, that the purpose of making money is to spend it, and that a principled self-denial makes sense only if you want to withdraw from the world. It is hard to understand how such a break could come about unless we read Max Weber's *Protestant Ethic and the Spirit of Capitalism* as the record of one of the great accidents made possible by human irrationality, the conversion of the trading classes to a religious doctrine that the spiritual benefits of self-denial can be won without retiring from the world, by practicing your trade honestly and industriously without enjoying the fruits of it, which by a curious chance contributed to the growth of rationality and decay of religion through the calculations of utility in commerce and manufacture. Inside what we shall continue with Bataille to call the bourgeois world, it appears natural to infer that if in the twentieth century, as so many complain, the meaning has been draining out of life, the cause must be the discrediting of religious dogmas and the failure of philosophy to put anything in their place. But if like Bataille we choose a viewpoint from outside the bourgeois world, it seems that a social group knows very well the things it would do for their own sake, and is inclined to take its values from the economically useless who are in a position to do them. Not of course that the *fact* that it wants these things confirms their value; but whenever we question that value, our only and sufficient grounds will be that we who feel differently are aware of more, see things from a wider perspective. If we ourselves lack the same assurance of having something to live for, we may indeed find it through conversion to a religion, philosophy, or political creed, but are the new ideas more than a guide to discovering for ourselves, whether with or against the social pressures of a flourishing market economy, just what it is we truly want?

Without things done regardless of further purpose, whether as sacred, glorious, honourable, beautiful, or pleasurable, a society would have no ends to be served by its means; and in stratified societies, with the limited resources of the pre-industrial world, the refinement of ends always depended on a leisured élite freed from the pressure of means, privileged to do things for their own sake and not for their consequences. Bataille calls attention to the startling extent to which ends socially admired as good in themselves have been not merely useless but positively wasteful and destructive, the warrior's glory, the rich man's extravagance, the ascetic's self-tortures. Aristocrats have traditionally distinguished themselves from the useful classes by the reality or show of treating possessions not as commodities to be earned and traded but as privilege or plunder, riches to be spent, wasted, lavished as largesse, giving without calculation of cost or of usefulness to the recipient, gambling away their estates, getting killed in duels on tiny points of honour, going to war not because the cause is just or practically advantageous but for glory and the joy of battle. These absurdities for reason intensify the spell exerted by the fortunate few on the imaginations of the many. The social estimate of a man's worth may be enhanced by even stranger forms of self-immolation; anthropologists know societies in which destruction of one's own wealth in the potlatch shames rivals into doing the same, or in which trade is conducted by the gift which demeans unless returned by an equal or greater gift—according to Bataille, following the *Essai sur le don* of Marcel Mauss, the origin of all trade, which only later degenerated into the striking of bargains. These last customs are Bataille's strongest examples, used in both *La notion de dépense* and *La part maudite*, of an aimless loss or ruin which enhances one's worth in others' eyes. They convince him that except in modern societies, which lose sight of ends in competition for means, the virtue everywhere fundamentally most valued is the courage to fulfil the universal desire to plunge from a plenitude of being into nothingness, at its highest in the spectacular self-combustion of hero and martyr. Thorstein Veblen analysing in his *Theory of the Leisure Class* the social role of conspicuous waste, or any rationalist criticising the ascetic ideal, assumes that in exposing its irrationality he also discredits it. Not so Bataille, for whom in *La notion de dépense* the whole point of rational endeavour is to maintain a sufficient supply of people and goods to be gratuitously squandered or slaughtered.

But in rehearsing Bataille's examples, we need to isolate the thing done for itself from the elements which he has inherited from a decadent Romanticism, the grandeur of Evil, the equation of value with intensity and of love with death. That mankind has a lust for death as well as for life, the Thanatos and Eros of Freud's *Beyond the Pleasure Principle*, is a thesis much enriched by Bataille's insights, and we can acknowledge that a blind will to destruction is active in many of the social customs he adduces. But death being the single goal which cannot be attained without renouncing all others, it is rational to resist Thanatos until all the possibilities of Eros are exhausted, and be on watch for and eliminate any morbid impulses involved in the activities he offers us as models of the end in itself. We may take from *La notion de dépense* the example of gambling. For economic man, the gambler is trying to make money without working, and usually is justly punished for it. Many gamblers, however, fit Bataille's analysis by being obscurely driven to destroy themselves; some are even conscious of it, and confess that the supreme thrill is not in vast winnings but in a catastrophic loss. But this is not true of such as the illustrious American gambler Nick the Greek, who is said to have lived all his life out of suitcases, used enormous gains for nothing but to play again or for extravagant tips and private benefactions, enjoyed the game for its own sake however much he won or lost, calculated meticulously by the laws of probability, and diagnosed and despised gamblers bent on ruin. If this personage has some appeal to one's imagination, it is surely because, unlike the rest of us trapped in the mundane, he pursued a mode of life, useless or only incidentally useful to beneficiaries of his generosity, which centred on the supremely skilful conduct of an activity worth so much in his own eyes that he would take unlimited risks for it, proving his perfect independence of the need or greed for money which confines others in the world of means.

Since for the life one thinks good in itself it is necessary to command the means, and not sink into subjection to them, still less to the means to mere survival, necessary also to renounce what interferes with the good life, there is indeed an intimate connexion between the good in itself and, not loss or destruction, but the capacity to risk or accept them, and many Bataillian themes may be taken up and reinterpreted from this angle. His later formulations do approach this position, for example, "Sovereignty is the power to rise, in indifference to death, above the laws which assure the maintenance of life".[57] The hero in battle, the celibate priest, the ascetic starving himself, all illustrate this pursuit of sovereignty, which may or may not be reinforced by some morbid drive. We may agree with Bataille that the meaning of the end in itself is obscured if we appeal only to high-minded examples, to a disinterested goodwill or to a refusal to besmirch honour or betray principle whatever the cost. Even the recklessness, so distressing to the prudent, with which the most wretched will waste the earnings of months on a festival or an individual night out, with a self-abandonment which risks ending up in gaol, does after all testify to the meagreness of life unless now and then one can submerge in present experience without reserve, escape altogether from the prison of means. There is something in us which refuses to admire a person solely for acts useful to himself and to others, which insists that there be something he finds valuable enough in itself to be worth suffering or taking risks for, if not a principle or ideal then his desires of the moment—a demand seen at its most elementary in derision of a drinker too cautious to down another glass or pay for another round. Is it really as an orgiast of self-destruction that the Indian of the American Northwest won prestige in the potlatch, or rather by the public demonstration that he had the courage and the resources to throw away the things which trap the majority in dependence, that he was the master and not the servant of his means? It is necessary to distinguish very clearly the respect due to a proof of personal sovereignty from Bataille's fascination with its lurid halo of death and disaster.

Granted that a thing being done for its own sake is no proof of its value, it is a condition of being valuable for itself; and it is only from the things it approves even if they serve no further purpose that a civilization can with growing awareness develop its fundamental values. Since life can be lived as pure end only by those freed from subjection to means, whether by abundance of wealth or by indifference to it, complex societies have regularly derived their ends from élites either supported by the economic surplus or dedicated to poverty, nobles, priests, poets, thinkers, who can pursue a mode of life for itself, and who tend to disdain the useful life as sordid. A happy outcome of technological revolution is that we have already begun to break out from the restriction of leisure to a fortunate few. Bataille himself in *La part maudite* acknowledges this change as decisive; it is economic abundance which lays the curse on obsolete ways of disposing of the surplus, and demands "refusal of war in the monstrous form it disguises, refusal of the wastefulness of luxury, which henceforth in its traditional form signifies injustice".[58] Up to the present, however, a sophisticated culture has always depended on economically useless élites. Their authority to define ends for the majority preoccupied with the means to survival derives, not simply from possessing the social power to impose their will, nor even from the high value of those ends in the eyes of the most aware, but from having visibly escaped the common lot, becoming empowered to do things for their own sake. Such honoured élites are not necessarily very different from the other useless elements which a community casts out; in the noble only a generation or two from the bandit, in the borrowing poet, begging saint or glamorous criminal, one is impressed by the ease of passage between the revered as sacred and the spurned as obscene. In feudal society the noble as conspicuous consumer could provide, not the highest (he left that to the priest), but the simplest and most appealing model of the good life, a life which his inferiors could enjoy only through his acts of bounty or as spectacle or fantasy. For those content to participate so humbly, having no more to hope for, the life of the noble enhanced the value of their own, assuring them of serving ends both easily comprehensible and fuller than those available to themselves. The "glory" of the noble or hero (and of God), a peculiarly difficult concept for the modern mind, for some no more than the prestige of social power, for Bataille the splendour of dealing or suffering death, may be understood as the radiance in imagination of things done as ends in themselves, revealing richer possibilities of life to those without the opportunity to share them.

The noble despised the bourgeois, not only for making himself useful, but for the withering in him of the spontaneity at the root of ends, the shaping of his personality by prudential virtues which are no more than means to means (industry, practicality, thrift, temperance, caution), and by a morality which amounted only to helping others to the means. The bourgeois for his part saw no point in deeds of no practical use to oneself or anyone else, and therefore dismissed aristocratic codes as obselete and irrational. Yet the value of the useful derives from what it is useful *for*, the value of which is degraded by confusing it with the useful and shows up unequivocally only in the useless. For the scientist, especially treasured for his utility by the bourgeois world, that may be the value of truth for its own sake and of the beauty of logical relations. But the value is not in these ends as abstractions; if the scientist is sometimes puzzled by the revulsion which that beautiful world-structure excites in so many, he is forgetting that others do not share in what gives meaning to his own life, that work which is one of the most satisfying for which a market economy finds room, informed at its best by a creativity ignited without warning by—not his word—the "sacred"; others see only the result, another abstraction which, if science as it is inclined to claim is all the knowledge there is, contributes to "blindly emptying the world of its human content". Nowadays the popular image of the flamboyantly useless life open to all possibilities has settled on rock singers, actors, and sportsmen, while the conscious care of values becomes the business of an intelligentsia also supported by or plundering the economic surplus, who by the mere fact of being freed to pursue thought or art for its own sake may become disdainful of the marketplace and bite the hand that feeds them, whether they are respectable academic reactionaries and revolutionaries or of the aggressively anti-bourgeois Bohemia on the edge of criminality which first emerged in nineteenth-century Paris. The lasting disaffection of a large part of the intelligentsia, always hankering after idealised pasts or futures in a society unprecedented for material abundance and freedom of thought, and their vulnerability to the temptations of Fascism and Communism, which in practice turn out to make things very much worse, testify to the continued starving in a means-oriented society of the hunger for modes of life satisfying in themselves. That hunger drove Bataille to the desperate quest for Acéphale.

NOTES

1. Cf. pp. 32–36 above.
2. Georges Bataille, *"La part maudite" precede de "La Notion de dépense"* (Paris: Editions de Minuit, 1967), 26f.
3. *L'érotisme,* (Paris: Editions de Minuit, 1957).
4. Bataille, *Oeuvres complétes,* (Paris: Gallimard, 1970ff.), vol. 1, 79–86. vol. 2, 13–47.
5. Ut sup., vol. 2, 22.
6. Ut sup., vol. 2, 22f.
7. Ut sup., vol. 2, 23.
8. Ut sup., vol. 2, 23f.
9. Ut sup., vol. 2, 414.
10. Ut sup., vol. 2, 420.
11. Ut sup., vol. 2, 24.
12. Cf. ut sup., vol. 1, 612.
13. Ut sup., vol. 45. For *Oeil* cf. 187–89.
14. Ut sup., vol. 2, 15.
15. Ut sup., vol. 1, 86.
16. Ut sup., vol. 2, 58–60.
17. Ut sup., vol. 1, 251n.
18. Ut sup., vol. 1, 523n.
19. Ut sup., vol. 1, 491.
20. Ut sup., vol. 1, 96.

21. Ut sup., vol. 1, 524.
22. Ut sup., vol. 1, 531f.
23. Ut sup., vol. 1, 532.
24. Ut sup., vol. 1, 533.
25. Ut sup., vol. 1, 535.
26. Ut sup., vol. 1, 533.
27. Ut sup., vol. 1, 445.
28. Ut sup., vol. 1, 644.
29. Ut sup., vol. 2, 278.
30. Roger Caillois, *Instincts et sociétés* (Paris, 1964), 67.
31. Hans-Georg Gadamer, *Truth and Method*, 2nd ed. (London: Sheed & Ward, 1979), 273f., 337f., 358.
32. Bataille, *La littérature et le mal* (Paris: Gallimard, 1957), 32.
33. Ut sup., 84.
34. Sade, *Justine ou les malheurs de la vertu* (Paris: Le Soleil Noir, 1950), xi.
35. *La littérature et la mal*, 13.
36. *La part maudite*, 75.
37. Ut sup., 68.
38. Ut sup., 52.
39. Ut sup., 50.
40. Ut sup., 52.
41. Ut sup., 51.
42. Ut sup., 50.
43. Ut sup., 59.
44. Ut sup., 60.
45. Ut sup., 71.
46. Ut sup., 83.
47. Ut sup., 76.
48. Ut sup., 83.
49. Cf. *Disputers of the Tao*, Appendix 1.
50. Cf. the title of Bataille's *Somme athéologique*, comprising *L'expérience intérieure* (1943) and *Le coupable* (1944) (Paris: Gallimard).
51. *Oeuvres*, vol. 1, 443.
52. Ut sup., vol. 2, 61f., n.
53. Cf. *Somme athéologique*.
54. Bataille, *Théorie de la religion* (1948), first published (Paris: Gallimard, 1973), 39.
55. Ut sup., 66.
56. Cf. "The Sacred and the Obscene", *R & S*, ch. 2, section 2.4.
57. *La littérature et le mal*, 212.
58. *La part maudite*, 79.

13

Two Perspectives on Present Mythopoeia

1. The Tiktaktok, "Record of Things Seen"

> Of the survival of certain myths, and some other myths in growth or in formation . . .
>
> —André Breton

In the beginning of things three gods, Vadla, Vadlam, and Vadikaliam, came out of the Cave and breathed the dust. After a thousand years these gods died.

The brothers Jehovah and Dracula came out of the Cave and breathed the dust. Jehovah flew up above the dust, Dracula flew low and said in his heart, "I shall die." Jehovah is the blue, the sun is his eye. When the eye opens, his brother sleeps. Dracula is the bat that flits at twilight.

After a thousand years two apes came out of the Cave and breathed the dust. The hairs dropped from their bodies one by one and became the leaves of the forest. They stood upright, a man and a woman. They each had one head, two arms and two legs. The bat came in the night and flew down to their throats. He sucked once, sucked twice, sucked thrice, and said, "I shall live."

They picked the fruits of the forest and swung on lianas from tree to tree. They built a house in the treetops and chattered to the chimpanzees. When they looked around them they saw that all things have names, mammoth, pterodactyl, flower, bird. They knew that their names were Tarzan and Jane.

The man hunted, the woman roasted the flesh and sewed the hides. They said to each other one day, "We too shall die." The bat that hovered by their throats said, "Live while there is blood of others to drink." They clung to each other and looked up at the white clouds. The blue between the clouds said to the man, "Go into the cave of the woman." Three sons and ten daughters came out of her womb and she died. The man said "Where is she?" The blue of the sky said, "She has gone back into the Cave."

The sons of Tarzan and Jane were America and Russia and Japan, whose children peopled the earth. America begat Jesse James the first warrior, and Jesus of the golden beard who was the first shepherd, who begat Solomon the wise who saw the first city in a dream, who begat Einstein who heard the secrets of Atlantis from the Magi of Jupiter and Frankenstein who invented moving skeletons of iron, who together commanded the giants to stand up the stones of New York, which is the city on seven hills in the desert south of Vitepka.

Frankenstein envied his brother Einstein the secrets of Atlantis. They fought in the fields from morning to evening, and as the sun set Einstein fell. The herbs that cure ills sprang from his blood. Frankenstein ate his brain and said in his heart, "I shall be wiser than Jehovah." A bat flew in through the window. When the bat speaks you do not know you heard. Frankenstein said, "I want to know everything." The bat said, "Let me drink your blood. You will think more clearly." The bat sucked once and he knew the number of the stars. The bat sucked twice and he knew how to measure the sky. The bat sucked thrice and he knew how to make a man. Frankenstein said, "Now I know there was no Cave." Then he killed twelve men, chopped them to pieces, and stitched together a thing with one head, two arms and two legs. He commanded the lightning to shoot fire through its veins. The thing stirred, grunted, stood straight up and walked. Frankenstein cried out, "My son!" It took him by the throat and he died. At the sight of it all the people fled New York, which is empty to this day. It begat Nismemi, who begat the Atalanka, who cannot speak and have a stitch down their necks and walk unharmed in the dust.

After a thousand years an ape seven miles high came out of the Cave and breathed the dust. He did not become a man, he waded through the sea to an island and sat down in the forest. There came a ship with a thousand men and one woman. He lifted the woman in the palm of his hand and loved her. She took him over the sea to the city of Babylon. In the city civilization had been going on so long that many were born without claws or tusks. Pharaoh the mummy who unwound and rose from the tomb, and the Zombies who refused to die, and the moving skeletons of iron, came down to see him from rows of tunnels in cliffs a thousand miles high. They sat him in a cage with a sign above it, "Ten dollars to see King Kong." King Kong roared and burst the bars and trampled the crowd. He put his left foot in a tunnel, he put his right foot in a tunnel, and climbed with the woman wriggling in his hand towards the blue of the sky. The crowd called up to him, "Come back! We shall teach you the secret of eternal life!" King Kong stood up on the Tower of Babel and beat his chest. They saw that in his rage he would trample all mankind. The most valiant stole the ships of aliens from the moon and flew up to fight King Kong. When his chest was full of arrows he laid the woman gently down, and fell crushing the towers of the city flat. Their children were the black Rastifari who discovered music.

Afterwards a great fog fell over all the cities of the earth. Holmes the subtle tracker said to his friend Watson, "The world has grown so dull. What is there to do but strum the guitar and sit smoking grass all day?" There was a knock on the door. It was the Emperor of Rome and the Pope. Bowing to the ground they said, "Holmes, only your eye can pierce the darkness. While the city of Rome sleeps the Master Criminal plots. He is the puppetmaster in the shadows whose hand is on all the strings." Holmes flung down his joint and his guitar and cried, "What does he look like, this man?"

"Like you, like me. He is a master of disguises. Not a detail to distinguish him."

"Is there always a bat that hovers by his left ear?"

"There is."

Puzzled by his question they departed. Holmes cried out in his joy, "It is Moriarty! Life becomes interesting again. Watson, the hunt is on!"

They ran out into the fog. On the doorstep lay the bodies of the Emperor and the Pope, their tongues torn out at the roots. "The trail is fresh!" cried Holmes. He went down on hands and knees, sniffed and cried, "Look!"

"At what?" said Watson.

"Do you not see? It is the footprint of Moriarty." They ran on through the fog. Holmes stopped, picked a tiny grain from the wall, and cried, "Look!"

"I see nothing."

"Have you no eyes? It is a fragment of the tusk of Moriarty."

They came out of the fog on the brink of Niagara Falls. Below, a giant octopus groped with its tentacles towards the ledge. "There is no one here", said Watson.

"Look!" cried Holmes, "The bat above its head!"

The octopus shrank back into the water. Holmes's keen eye scanned the rocks. "That was not here before", he said. It was a giant spider squatting in a web stretched over the face of the cliff. A bat hovered above its head.

"Moriarty!" he cried, "Enough of these disguises! Stand up and fight like a man!"

Moriarty stood forth as a man like other men. They grappled, slashing each other with their tusks, then fell in each other's arms down, down into the abyss.

Watson walked sorrowfully home through the fog. "Good and evil have died together", he said as he opened the door.

"No", said the voice of Holmes through the fumes of marijuana, "I never die. But it will be a duller world than ever without Moriarty."

After that time there was no more hunting and fighting in the world. There lived among the skeletons of iron a respected man in a top hat and black coat named Doctor Jekyll who knew everything. (His mother was Marilyn Monroe the princess from Venus, who when the dust entered her womb gave birth dying to the Robots, who worked as slaves until the rising of the second sun.) Doctor Jekyll said in his heart, "I am wiser than Jehovah." A bat flew in through the window. When the bat speaks you do not know you heard. Doctor Jekyll said, "I am weary of knowledge. I want to be King Kong." The bat said, "Drink down this chemical. It is your own blood." He drank, fell shaking, staring, clutching his throat, and rolled on the floor. When he stood up and looked into the mirror, he saw a little ape. It was Mister Freud. From that day men did not know their true names. The ape took a surgeon's knife in a black bag and went out at night into the corridors of Whitehall. Doctor Jekyll, resuming his shape, said to Jehovah, "I went out to punish the daughters of Dracula." In the silence a bat squeaked. Doctor Jekyll said, "Why did I say 'I'? Who is it, if both are one?" He started out of his chair, reached up, and weighing on his head was the crown of England.

The bat said aloud, "Look into the mirror again. Thine is the power.

The fat man is bluff King Henry the Eighth, founder of the Church and the Navy, and there is the lady who walks the Bloody Tower."

In the last times Dracula was incarnate of a virgin in the black forests of California. No one recognised his name. He said to women, who said to men, "Love is insipid without the sting of the bite." Plague spread over the earth. In the black forest a good man came to an inn and asked, "Where is the castle of Count Dracula?". There was a hush, heads spun round, then all slapped down their tankards and fled. The good man came at night to the castle and saw the doors wide open. At the head of the stair a giant phallus swelled and stood up inside a black cloak. The top of it was a fanged face rotted by the plague. At the sight the good man's soul cringed from his own flesh and the womb that bore him, and the Cave for which it yearned became a nothing with a line around it. Count Dracula said, "I see you understand. Only Nothing does not change and decay and disappoint. I am but a short time on earth and bring one message. Desire quickens as it sees the way to Nothing. Evil is energy, intensity, life, joy." The good man said, "Energy, intensity, life, joy are evil." "My brother", said the Count, "We agree in everything."

Next day the good man did not dare to leave his chamber. At nightfall a crowd of women came, with open wounds in their throats, and faces on fire with energy, intensity, life, joy. He cringed back to the window, where their poxed hands and dripping blind eyes could not find him, and looking down saw the Count crawl upside down along the wall and fly off on bat's wings. All the women flew through the window after him. Towards daybreak the good man heard the beat of returning wings, but when he walked through the castle there was no one there. He went down into the crypt and found the Count asleep in his tomb, black buboes swarming on his face and his crossed hands. The good man sharpened a stake and drove it into the vampire's heart. The vampire shuddered and shrieked. Before its flesh rotted the fanged mouth spoke: "Brother, take our message to the world. Nothing else has taste when you know the taste of death."

From that time the witnesses of Jehovah forgot the Cave and aspired to fade into a white sky. Kings arose who were witnesses of Dracula. Only the poisoned in blood had an end in sight, the rest sat down with their heads between their knees. There was no hunting or fighting anywhere in the world. The dreams floated out of their heads and melted the walls. The skeletons of iron ran wild and murdered their masters. The moon rose by day and jostled the sun in the sky. Volcanos undersea erupted into America, lightning over Siberia struck in Japan. The Mad Scientist, whose name it is forbidden to utter, divined a reason and said in his heart, "I shall be master of the universe." In a cellar of the castle with tubes and wires and bubbling bottles he invented a second sun. (The number on his brow is 666, may he that listens understand.) The witnesses of Jehovah proclaimed from door to door, "The end is near! A chariot from the stars will carry the faithful to the sky!"

There was a man named Noah who knew nothing, but knew his true name. The blue of the sky said to Noah, "A second sun will rise and put out my eye. With the perfect in ignorance, and the animals two by two, go down into the Cave. Build a chapel within with a sign above it, NO FARTHER DOWN. From the chapel to the doors is the Ark of the Covenant. After a thousand years, when my eye has grown again, come back into the world. Let no one in who knows anything, that knowing may begin anew."

Then Noah and the perfect in ignorance and the animals two by two went down into the Cave. All the bats of Dracula hung asleep in the roof. They hurried to kill them before nightfall. Noah said, "Leave two alive, or they will fly up in swarms from the heart of the earth".

They measured out the Ark and built the chapel and shut the doors. When the work was accomplished Noah said goodbye to them all, and died. The men lay with their feet up, drank cans of beer, looked at strips of pictures telling stories, made lazy fun of a witness of Jehovah who preached. A black man with dreadlocks sang to a guitar. The women gossiped and looked at themselves in mirrors. Suddenly there was a flash and a rush of wind. Then they saw through the keyhole the rising of the second sun, and the people outside who beat on the doors and sank dying in the dust.

They lit a fire and lay down, and with the two bats in the roof slept for a thousand years. When the time was fulfilled they woke and stirred the ashes and blew on the faint glow. They knew that knowing was beginning again. They threw open the doors and saw the first sun in the blue of the sky.

That the truth of things seen be not forgotten, we that heard it from the mouths of their children's children pass down to our children the memory of the ancient world.

SETI PIATVAM JEHOVA SAVATAI DRAKULA

2. The Myths of a Modern Fall

It is a familiar thought that many of the more lasting tales of popular entertainment have something of the look of ancient myths. In an age when even the theologians want to "demythologise" Christianity, it is to be expected that the mythopoeic impulse will find scope only in the realm where we allow ourselves a holiday from reason, maturity, and reality. But how seriously are we to take the resemblance?

Let us say that myths are stories which relate man to forces independent of his will and reason, forces which he experiences as sacred when they lift him above the capacities which are fully at his command, and as obscene when they drag him down below them.[1] For the religions these are external powers divine or diabolic, for psychology they are subterranean drives untamable until brought to consciousness; but however interpreted they are outside the acknowledged self, and crystallise in images of beings who are either more or less than human, and free of the restrictions of the real. The stories which recur in popular entertainment include of course tales of love or adventure which are about persons recognisable as human in situations acceptable as real, but these would fall under the heading of legend rather than myth. A modern presence that is truly mythic must in some way or other, not necessarily sinister, be a monster—Frankenstein's, Dracula, Mr. Hyde, Tarzan, King Kong, Superman. He may reappear under his own name through generations of novels, plays, films, and strip cartoons. He may change his name at every reappearance, like the Mad Scientist, the Extra-terrestrial, or that Master Criminal who fought Holmes as Moriarty, fascinated the Surrealists as Fantomas, haunted the German cinema as Fritz Lang's Mabuse. He may appear just once as supreme representative of a genre, like King Kong, greatest of the animal rebels against man, identified for ever with a single film which remains strangely memorable after fifty years of the technical progress which should have made it obsolete. He may emerge from one corner of what is otherwise legend, like Moriarty, whom we are tempted to forget appears only in a couple of the Holmes stories. Since it takes time for the monster to root himself in the social imagination we had better stick to the old and tried names with the imprimatur of Hollywood, many from the nineteenth century with their roots in the Gothic novel, nothing less than half a century old. As for his story, much as nowadays we prefer a veneer of scientific plausibility to help the suspension of disbelief, a myth must be of events which defy reason, impossible or else possible only in the primordial age (for the ancients) or the future (for ourselves). However rationalised, it must have something uncanny at the centre of it, still visible through any scientific disguise. Even Tarzan, in spite of all efforts to keep him human, the hero of a wish-fulfilment fantasy of returning to nature, betrays the mystery of the man who is also animal in his blood-curdling call to the beasts of the jungle. The Master Criminal too, however realistic the background, becomes more vivid as a mythic presence the nearer he is to persuading that he can walk through walls, read your mind, transform himself in an instant by another unfathomable disguise. Finally, a modern myth has to be popular, not to say downright vulgar, childish. It may have originated in an individual and distinguished mind, Mary Shelley's or Robert Louis Stevenson's, but it can fulfil its social function as myth only if ordinary people, through impressions at their most receptive age or in their most relaxed moments, are unthinkingly influenced by it in interpreting the superhuman and subhuman within and beyond themselves.

The worldview of science allows us a holiday zone for mythopoeia, but in one direction only. Modern rational man, whether or not he professes a religion, has little experience of the sacred which uplifts, but is much aware of the obscene which will overwhelm him unless he stays on guard. His inborn talents and spontaneous flights of love or creativity are largely independent of his will, and once seemed of divine origin, but he now takes all the credit for them as his own. He does however recognise and fear the dark forces which reign when he is "not himself", and which can topple him into madness. Our mythology is therefore godless, inhabited only by humans and by the monsters which they fall before, or vanquish, or themselves become. If there is any place for gods in our mythopoeia it is in fantasy of being gods ourselves, like that modest newspaper reporter whom everyone condescends to, unaware that he is Superman. There is Christian symbolism in *Dracula,* but the Cross is no more than a practical weapon against the vampire, like the garlic and the stake through the heart. What an anticlimax if the story had ended with a last minute rescue by St. Michael and his angels! The UFO craze has generated quasi-religious cults, and sooner or later perhaps we shall meet in space fiction the obsessively recurring figure of a Saviour from some planet, as vivid as Dracula and a great comfort to us all, but he has not to my knowledge yet taken hold.

It may be objected that in the fifty years we have excluded by our time limit for fully established myth, "modern rational man" has lost much of his authority, and there are now other sources of mythopoeia than the underground defence of reason against the obscene. The gods have certainly returned in music and dance, a road to the sacred ecstasy no longer closed by the rational man's fear of losing his identity by relaxing self-control. Unlike the stars of the old cinema who were no more than idealised humans, the rock stars are unmistakably gods, androgynous monsters transfigured in glory by freaky dress and psychedelic staging, the Extra-terrestrial David Bowie, the Rolling Stones whose Satanic postures disclose the terrible aspect of the sacred. But the divine in pop culture is manifest in instant experience, through hypnotic rhythm and vertiginous lighting which dissolves individuality in collective trance, and its gods, with their message of absolute freedom, sensual fulfilment, "I want it all and I want it now", must be physically present, in the flesh or on video. There is still room for sacred myth in the exemplary lives of the stars, which one prefers to be cut short by a sacrificial death symbolic of living in the fast lane, by car accident or drug overdose. But biography and hagiography do not much matter when the disposable and instantly replaceable gods are always before the eyes of their worshippers. The indirect approach through mythopoeia remains important only for coming to terms with experience we do *not* want here and now. When the rock singer does display himself in a story not his own it tends to be, if not in a *Jesus Christ Superstar* about the one star of traditional religion still mythic for the rock culture, then in a *Rocky Horror Picture Show* drawing on just the mythology we are examining.

The lifting of the rationalistic ban on the sacred does not therefore affect the persisting orientation of popular mythopoeia towards the obscene. In consciousness of spontaneous forces pulling us up or down we experience both the attraction of surrender and the dread of dissolution; when they uplift, the combination is numinous awe, the terror and fascination of the sacred; when they degrade, drag down towards death and corruption, the combination turns to horror, the mingled desire and repulsion of the obscene. Horror stories should therefore be the purest among our myths. But in all of them, not only the explicitly morbid, we lean a little over an abyss, drawn by the spell of Dracula or the Master Criminal while clinging to the side of Van Helsing or the detective. While the sacred offers an exaltation beyond the reach of any act of will, the obscene invites a self-indulgence into which we sink comfortably but dare not sink too far (we are of course using "obscene" in a sense which has little to do with the sexual and excremental). A grown man is a little ashamed of still enjoying this crap, unless he can disguise the appetite as a sophisticated taste for camp; even Tarzan, who has nothing morbid about him, and with whom he can identify freely knowing that in living as a wild animal Lord Greystoke retains the instincts of a gentleman, is regressing him into a dream proper to childhood.

How do the obscene myths ascend into the world? By the same route, of course, by which the sacred myths descend, by inspiration. The fully inspired work which writes itself word by word, as Coleridge reported or pretended of *Kubla Khan*, and the Surrealists cultivated by automatic writing, is not very common in high art. But the metaphors of poetry, and for that matter the paradigms of science, do come in a flash from nowhere, and a myth is in the first place a constellation of images, as effective in one medium as another, and as fully present in the feeblest strip cartoon as in the prose of Stevenson or cinematics of Lang. Both of the popular myths which originated in the high culture, Frankenstein and Jekyll-Hyde, belong among the few well authenticated cases of fiction taken directly from dream. Stevenson was woken screaming from the nightmare in which he saw the story of Jekyll and Hyde, and finished his first discarded draft in the next three days. Mary Shelley, as she tells in her preface, tossed in bed looking for a theme for a Gothic story, and tried to push out of mind the compulsively vivid "waking dream" of a scientist and a monster which at first she refused to recognise as the story she was looking for. Popular entertainers are seldom so informative, but *La révolution surréaliste* picked up and reprinted an account of how the creators of Fantomas wrote in hallucinatory excitement without remembering what they had written. Yes, our myths too come as messages from beyond.

Myths relate a whole people to the most fundamental truths through the medium of what for moderns are the most transparent lies. Do the disreputable stories we claim to be myths stand up to this further test? Entertainment though they are, only one of those we have mentioned, Superman, is the pure wish-fulfilment fantasy of a story of romance or adventure. The most truly mythic, the ones which evoke horror, the counterpart of numinous awe, nearly always, even in some tired B picture by Boris Karloff in his decline, touch profound issues strange to any other kind of entertainment, the dangers of knowledge, the mystery of personal identity, the conquest of death, the disquieting affinities and repugnances of man to animal and to machine. The modern myth, however, relates us not to eternal order but to disruption and change. In its thirst for the ultimate terror it searches the foundations of our world for fissures ready to open, with an insight which can be prophetic, in that it centres on a fear occasion for which will grow. That sensation, which became real in 1945, that because of a new invention everything, the survival of life itself, from now on and for ever hangs by a thread, was already familiar through the myth of the Mad Scientist. Modern, like ancient, myths have an oblique relation to reality, and may be pointing to the truth just when we take them least seriously. Recognition of the power of the Mafia in the United States seems to have been delayed for decades by the assumption that the vision of a secret empire of crime belonged only to cheap fiction, which had revelled in the Italian secret societies since well back in the nineteenth century. On the other hand taking prophetic fantasy too literally can breed delusions which break into the real world of politics. In the nightmare of a secret international conspiracy against religion, the state, and private property, which sprang up among reactionaries during the French Revolution, paranoia seems to glimpse the Internationals a century in advance, yet focusses crazily first on the Freemasons and later on the Jews. When we meet the Masonic or Jewish conspiracy in an old adventure story by Buchan or Sapper, it disgusts by reminding us of the outcome in Fascism. Yet it also, like Moriarty, gives an otherwise prosaic adventure the touch of myth, by transforming a merely local into a cosmic danger.

How is it that by an imaginative indulgence which is childish (and when it enters politics, dangerous) we move not into but away from the wish fulfilment of more reputable entertainment, towards insights which can be profound and even prophetic? We may find an answer in the reversal of the normal tendency to shut out the personally threatening, the switch to a positive desire for what terrifies most. Here, too, horror shows its affinity to the blended terror and fascination of numinous awe, of which it is the obscene parody. The crucial instance of a fact from which awareness shrinks is the certainty of death. There seem to be only two ways of sustaining this awareness, which eludes a mere effort of will never to lose sight of the worst. One of them is to be drawn into and beyond the terror of death by the attraction of future life, whether as personal immortality or as oneness with posterity or with Nature generating new life by sacrifice of the old; the other is to look directly at death by surrendering to the pull of a morbid desire. The sacred lifts through death to coming life, the obscene attracts to death itself, even to organic decomposition. Other entertainments, however bloodthirsty, show only fresh corpses or clean skeletons; the spectacle of a rotting carcase is a pleasure of the horror genre alone. This peculiarity is the proof that, as much as with the sacred, we have stepped altogether outside the limitations of personal ends. Vision is cleansed of everyday evasions and consolations by the pure appetite for the obscene itself.

It is sometimes assumed that to recognise the mythic under its modern disguises is to discern the fading outlines of primordial images and themes. But the mythopoeia submerged since the Industrial Revolution has been growing underground shoots towards the future; instead of celebrating a traditional order it confronts a sterility and a disorder which are qualitatively new. Let us then listen seriously for a moment to the Gospel according to King Kong, Tarzan, and Dracula. The message of these stories is simple and coherent. It seems that the power which spoke through the dreams of Mary Shelley and Stevenson has very decided

262

opinions about what has gone wrong with the world. The stories we have identified as myths (with the exception once again of Superman) all tell of the consequences of a Fall, not quite the same as the one in the Bible. By this Fall man cut himself off from his roots in nature to direct himself solely by reason, and the schism cast both into chaos. Those mutants, side effects of genetic or nuclear experiments, which in contemporary fantasy rise up in swarms to exterminate mankind, are a characteristic result, but we shall stick to our decision to admit nothing less than fifty years old. Frankenstein, Jekyll, the Invisible Man, all pried into secrets man is forbidden to know (the sacred does enter these stories as the dread of sacrilege), and in interfering with nature perverted it, raising up or themselves turning into monsters. Offended nature generated a giant ape, which insulted by man ran wild in the streets of New York. Reason by its successes became itself a road to madness, when the Mad Scientist, inventing a death ray which can depopulate the world, surrendered to the dream of absolute power. One rash experiment too many, and rebellious nature split the respectable Dr. Jekyll in two, to emerge rampant as Mr. Hyde. (How many of these enemies of mankind exhibit in their very names the perils of higher education, Prof. Moriarty, Dr. Mabuse, Dr. Fu Manchu!) Worst of all, the demons of superstition which reason denies still reign in the forests of Transylvania at the bottom of the heart, where the generative force of nature is now perverted to a lust for blood, so near the surface that a single bite of Dracula will turn any of us into a vampire.

What then is the answer? To abandon reason? No, it seems that our precarious civilization is saved from underground subversion by the Master Criminal only through the untiring dissipation of mystery by the reasoning mind of Holmes. But for more than a temporary respite modern mythopoeia has so far come up with only one constructive proposal. By a judicious compromise revert to the animal without giving up the best of civilization, like Tarzan, English lord and honorary ape.

NOTE

1. Cf. my *Reason and Spontaneity*, 113–55.

Mysticism and the Question of Private Access

14

(To Herbert Fingarette)

The great obstacle to the man of reason in coming to terms with mysticism is its appeal to the authority of an experience outside the public domain, and least accessible perhaps to the analytic cast of mind. He may be struck by the apparent agreement of so many East and West whom it is customary to call mystics that in the ultimate enlightenment everything turns out to be one, or rather perhaps that all distinctions fall away, between the one and the many as well as between self and other, and in theistic doctrines between the soul and God. He may also wonder whether post-modern questioning of dichotomies and dissolution of categories may be leading in the same direction through a breakdown of Western rationality which he cannot welcome. But what meaning can he ascribe to mystical claims, admitted to be no more than approximations to a finally unverbalisable revelation? It is true that we acknowledge the formulas of quantum mechanics as meaningful to a privileged few although meaningless to most of us, lacking as we are in, not only the knowledge, but possibly the innate mathematical ability as well; this, however, is a matter only of a more complicated use of a language which, at the level of $2 + 2 = 4$, we all understand. It is not plain that mystical affirmations would assume a meaning for the critical mind even if he did share the experience. He may concede in theory that he may lack the equivalent of a sixth sense possessed by mystics, as a person blind from birth lacks even a conception of what sight is. But the blind man learns by experience that others have an independent and superior access to the same world which he discerns by hearing, touch, taste, and smell; what is a philosopher to make of a sense giving access to a world otherwise inaccessible? It is as though one were to make the vacuous claim that dream is of real events occurring, not even on some remote planet where in principle a space traveller could witness them, but in a realm unvisitable except in dream itself.

The objection assumes, however, the traditional Western conception, with neo-Platonism at the back of it, of mysticism as the quest for Being, Reality, conceived after the analogy of a search for propositional truths even when the mystic explicitly refuses to verbalise. Granted that Indian philosophy may be fitted to this conceptualisation, the Far Eastern doctrines such as Taoism and Zen have nothing to say about truth or being; they promise only that with the liberation from all dichotomies we shall find ourselves moving spontaneously on the Tao, discovering not an ineffable Reality but an unformulable Way on which to navigate the reality we already know. They turn our attention from the supposedly experienced to the experience itself, dimly evoked through poetry, aphorism, and parable, and offered as attainable by ourselves through prescribed techniques of meditation. To the extent that the fact/value distinction applies—a point to which we shall return[1]—the illumination is not of reality but of value. But in that case a claim to private access need not worry us. In poetry and the arts we expect to meet unintelligible language or symbolism which will assume meaning if we happen on the relevant experience. The morally or aesthetically, unlike the physically, blind, have nothing to warn them that they are missing anything; their lack is manifest only to the morally or aesthetically perceptive, who—to stick to the same visual metaphor—have the same maddening assurance as mystics of the superiority of their own vision. Whatever the dangers of élitism, the conclusion that in matters of value some can see what to others is invisible cannot be escaped even by relativism. The extreme relativist too assumes on particular issues his superiority in valuation to those with less of the relevant knowledge and experience, including his own past self, and has likewise to concede in principle his inferiority to those with more. Then the mystically unqualified should be comparable, not with the sightless, but with the small boy who thinks his elder brother silly to waste his time with girls; he cannot yet know that after his own sexual awakening his present valuation will look silly to himself. In the Western tradition we tend to think of artistic creation and appreciation, although cultivated only by a minority, as inside the generally accessible mainstream of experience but of mysticism as outside, and of aesthetics as a rather uneasily acknowledgeable branch of philosophy by the side of ethics but of mysticism as too exceptional and too problematic for a classified place within the discipline. It may be, however, that our culture has been especially unfavourable to the recognition and education of the states called mystical. It is remarkable that in every philosophical tradition except our own the mystical is central and is not sharply distinguished from the aesthetic; indeed it tends to puzzle Westerners by appearing in such fields as martial arts and the government of the state.

But even if there is no objection in principle to accepting the private mystical experience as relevant to the philosophy of value, there remains the practical difficulty of introducing it into public discussion. In 1963, in his first book, *The Self in Transformation*, Herbert Fingarette proposed a direction from which the man of reason can begin to make sense of mystical discourse. He made an illuminating comparison between its paradoxes and those of the report of a woman on her self-reconstruction under psychoanalysis, and suggested that in spite of the glaring contrasts in theory and method mysticism and psychoanalysis pursue comparable states of psychic well-being. I shall here approach the problem from a different angle. Among the private experiences highly valued by those who share them there is one which seems especially well suited to verbal communication. I have the impression that a description of it is recognisable to most who are acquainted with psychedelic drugs or with meditative practices and to many who are not. It may or may not deserve the label 'mystical', however that word is understood, but those who claim to be on the mystic ladder seem generally to acknowledge it among the lower rungs, as 'nature mysticism' perhaps. To start with a crude summary, it is a state of exceptional tranquility and harmony with surroundings, in which attention detaches itself from one's habits and projects to become autonomous and intensely focussed, so that all perception is peculiarly lucid, detailed, and vivid. Its advantage for public discourse is that, being wholly extroverted, it is describable in terms of the things perceived. It perhaps belongs to common experience, but in our culture, which attaches little significance to it, is seldom noticed except by people with a pantheistic or other mystical vocabulary to identify it. To isolate it as far as possible from philosophical interpretation before discussing its philosophical significance, I shall appeal only to first-hand accounts by myself and others deliberately chosen as outside the standard literature of mysticism. The first is from Thor Heyerdahl's account of the earliest and best months of his flight from civilization to the Marquesas with a Girl Friday in 1937.[2]

> Sitting in the pool it sometimes happened that shades we are unaware of seemed to fall from our eyes, whereby everything around us took on a breath-taking beauty. Our sense of perception seemed to be tuned in to a different and clearer reception, and we smelt, saw and listened to everything around us as if we were tiny children witnessing nothing but miracles. All these little things were everyday matters, such as a little drop of water shaping up to fall from the tip of a green leaf. We let drops spill from our hands to see them sparkle like jewels against the morning sun. No precious stone polished by human hands could shine with more loveliness than this liquid jewel in the flame of the sun. We were rich, we could bale them up by handfuls and let them trickle by the thousands through our fingers and run away, because an infinity of these jewels kept pouring out of the rock. . . . It was good to feel the breeze, the sun, the touch of the forest on our skins, rather than to feel merely the same cloth clinging to the body wherever we moved. To step from cool grass to hot sand, and to feel the soft mud squeeze up between the toes, to be licked away in the next pool, felt better than stepping continually on the inside of the same pair of socks. Altogether, rather than feeling poor and naked, we felt rich and as if wrapped in the whole universe. We and everything were part of one entirety.

This is almost a description of any childhood day by the seaside, but Heyerdahl is aware of the experience as qualitatively different, "shades we are unaware of" falling from the eyes, and happening only sometimes. His concern is not with its meaning, merely with reviving in memory the best time of an adventure of his youth. He slips, however, into the kind of phrasing used by the mystically inclined: "we and everything were part of one entirety". The phrase 'tune in' suggests Timothy Leary's slogan "Turn on, tune in, drop out", still recent when the book was first published in 1974. Have we all experienced this tuning in, except for those of us unlucky enough never to have known joy? If so, it would be in spells of tranquility during otherwise excited states, in love, or in that first phase in a new country so packed with impressions that one recalls with amazement having got off the plane only yesterday morning; and since we are not in the habit of analysing joy, if only from fear of spoiling

268

it, its distinctiveness would elude our notice. There is, of course, the further question whether we can speak of the experience as the same before and after it becomes an object of attention.

The next example is from Georges Bataille, a mystic no doubt but a highly idiosyncratic one for whom the annihilation of self in the void is not a serene illumination but a convulsion of alternating anguish and rapture sustained only until terminated by exhaustion. Bataille knows the experience we are discussing, but as the "agreeable possession of a rather insipid loveliness".[3]

> At the moment when the sun sets, when silence invades a purer and purer sky, I happened to be alone, sitting in a narrow white veranda, seeing nothing from where I was but the roof of a house, the leafage of a tree and the sky. Before getting up to go to bed, I felt how much the loveliness of things had penetrated me. I had had the desire for a violent mental upheaval, and from this viewpoint I perceived that the state of felicity into which I had fallen was not entirely different from "mystical" states. At any rate, when I passed abruptly from inattention to surprise, I was more intensely aware of this state than one usually is, and as though another and not myself were experiencing it. I could not deny that, apart from the attention, absent from it only at the beginning, this commonplace felicity was an authentically inward experience, plainly distinct from project and discourse. Without giving more than an evocative value to these words, I thought that "heavenly loveliness" was in communication with me, and I could feel precisely the state which responded to it in myself. I felt it present inside the head as a vaporous flow, subtly perceptible, but participating in the loveliness outside, putting me in possession of it, making me enjoy it.
>
> I recalled a drive on which I had known a felicity of the same order with exceptional distinctness, when it was raining and the hedges and trees, hardly covered by the sparse leaves, stood out from the spring mist and came slowly towards me. I came into possession of each soaked tree and was sorry to give it up for the next. At that moment, I thought that this dreamy enjoyment would not cease to belong to me, that I would live henceforth guaranteed the power to take a melancholy joy in things and drink in their delights. I must admit today that these states of communication were only rarely accessible to me.[4]

For Bataille the experience on the veranda is immediately identifiable, not only with previous ones of his own, but with Proust's: "I recall having noticed the resemblance between my enjoyment and those described in the first volumes of the *Récherche du temps perdu*."[5] Leaving the veranda for his room, he wonders whether he has the right to despise "the state which I had just entered without thinking about it", to insist on preferring his "torturing joy"[6] to "possibilities a little different, less strange but more human, and, it seemed to me, equally profound".[7] In the quiet of his room he revives it, letting "the flow of which I spoke" intensify inside him.[8] But he is dissatisfied because "this plenitude of inward movement" does not abolish self. In starting to philosophise his language becomes abstract and strained. "It is true that in it I lose myself, attain the 'unknown' in being, but *my* attention being necessary for the plenitude, the self attentive to the presence of this 'unknown' is only partially lost, is also distinguished from that: its lasting presence still demands an opposition between the known appearances of the subject which I remain and the object, which it still is."[9] He decides to return "from a contemplation which referred the object to myself (as is usual when we enjoy a landscape) to the vision of that object in which at other times I lose myself, which I call the unknown, and between which and nothing there is no distinction which discourse can express."[10]

It will be noticed that Bataille, who despises happiness, attends to this "commonplace felicity", and recognises it as distinctive, only because he is in the mood for one of his self-lacerating ecstasies. Otherwise it would have passed unnoticed, as very likely it does for most of us. That Bataille, very unusually, describes it as, on one occasion at least, a *"melancholy* joy in things", is in keeping with his dark view of life. Here I introduce myself as third witness, with some background information to put my testimony in perspective. I am among the many who first noticed the commonplace felicity during the late sixties, when I had a few LSD trips and sometimes joined in smoking marijuana. It presented itself at its purest as the relaxation of body and mind and the clarity of the senses which persisted for a day or more after coming down from LSD. I shared the common impression that the calm lucidity was the effect, not of the drug itself, but of the unknotting by the drug of hardly noticed habitual tensions which only gradually returned with the pressures of ordinary life; and that there must be, if one could find it, a certain knack of relaxation which would restore the state without resort to chemical aids. Many with this impression proceed to try out some technique of meditation. I did not, judging myself (as I still do) temperamentally unsuited to mystical exploration; although fascinated by the Taoists whom I study professionally as a sinologist I have not read seriously in any other field of mystical literature, and have never practiced meditation. But from this time I had a new respect for episodes in which attention simply freewheels to sights and sounds—watching the shadows slant on a wall in the still and cool of late afternoon, or walking home late at night from a party a little drunk and peering into the reflections in a darkened shop window of lighted windows opposite and passing cars in between, or lolling in a chair listening without discrimination to birdcalls, barking dogs, wind in the trees. These seemed tantalisingly close to the experience without reaching it. During the same period another gain from the sixties, awareness of habitual tension, led to informal ways of easing it; neck and shoulder muscles loosened, various longstanding aches disappeared, my jerky awkward swimming and dancing became freer with the trusting of the body to make its own decisions. For some years the exhilarations of sensory vividness and bodily spontaneity remained unconnected. Later they occasionally came together, for example, on a warm night swimming in the blackness of air and water through phosphorescence, starlight, and lamps of fishing boats. Eventually in 1979, by the completion of some underground process of maturation, they quite suddenly fused, with the movement of attention becoming autonomous, and awareness and responsiveness interacting and enhancing each other. For the next three weeks, the last of a vacation, I had the knack of reaching this state almost at will, and did so for some or most of nearly every day. As was the case with Bataille I thought that "I would live henceforward guaranteed the power . . .", but afterwards "these states were only rarely accessible to me." Nowadays they are generally less vivid and are coaxed back perhaps twice in a year, but I have never ceased to be grateful for them. I still feel more honest speaking of them in the psychedelic slang of the sixties ('trip', 'turning on') than in a mystical vocabulary the right to which I have not earned. The experience is indeed a sober version of the wholly extroverted type of LSD trip, with undisturbed lucidity and full self-command, and anyone who wishes to think of me as having learned a knack of reviving a mild LSD intoxication without the expense and trouble of finding the drug is at liberty to do so. The point would be significant only for those who judge unusual states by their claim to uncover Reality, an enlightenment of which drugs treacherously give the illusion. But if the issue is not of reality but of value, approval of the experience is no more affected than would approval of present moods of confidence, cheerfulness, and friendliness if they improbably turned out to be after-effects of a brand of whisky one was drinking ten years ago.

In my own case, which like any other will have idiosyncratic features, the experience generally starts on the visual level from the "disinterested vision" of aesthetics, surrendering to whatever attracts the eye without discriminating in favour of the practically relevant. There is, for example, that equalising of interest in objects and their shadows or reflections which may accompany the suspension of practical concerns. In a dirty pond with wooded banks you at first see only muddy water, then the upside-down reflections of the trees becoming as plain and solid to the eye as the trees themselves, then sun, blue of the sky, moving clouds, quite distinct underneath the inverted treetops. The multiplying images enormously enhance the pleasure in the scene, but since for practical purposes most reflections are useless if not dangerous distractions, the mind in normal conditions shuts them out. When in this mood, I try to make, or rather to relax in order to *let*, the disinterested attention to sensation spread from sight not only to sounds, smells, tastes, feel, but to my own breathing, my own movements. (This is not a meditation in which one sits still.) Too exclusive concentration on the visual hinders the play of attention from keeping up with the changing scene, because sights departing without leaving time to assimilate them tempt one to cling to them as they pass (Bataille's "I came into possession of each soaked tree and was sorry to give it up for the next"); sound on the other hand, having temporal duration without spatial distribution, pulls attention along with it. If everyday stresses are not quite released, the nerves not quite unjangled, nothing more happens, and you get bored with looking purposelessly into the spectral colours radiating from carlamps or sun, or heeding the feel and sound of your own footsteps. But once you hit on the rhythm at which attention keeps pace with change, the takeoff is unmistakable (except perhaps during a brief interval of instability). The flow of attention becomes autonomous, pulling you, not pulled by you towards goals, which is presumably that "vaporous flow, subtly perceptible", that "plenitude of inward movement", which puts Bataille into communication with the external scene and which resumes when he returns from the veranda to his room. Attention no longer depends on pre-existing goals to give it purpose, and anything on which it focusses, the band of light along the edge of the bathwater, the brown discoloration of an old newspaper, becomes inexhaustibly interesting for its own sake. The texture of experience, when without memory or anticipation one is absorbed in the moving present, becomes so rich, varied, and transitory that the only alternatives in confronting this plethora of riches are either to turn to something new or to plunge farther and farther into the detail of the same thing. Blake's dictum, "If the doors of perception were cleansed everything would appear to man as it is, infinite", assumes a straightforward, almost literal meaning. There is no longer any such thing as monotony because your own kitchen is from moment to moment as new to the eye as Venice the first day you saw it. It is hardly the mystic oneness with everything—Bataille justly complains of the continuing separation of subject and object—but in surrendering to spontaneity one is as though breathing and moving in harmony with a bee settling on a flower or water rippling over stones (Heyerdahl's "We and everything were part of one entirety"); it becomes intelligible that with experience further on in the same direction the language of mystics would deepen in meaning like Blake's "If the doors of perception . . .". The illumination waxes and wanes but, unless abandoned for practical reasons, lasts until the senses tire at the end of the day, and is then relatively easy to resume the next morning. It is not a matter of an ecstasy from which one must sooner or later come down but of a dishabituation, Heyerdahl's "shades falling from the eyes", the putting back of which can be delayed indefinitely. (But nowadays I lose interest in it about the fourth day.)

Has this semi- or sub-mystical state any philosophical significance? Better still avoid the language of conventional mystical discourse, which is inevitably, even more than other languages, debased by usage in excess of the experience which gives it meaning. One might be tempted to take a Bergsonian line and acclaim the insight as a disinterested vision of the universal flow as it is in itself, not as the intellect abstracts and classifies for human ends. Certainly this liberation from what Bataille calls "project and discourse" involves a deconceptualisation of experience, a suspension of language. At one moment, in grinding coffee let us say, there is an equally vivid consciousness of a cobweb wavering in the breeze and throwing a shadow on the window, the red and white lights and the engine hum of a plane receding in the sky behind it, and the new-ground smell entering the nostrils with the feel of metal on the palm and of winding against the resistance of the crunching beans. To find words to fix the complex of sensations you would have to withdraw from the flow, and by the time you found them you would have been left behind. Reversing Derrida's slogans the illusion of presence and "Nothing outside the text", there is no text to be inside and whatever is perceived is fully present. In this heightened awareness one does not become more *observant,* more alert to the useful or dangerous; it is simply that one perceives a leaf as moving however slight the breeze, hears by day the creaks and squeaks which worry the sleepless at night, knows anywhere in the house that outside a cloud is passing over the sun. In shifting to this unutilitarian viewpoint the most familiar scene becomes full of marvels. In your own sitting-room, when free of the practical necessity of remembering that among reflecting surfaces things may not be where you see them, you enjoy the sight of blossoms and creepers growing from the walls, the washing on the line in the garden behind hanging unsupported in the air in the street in front, cars driving straight through the house. The effect of opening the senses to the irrelevant image is most spectacular in the city by night, whether indoors or in the street, in a tumult of mirrors, wide windows, polished metal and plastic, contrasting colours, and glaring lights. Nothing that architects plan has the complex beauty of the astonishing collages, the endlessly changing mobiles, springing from chance conjunctions to transform the most commonplace building. It may seem surprising that a vision associated primarily with the countryside, indeed often called "nature mysticism", adapts so easily to the landscape of the city, for this witness at least. But a man-made environment seen in a dull and even light does remain peculiarly resistant to this vision. The "state of communication", as Bataille calls it, seems to be nourished by the interaction of the spontaneous within and without. At night one is gazing into fortuitous blends and clashes of light, glass, and colour, at the city not designed by man but recreated from moment to moment by the Surrealists' "objective chance", which might be claimed as the characteristic mode in which modernity apprehends Nature.

But in pursuing these flights of fancy it is already plain that the vision is *not* of things as they are in themselves. The doors of perception may be cleansed, but attention always takes the direction which is spontaneously pleasing, and pleasure just as much as utility is a selective human interest. The Commonplace Felicity (we need a label from neither the mystic's nor the psychologist's argot, and Bataille's phrase will do as well as any) never in my experience comes except in favourable conditions, leisure, comfort, warmth, light, and the awareness which it enhances is of the nice but not the nasty things in life, by a paradisiac vision as one-sided as the infernal. In this respect it is narrower than aesthetic vision, which can be as much or more at home in the infernal, being safely detached from the present experience in which spontaneity cannot do otherwise than flinch from the displeasing. If a visit to paradise makes some people want to climb the mystic ladder still higher, it must be because it suggests the possibility and the direction of some still higher state embracing or transcending the dark side as well as the light. It may be noticed also that granted that the experience approaches the ideal of the shedding of all verbal concepts, it is certainly being shaped by preconceptions about the aesthetically pleasing. Looking at dew on a cobweb or rust on an abandoned car, colours and textures clarify and interrelate as though in a painting in the National Gallery. To my eyes, at least, a scene will look Impressionist (waterlilies in a pool as though painted by Monet), or Cubist (diverging lines and planes of a table top and the corner of the wall), or Surrealist (that car driving through the sitting-room), all of them styles which start from an unlearning of the conceptualisations shaping conventional vision; but how far would I be seeing like that if I had not seen the pictures before? The same question comes up when the ear discovers consonances in the clink of ice in a glass, a creak on the stair and the whirr of a neighbour's lawnmower, as though I were listening to Stockhausen or John Cage.

But the awareness, although one-sided, is relevant to the question why the experience seems to impress everyone who shares it as self-evidently valuable, not merely as enjoyable recreation but as an illumination of life.

Indeed it invites the language of sacred authority; Bataille speaks, "without giving more than an evocative value to these words", of a "heavenly loveliness", and I would myself not be more than slightly embarrassed to call its peerless serenity "blessedness" or the "peace which passeth all understanding". Bataille's testimony is especially remarkable, since even his qualified approval of it is hard to reconcile with his extremist, to some tastes positively sinister philosophy, which equates value with intensity, and conceives all intensity as expenditure of life, inherently destructive and self-destructive. The explanation of its apparently impregnable authority is, I would suggest, that you are surrendering to pure spontaneity but in abnormally intensified awareness of the things around you, on occasions when only the immediate surroundings matter. It becomes idle to dismiss the assurance of high value as a treacherous subjective conviction; you are judging not deliberate action but spontaneous reaction, and to judge the most aware reaction to be the best requires no further authority than the value of awareness itself, which will be just that which in propositional knowledge you ascribe to truth. Pronouncing it best no doubt demands the qualification 'Other things being equal', but in a state limited to occasions when no issue of prudence or morals arises, what other thing is there to take into account? This argument, which if valid undermines the fact/value dichotomy, I have elsewhere put in quasi-syllogistic form and debated with Professor Fingarette.[11]

But is not this high value relative only to spontaneity in lesser awareness, not to the ethical value of deliberate action? It might plausibly be claimed that the episodes into which no practical or moral consideration enters are the very ones it is least important to evaluate. The experience does not merely lack the value proper to deliberate action, it is actually incompatible with prolonged deliberation. Not that it is abandonment of self-control, reversion to animal instinct. The submergence in the spontaneous as it is acted on from outside is, if one wishes to put it in these terms, a re-incorporation into Nature; yet one is never more in control than when both spontaneous and highly attentive, as in athletic performance. If this seems a paradox, it is of the sort (at the same time having and lacking self, desire, thought) which Professor Fingarette notices as common to mystical discourse and the report of the psychoanalytic patient whom he quotes.[12] In this reincorporation into Nature we have an answer to why the experience seems sacred; although the human capacity for awareness is raised to its highest pitch, one is being moved by forces from outside Man. In spite of the resemblance to the LSD trip one is not in ecstasy or trance; one is simply doing what from moment to moment one spontaneously prefers, with no need to deliberate until some opportunity or danger arises. One still thinks (including the thinking about the experience itself exemplified in this essay), and if it turns cold can walk across the room to shut the window without heeding every perception on the way; but thoughts straying too far from present sensation, or goals too long deferred, disturb the spontaneous flow until eventually it loses momentum. It is plain that to maintain permanently this immersion in a solipsistic stream of impressions would not merely be impossible in practice, it would amount to a sacrifice of most of life. This, however, is to say no more than that we cannot remain for long in the contemplation of attained ends forgetful of means to further ends. Here we may recall a surprising touch in Bataille's reluctant tribute to the Commonplace Felicity, his recognition that compared with the agonised intensities which he prefers it seems "equally profound". 'Profound' is an unexpected word for an experience which, not only for Heyerdahl and myself but for Bataille (with his rooftop seen from the white veranda and trees approaching through the mist) is not of depths but of surfaces.

But there is a sense in which the experience is indeed profound. It is a return to the foundations on which one's personal code of means and ends is built. Deliberate action as means depends for its value on ends valued for themselves, without which one is caught in that infinite regress of means to means which empties existence of all meaning. To the extent that we lose faith in the religious or philosophical grounding of ends, we seem to be left with nothing but our own spontaneous likes and dislikes. We are not in practice deterred from acting on these by the theoretical ban on inferring the value of something from the fact that one likes it; but with attention concentrated on choices of means, on the one hand the rigidifying ends come to be taken for granted, and lag behind and obscure spontaneously changing preferences, on the other choice of new ends is stultified by the habit of seeing in anything only what is useful to the old ones. The arts are the most easily available source from which to replenish ends. But the Commonplace Felicity, in spite of its more restricted scope, has one advantage over learning from the arts; it is not the sharing in imagination of another's experience but an intensification of one's own. For a few hours, as an individual at leisure in that particular time and place, you have the assurance that without reflection you are from moment to moment living exactly as you should. It would not be to the point to object that an enhancement of selfish enjoyment however intense is of negligible value compared with moral ends. Moral action is a means to others' ends, self-regarding to one's own, and both require an education in ends valued for themselves, whether through ordinary experience, the arts, the Commonplace Felicity or whatever higher mystical states there may be.

To dismiss any suspicion that this approach to ends encourages an amoral aestheticism, let us take a story by Tolstoy, severe moralist and public enemy of "Art for Art's Sake". In *The Death of Ivan Ilyitch* the dying man asks "Why these agonies?" and finds no answer but "For no reason—they just are so." "Beyond and besides this there was nothing." But he is not in the existentialist void without values other than those which the sovereign individual freely chooses for himself; on the contrary, in his new self-awareness on the verge of death new valuations are forced on him against his will, not by his standards (all of which justify "the law-abidingness, uprightness and respectability of his life"), but by an irresistible revulsion against his stultifying marriage and "that deadly official life and the preoccupation with money, a year of it, two years, ten. . . .", a revulsion which extends progressively to almost the whole of his life. Ivan Ilyitch tries to recall his best moments. "But oddly enough none of those best moments of his pleasant life now seemed at all what they had seemed at the time—none of them except his earliest memories of childhood", a few more from his student years ("There was still something then that had been genuinely good—gaiety, friendship, hopes"), and a last trickle from the start of his career ("again some good moments: they were the memories of love for a woman"). "The farther he looked back the more life there had been. There had been more of what is good in life and more of life itself." As for the earliest and least discredited by time, the one memory which Tolstoy elaborates has just that inconsequential value justified only by authenticity in vivid awareness which revives in the Commonplace Felicity: "the raw, wrinkled French plums of his childhood, their peculiar flavour and the flow of saliva when he got down to the stones." His choice of ends in the void, after all standards have broken down, is through the pursuit of the most genuine impulse in the unwelcomed blaze of self-awareness. He begins to suspect that "those scarcely detected inclinations of his to fight against what the most highly placed people regarded as good, those scarcely noticeable impulses which he had previously suppressed, might have been the real thing and all the rest false."

" 'But if that is so', he said to himself, 'and I am leaving this life with the consciousness that I have lost all that was given me and there's no putting it right—what then?' "

For three days, "during which time did not exist for him", Ivan Ilyitch lies screaming, in an anguish as though endlessly being forced down resisting into a black hole. He goes on resisting as long as he clings to the last remains of his illusion that he has lived as he should. His salvation comes an hour before death; ceasing to resist, "he sank through the hole and there at the bottom was a light."

" 'So that's what it is!' he suddenly exclaimed aloud. 'What joy!' "

Shall we say that he has a vision of the divine symbolised by the light? As a religious thinker Tolstoy would no doubt have said so, but as a writer he is meticulous in describing only the human event without interpreting "the meaning of that instant" in theological terms. The event is the final letting go of illusions about himself, and simultaneously an impulse of sympathy as Ivan Ilyitch is suddenly aware that his wife and child are suffering too, releasing him from imprisonment in his own pain. Whether or not one calls this a "mystical experience" it is plainly different from and far greater than the solipsistic vision of the Commonplace Felicity, but describable in similar terms. It is a breakout from awareness contracted to his own suffering into awareness from other viewpoints, by which his pain and death lose their unique significance for him, and it becomes possible for him to think "They are sorry but it will be better for them when I die". The light is the illumination of instantaneously expanded awareness which in the first place is of what is happening around his bed. In the spontaneous sympathy which carries him outside himself he has at last rediscovered "the right thing", following from the expansion by mere causality (as despair followed the contraction), and so sharing the self-evident value of the awareness itself.

The Commonplace Felicity on a sunny day is a very minor affair compared with the agony and salvation of Ivan Ilyitch. But in principle it has the same claims to be a source of non-propositional knowledge, enabling its enjoyer to liquidate, reconstitute, and revitalise ends, and see the means to them in a new perspective. Speaking personally again, I had never before catching on to this knack guessed how much one sacrifices by immersion in the realm of means. Granted that, as moralists and practical people have always insisted, there are for much of the time compelling reasons to deny oneself the pleasures of the moment, as soon as one appreciates how much joy is being lost one begins to count up just how much one is getting in exchange. An enormous range of experience commonly dismissed as neutral, mere fodder as means to something else, or even as positively unpleasant, is revealed in enhanced awareness to be highly enjoyable. It is not that the world is disclosed to be a beautiful place after all, but that the beauties which it has seem inexhaustible. Heyerdahl and his friend letting "drops spill from our hands to see them sparkle like jewels against the morning sun" are getting more from them than many get from the possession of real jewels. During the three weeks when I first explored the possibilities of the experience I was living in a flat right up against a railway. I listened with fascination to the rhythmic clang and clatter of trains passing the house, distinguishing while in one room or another the differently arching sound of arriving and departing—a noise which originally had almost deterred me from taking the flat, which I learned not to hear soon after moving in, and which I still did not hear except in this state of sharpened sensitivity. I had also not appreciated how tastes can change decisively but temporarily at peaks of awareness one is unable to sustain, and how this calls into question the value of the taste mortified by habit to which one reverts. On most mornings of my life I hurry through a breakfast which varies little and is hardly tasted. But on occasions when I have coaxed open the doors of perception while in my morning bath, I do not breakfast until the quickening of hunger, and pick only what that morning stirs the appetite. Whatever it may be, fruit, unflavoured yogurt, wholemeal bread (my tastes shift in the simple-lifer's direction), I linger over every mouthful with acute enjoyment, much more than at most banquets. It is not, however, that every flavour becomes enjoyable. Certain positive distastes emerge, for example for processed fruit juices, and for sprinkling too much sugar. Next day, in a hurry to leave the house, I shall be swallowing juice and sugaring corn flakes as negligently as ever, but with a distinct sense of *Video meliora.* . . . "I see and approve the better, I follow the worse." This is not one of the more significant life-choices, but it illustrates how one may be led to revalue one's ends and consequently one's means also. Why would it be more rational for me to work for the money to pay for meals in more expensive restaurants than educate myself to become more conscious of the flavours of fruit, yogurt, and wholemeal bread?

This is the sort of question which, although of course asked in the West, not least by explorers of psychedelia and mysticism, goes decidedly against the grain of our culture. The technological progress of the West over the last few centuries depended on a choice *not* to live for the moment but for the future, not to spend but save, not to relax but stay on the move, not to trust to spontaneity but to thought and will. In terms of this basic choice there was no point in being aware without being observant, no point in spontaneity except of the sort rationally directed to a goal, such as manual dexterity—and no point in the goal, without calling on some dubious religious or philosophical principle to support it. As for the joy in which awareness and spontaneity evoke and enhance each other, it still happened, but without a commonly recognised category into which to fit it, except that of the pleasure which rewards work done and refreshes for doing more. Much of this has survived the puritanism which once gave it a moral meaning. Might it be that in philosophy of value our culture tends to cut us off from one of the main sources of knowledge? The fact that, for example, we find Chinese thought logically undeveloped in comparison with our own is a reminder that we have no assurance whatever that all sources of knowledge are equally open to us. A Westerner at the seaside sharing Heyerdahl's experience might miss its significance as in traditional China a thinker whose argument happened to make explicit both premises of a syllogism would not recognise in its logical form the necessity lacking in his looser reasoning. I suspect that some states that we call mystical are as natural as the relief of sorrow by tears, and are suppressed by certain cultures much as grown men may be forbidden to weep.

NOTES

1. Cf. pp. 275–76 below.
2. Thor Heyerdahl, *Fatu-Hiva: Back to Nature on a Pacific Island* (New York: Penguin Books, 1976), p. 62f.
3. Georges Bataille, *L'expérience intérieure* (Paris: Gallimard, 1954), p. 177.
4. Ut sup., 173f.
5. Ut sup., 175.
6. Ut sup., 88.
7. Ut sup., 175.
8. Ut sup., 175.
9. Ut sup., 176.
10. Ut sup., 177.
11. *Reason and Spontaneity* (London and Barnes and Noble, Totowa NJ: Curzon Press, 1985), ch 1. "Value, Fact and Facing Facts", ch. 1 above. Fingarette, "Reason, Spontaneity and the *Li*", and my rejoinder, in *Chinese Texts and Philosophical Contexts*, ed. Henry Rosemont, Jr., (La Salle, IL: Open Court, 1991).
12. Fingarette, *The Self in Transformation* (New York: Basic Books, 1963), ch. 7.
13. Leo Tolstoy, *The Cossacks, Happy Ever After, The Death of Ivan Ilyitch*, trans. Rosemary Edmonds (New York: Penguin Classics, 1960), 152–61.

NAME INDEX

SUBJECT INDEX

287